CHARLES MOORE
Buildings and Projects 1949–1986

CHARLES MOORE
Buildings and Projects 1949–1986

Edited by Eugene J. Johnson

*To Chris Turley
with our deep
appreciation to our
favorite Tech Weenie*

*Charles Moore
Aug '91*

RIZZOLI
NEW YORK

First published in the United States of America in 1986 by
RIZZOLI INTERNATIONAL PUBLICATIONS, INC.
597 Fifth Avenue, New York, NY 10017

Designed by Abigail Sturges
Composition by Rainsford Type, Ridgefield, CT
Printed and bound in Japan

Library of Congress Cataloging-in-Publication Data
Charles Moore: buildings and projects 1949–1986.
   Bibliography: p.
   1. Moore, Charles Willard, 1925–   —Criticism
and interpretation.   2. Architecture, Modern—
20th century—United States.   I. Johnson, Eugene J.,
1937–
NA737.M65C43   1986   720'.92'4   86–42734
ISBN 0–8478–0746–0
ISBN 0–8478–0759–2 (pbk.)

Contents

Preface

What started out to be a modest exhibition of a few buildings and projects by Charles Moore has turned into this book. Along the way, a lot of funny things happened, many instigated by Mr. Moore himself. He has been both extraordinarily generous with his time and energy and extremely careful to see that this book represents in some way his buildings as he would like them to be known. The splendid set of drawings, specially made for this publication and its attendant retrospective exhibition, of a group of works he chose himself are his most obvious contribution. For them, and for countless other things, my profound thanks.

The buildings illustrated in this book are a select group of the many in which Moore has had a hand. Partly, this fact can be attributed to the chance preservation, or the thoughtful preservation, of original drawings. Buildings that might have been illustrated, because of their importance in his career, may not have been, simply because none of the original visual material, particularly drawings by Moore himself, is preserved. Thus one gets here both a somewhat skewed view of his career and a rather clear sense of his design methods from the chance to study the evolution of at least a few of his designs in some detail. Of course, our view of the history of architecture is always skewed by chance preservation of buildings or drawings. Why should it be any different with history that has scarcely happened? On the other hand, I would like to pay particular tribute to two men who have worked with Moore and have carefully preserved some of his history for us: James Volney Righter and Stephen Harby. They are among the blessed of Clio.

Bringing all this material together has been exciting, particularly for an architectural historian who cut his teeth on Alberti, from whom we have two miserable drawings and about six magnificent fragments of buildings. The wealth of it all was quite overwhelming. I have also learned something about the study of history that I think I would never have understood so well, had I not been working on a contemporary topic. Time and again I would work up a hypothesis, based on the material that has been preserved, only to find out how disastrously wrong that hypothesis was. The mistake was generally not to be attributed to faulty reasoning, based on what I had in front of me. Rather, the mistake was caused by not knowing what actually had happened. Usually when I found out what actually had happened, through some chance remark of someone who had been there, the real circumstances were so bizarre or improbable that had I hypothesized them, I would quite rightly have been disbelieved. So much, then, for the reliability of the history we painstakingly create from the fragments that come down to us. What we do create is often wonderful and imaginative, and even sometimes intelligent, but it is almost never a re-creation of what really took place.

The drawings and models presented here, with the exception of those newly made by Moore and his associates, have been retrieved from the files of the firms with which he has been associated. The MLTW file is maintained in San Francisco by William Turnbull, even though the name of the firm has now disappeared from his door. There are two archives in Los Angeles, those at Urban Innovations Group and Moore, Ruble, Yudell. In Essex, Connecticut, are the records of Centerbrook, formerly Moore, Grover, Harper. In addition, there is the remarkable cache of drawings preserved by Jim Righter from his days of working as Moore's assistant. Even as I write, of course, a whole new treasure is being created in his new center of activity, Austin, Texas. Almost no project, except for some of the earliest and most recent ones, can be tracked down in its entirety in the files of any one office. To study Moore, one must become somewhat as peripatetic as the master himself.

The essayists who have contributed to this publication have done so under severe time limitations. That they have performed, nevertheless, with grace and wit should not be surprising. I am very grateful to them for the considerable efforts they have each expended to help in the explication of an architectural career that will never be simple to understand.

At the end of the book is a bibliography that attests, if nothing else, to the ever growing interest in Moore's work. Indeed, one might think of publications on Moore as a growth industry. Also, Moore is a very productive author. Although the bibliography is lengthy, one should be cautioned against thinking it could ever be complete. His work has been published in the most obscure places, so that even the most diligent of bibliographers will find it difficult to track it all down. What one finds here, with its faults, may, one hopes, prove useful to future students of Moore's work.

Moore, like Christopher Robin's Rabbit, has numerous friends and relations. Many of them have been kind enough to stand or sit still long enough to answer questions or to show me drawings or to perform any number of helpful and generous acts. I recall them here, more or less, in the sequence and places in which I encountered them. Peter Becker, Richard Peters, and Dmitri Vedinsky at Sea Ranch. Chris and Sally Noll in Berkeley, Mary Winters in San Francisco. Mimi Weingarten, Moore's sister, and Roger Bailey in Pebble Beach. Stephen Harby and Marilyn Zuber, then Tina Beebe, John Ruble and Buzz Yudell in Los Angeles. In Essex, Bob Harper, Chad Floyd, Jim Childress, Bill Grover, and Emay Buck. Once again in San Francisco, Wendy Libby, and most particularly Don Lyndon and Bill Turnbull. In Boston, Jim Righter, and his associates Jacob Albert and Kemo Griggs. There were also a number of people outside the Moore circle whose help has been crucial to this work. David Littlejohn, author of a biography of Moore, sent me, in a great act of scholarly generosity, his painstakingly created list of Moore clients, with addresses and telephone numbers. Some of those clients greeted my asking to see their houses with extraordinary graciousness, particularly the Klotzes and Mrs. Licht. My colleagues have also given advice and counsel when asked for it, and sometimes they have even volunteered it when I hesitated to impose on them. Particular thanks in this regard are due to Whitney Stoddard, Zirka Filipczak, William Pierson, Sheafe Satterthwaite, and Andy Burr. There have also been two groups of students who have worked on this project with me, one when it was just beginning, and one as it was coming to a close. What I learned from them is, in good part, found herein. Of those students, I want particularly to mention Richard Song, who has followed the whole process with equal parts of interest and bemusement, and whose comments on the manuscript were the most helpful I received, because he asked the toughest questions. Mark Stansbury-O'Donnell has helped in numerous ways. He is that rarest of creatures, an assistant in whom one can have total confidence. I would also like to acknowledge the help of members of the staff of the Williams College Museum of Art, particularly Tom Krens, Rod Faulds, Vivian Patterson, Beth Miller, and Linda Barnett, and of former members of the staff, Russell Panczenko and Lisa Holst.

Eugene J. Johnson
Williamstown, Massachusetts

Foreword

Charles Moore is an important architect because he has over the past three decades produced an architectural oeuvre that reflects, perhaps better than any other, the conflicting tendencies of our time. He has done this with a grace, wit, and consistent intelligence that has made his achievement all the more remarkable. Moore's buildings are deceptive. The obvious playfulness, the drama and surprises, the allusions that make his buildings thoroughly accessible also suggest a sensibility that is perhaps too attuned to a casual or populist gesture. It is hard not to like a Charles Moore building just as it is hard not to like Walt Disney. Good-natured fun sticks out all over at the expense of an obvious and inflated self-importance.

As accessible as Moore's work is, there is also far more to it than first meets the eye. It is precisely his perceptive recognition of the utilitarian nature of architecture in the context of the transitional elements of human nature that guides him in the design of spaces. His acute awareness of his time, reflected in both design and process, makes his work far more profound and complicated than it initially appears. Moore has understood better than any other architect that the building of habitable structures is not an exercise in theoretical design. He knows that the shapes of buildings are probably determined more by the variety of attitudes and pressures of a given culture than by a prescient inspiration of an individual designer. He works with rather than against that understanding.

Charles Moore may be unique among contemporary architects in his ability to incorporate process and culture in his work. For more than thirty years he has surveyed the landscape and seen a society emerging that no longer feels compelled to assert, through its architecture, control *over* its environment, but rather harmony *within* it. Harmony for Moore is not measured in terms of a romantic balance with a traditional and mythical Mother Nature. Rather he sees it as consistency with the changing attitudes and artifacts of contemporary society that comprise our regular experience of the world. In this sense Moore is the quintessential contemporary architect. The neoclassical elements in his vocabulary come more from the vernacular of Caesar's Palace in Las Vegas than from the Parthenon in Athens. His choice of materials is guided more by his unsurpassed ability to find unique combinations of the feasible and available than by a reliance on the sleek or the distinctive. His method of working is tuned more to a flexible collaboration between client and designer than to the authoritarian attitudes of a genius.

Architects have been popularly represented as strong-willed visionaries who impose a personal concept of design and order that transcends existing canon. Moore's strength is that he works with culture, not canon. His surpassing importance as a practicing architect is grounded in the fact that he does not find contemporary society threatening. He positions himself to intuitively embrace change rather than seek shelter under the protective umbrella of a handful of well-formed ideas. He intuitively understands that the fundamental division in contemporary society is between that which is known and that which is not known. Through his work he seeks to bridge this gulf in a gentle manner by remaining open, noniconoclastic, nondogmatic, irreverent, and available. As a result, his buildings are humorous and colorful, ironic and complicated, and they inevitably convey a sense of lively and vibrant accessibility. In short, he is the perfect architect for a contemporary art museum.

Moore began work on the addition to the museum and art building at Williams College in 1977, almost a decade ago. The process of design development never really abated through most of that time. He was selected in large part because it was felt that he could provide a sensitive addition to an existing Greek Revival building, on a difficult site, without sacrificing the excitement of an original solution. It was for Williams an excellent choice. The design and renovation produced by Moore and his associates at Centerbrook has resulted in an almost seamless integration of the old and the new in a single concept—which may ultimately prove to be one of the most distinctive aspects of the Williams project. Despite feeling occasional exasperation at first in dealing with an architect who was so open and receptive to modifications in his plans, I must confess to being finally and convincingly co-opted by Moore. I have come to see that his fundamental ideas about architecture are larger than just the design of buildings. Moore uses his clients and his opportunities to maximum advantage to orchestrate buildings that reflect the scale of his ambition for architecture and its role in society.

It is perhaps fitting that an academic institution play a significant role in the analysis and presentation of Charles Moore's architectural oeuvre, and fitting that it happen at Williams. The Williams College Museum of Art was the first art museum designed by Moore; he briefly taught here in the 1950s and he has subsequently had distinguished academic associations with some of the major colleges and universities in this country; and for him the process of making structures is inseparable from the processes of teaching and learning. Professor Eugene J. Johnson, who initially proposed the idea of a Charles Moore retrospective and collected the materials and produced most of the writing that comprises this publication, has made Williams a modest center of Charles Moore research. We are proud to have this association with Charles Moore and his work.

Thomas Krens
Director
Williams College Museum of Art

CHARLES MOORE

Buildings and Projects 1949–1986

Arch is "making places"

Suzanne Langer. "ethnic domain" { steamships
· doesn't need to be in one place { gypsie caravan

"taking ~~takes~~ possession"

imagine our body in the space.
up, in, and through

act of making a place
starting of separating an inside, (not necessarily indoors.)
    from the outside
    as in a plaza.
ordering of the inside
so that it makes sense.

came from natures and then recreated them – pyramids
also the cave – endless.
column - counter to the cave with its obvious symbolism.
2 columns can get extended into an arcade.
    or porch.

window of appearances

archs + columns

towers + columns + pediments + domes

walled compound
with water

house   and then back to 4 poster bed.

then a matter of positioning all of these items   axis
                                                     path
                                                     distance.
                                                     progression

The Yin, the Yang, and the Three Bears

Charles W. Moore

Earlier in this aging century, architects were given to writing ardent manifestos proclaiming the death of a shackling past and announcing the onset of a modern architectural salvation. Just over twenty years ago, Robert Venturi, speaking for members of another generation (his own and mine) presented a "gentle" manifesto in favor of pluralism and history, noting that the American Main Street was "almost all right." That gentle manifesto triggered howls of rage from the orthodox Moderns, and even Venturi's own position hardened into defense of the "ordinary" against the "heroic" modernists. An exhibition, new in 1986, called "Modern Redux," picks up the competition in previous centuries between the Moderns and the Ancients, and picks up the cudgel again in favor of the Moderns against the Ancients, by now marshaled under the banner of postmodernism.

I have believed for some time that sense might be made of the opposing views in the terms of "yin" and "yang," the Chinese diagram of opposites complementing one another. If our century's predominant urge to erect high-rise macho objects was nearly spent, I thought we might now be eligible for a fifty-year-long respite of yin, of absorbing and healing and trying to bring our freestanding erections into an inhabitable community. I like that, but am growing impatient with fifty-year swings, and wonder whether a more suitable model for us might be Goldilocks, of Three Bears fame, who found some things (Papa Bear's) too hot or too hard or too big, and other things (Mama Bear's) too cold, too soft, or too small, but still other things (Baby Bear's) just right, inhabitable, as we architects would say. The early modern polemicists disliked the world they saw and expected the opposite to be an improvement (like Goldilocks part way through her testing); but their panacea turned out to have its drawbacks, too, and it seems more accurate to note that, even as humans have yearnings—for place, for roots, for changing sequences of light and space, for order and clarity, for reverie—just so, when each of these yearnings is satisfied, we can feel surfeit, and seek to head another way, to mobility, or ambiguity, or surprise.

But there is one architectural circumstance more universal than our yearnings and surfeits. Buildings, Donlyn Lyndon pointed out to me years ago, are receptacles for human energy; if they receive enough of it, they can repay in satisfaction for the occupants, as in the biblical image of bread cast upon the waters. It behooves architects, it seems to me, therefore, to do everything we can do to increase the human energy put into "our" works, so those works can repay it. The care and love, then, of everyone involved—architects and builders and inhabitants, even the bank loan officers—should be invited. I still remember visiting some of Louis Kahn's building sites with him; everyone there from the guard at the gate on forward seemed vitalized by his part in the work. I don't make any parallel claims for the buildings in this book, but they do represent attempts increasingly pointed, I think, as time goes on, to collect as much energy as we can, starting with our own care and then trying to include the energies of the site (as at the Sea Ranch) and of the local history (as at the University of California at Santa Barbara Faculty Club) as well as the spirit of the inhabitants, their dreams and images and ambitions and care (as at the Hood Museum and St. Matthew's Church).

The buildings in these pages, I submit, should not be seen as signposts to some Architectural Utopia or some Big Revelation, or to some perfectible style, but rather as attempts better to gather into structures the energies of people and places. These attempts come from a belief that the world contains an astonishing number of wonderful places, fancy and plain, large and tiny (or somewhere in between). My own most worthy contribution, I believe, is that I have encouraged (it used to be decried) looking at places and listening to

Opposite. Sketches from Kent C. Bloomer and Charles W. Moore, Body, Memory and Architecture, *New York, 1977*

Boldface numbers *referred to in the following essays correspond to projects illustrated in the* Buildings and Projects *section of this book.*

people, acknowledging the sources, even exulting in them, adding our own energies, care, and love, and even joy, if we have it in us.

Which is not to say that I decry learning and the rules. I stretched out my schooling as far as I knew how and have been involved with architecture schools, with hardly a gap, for the last forty-four years. I read *The Fountainhead* at an early age and identified with the supercilious bad guy Peter Keating, rather than with that dangerous baboon Howard Roark. And I value the limited formal geometries I'm about to describe, even as I value the caring that transcends limits.

The buildings themselves don't make a particularly orderly *oeuvre*; they were all done in response to a particular client, on a particular site, usually with particular design collaborators. I started organizing the work of trying to remove every project I didn't really need and I never could get the list below sixty-five buildings.

So, I started from the other direction, with four sections. I wanted to include my own houses, eight of them by now; a section called *Houses As the Center of the World* lets me include the geometries that have focused schemes for houses and housing; *Frivolous and Serious Play* allows me to describe some places meant as playgrounds which have offered chances for my most serious explorations; and *Fitting* is the chance to show buildings designed to be good neighbors to other buildings or friendly to a special past or a special site or to a special group of people.

the aedicula

My own houses have given me the chance to pursue chimera, to the possible discomfort of no one but myself. There have been eight of them, so far: my house in Pebble Beach, California, on a sloping lot with a view of Point Lobos to the south was really for my mother. It was built in 1955, with rooms in single file facing south to the view. The plan, very like one I had done at Torch Lake, Michigan, in 1948 (my first house), was 16 feet 2 inches wide, on a 2-foot 8-inch module carefully set up to minimize wasted lumber and to be within the $11,000 budget that the veterans' loan demanded. The scheme owes a lot to the Japanese buildings I had just seen for the first time, especially the gardens at Daitokuji in Kyoto.

The next house was a square pavilion across the hills from Berkeley, in Orinda, California. I had fallen in love with the site when Dick Whitaker, who was looking for a lot himself, took me one noon hour to see it. A slope thick with oaks had had a circular pad bulldozed years before, so it looked as if it had always been there, and I remembered a description by an early Chinese poet—I think Li Po—of his little square house on a round meadow. I had to have one, too. My square pavilion measured 26 feet 8 inches on a side. By the time the house was designed, I had bought several wooden columns from a demolition in San Francisco. They had cost only two dollars each and were over 11 feet tall, so I argued that they would keep me from thinking too small. They became two square aediculas within the larger square and had, I thought, to hold up the roof, on which I wanted a skylight. That left the outside walls structurally redundant, except that they were required for shear; so the sides became half wall, half sliding doors, with all the corners left open, to insist on the supporting role of the big columns. That allowed for symmetry about a diagonal axis, which pleased me.

My next house, built in 1964, and still mine, which makes it the longest inhabited of my own houses, was a condominium in a group designed by Moore, Lyndon, Turnbull, Whitaker for the Sea Ranch, north of San Francisco. Here was another four-posted aedicula inside a square barn structure with a two-story object beside the four-poster which contains kitchen below, bath above, and a sleeping loft above that, in what we thought of as a giant piece of furniture and have painted several shades, first of blue, later of gray to emphasize layers of shelter in a thrillingly exposed site on the bluff above a rocky bay.

The fourth house is in New Haven, Connecticut, a workman's little house of the 1860s bought in 1966. The standard procedure then was to gut old houses, but this one was so small that gutting would have yielded about one middle-sized room. I decided therefore to poke some vertical holes and line them with double layers of painted plywood. For reasons of code and preferences, the openings were staggered; the first one just inside the front door opened to the basement; the next one, in the living room creating the only room on the entrance floor, opened up to the roof; and a third one, under the one-story rear wing, opened to the basement again, which was kitchen, dining, and study. The vertical shafts, or tubes were named Howard, Berengaria, and Ethel, and the cutouts in their plywood linings, in an early case of supergraphics, played with making fragments of shapes too grand to fit in the tiny house—my East Coast version of the giant columns in the little house in Orinda.

We bought an old brick factory in Essex, Connecticut, in 1969. The property included a Victorian gingerbread wooden predecessor of the factory, which had been storage rooms, but became my apartment. An entry building was gutted and then partly filled with an object which contained kitchen below and bath above and a big stair, all of it painted with stars and stripes to match a spirited paper napkin I had chanced on. The stairs and a bridge led to a large upper room, the main living room, big, with ancient, dark, beaded board walls and ceiling. After some tentative moves, I finally seized on an Olivetti calendar that showed a section (like an ant farm) through an Egyptian pyramid, and decided to make a pyramid cut away on the front to reveal passages full of toy figures and a train, and cut away behind to accept my bed. Once I had the pyramid, I established an interest in the U.S. dollar bill with its pyramid topped with an eye (a witch ball would do) with ANNUIT COEPTIS NOVUS ORDO SECLORUM ready to be painted on the ceiling. The U.S. currency green, which was the obvious color to paint the pyramid, came off a touch too blue—just the color of a watermelon—which led to our painting the cut sections of the pyramid green into watermelon pink. We skipped the seeds. The first act of the new tenants when I left was to sweep all this away.

I moved to Los Angeles in 1975 and found myself looking for a lot, to build again. This time I joined two other academic families from UCLA, and we bought a vacant lot 50 by 125 feet not too far from the campus for three condominiums. The site plan is based on the reasonable premise that arrival in Los Angeles is always by car, so the place for the cars should be the main plaza, not a grungy dungeon below it. My own condominium is the smallest and fit in front, climbing up over three parking spaces. The whole place inside became a giant stair with landings: guest room, bath, and hot tub are below, opening onto the patio, which doubles as a required car parking space; on the middle level is a dining place, kitchen, and tiny passage to a master bedroom and bath; on the top landing is a living room and study. But it is the stair, all visible from the entrance which serves here as the grand act, like the columns in Orinda or the tubes in New Haven, to try to make a small apartment spacious.

The cabin at Pine Mountain, in the mountains north of Los Angeles, is the same scheme as the Los Angeles house, but smaller, a flight of stairs on a very steep slope with flat spaces along the way, and open decks to the sides. The interior painting here was the special act, with widening bands of soft dark colors which owe a great deal to the similarly painted dining room at Olana, Frederick Church's house above the Hudson, north of New York.

The most recent house, in Austin, Texas, was occupied in 1985, but at this writing it isn't finished yet. Here the grand gesture is a giant ellipse in plan, which sweeps through and opens up my house, and will eventually continue outside (as chain link) to screen off a pool, thence inside the house next door, where it is suggested on a fireplace wall. The original house on the wooded site, a rather nasty wood-floor cottage of 1936, had been enlarged in 1950 by an even nastier addition, on a concrete slab. This slab became rather attractive when the asphalt tiles were pulled off, revealing a grid of mottled mastic. I thought it would be archaeologically proper to reveal both and painted a loose net of lines and circles over them, on a scale grander by far than the house deserves.

What all these houses have in common (besides their modesty, and my residing in them) is a grand gesture, and since there was no client to offend but myself, they gave eight special chances to walk the thin edge of disaster.

The next section I'm calling *Houses As the Center of the World*, for what have been lifelong preoccupations of mine: to try to make each dwelling the center of the world for its inhabitants, and then to make groups of dwellings in

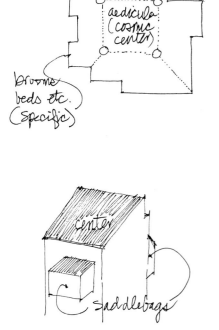

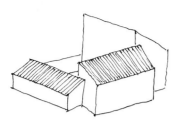

rooms around a court

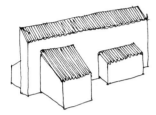

rooms along a spine

rooms in a row

which each place centers its occupants. Following an idea developed by Sir John Summerson in *Heavenly Mansions*, we found ourselves employing a four-posted aedicula which served Egyptian pharaohs and medieval saints alike as a dwelling, to enshrine (without too much confinement) contemporary inhabitants. The first clear aedicular house of mine was in 1961, for the Cyril Jobson family. Then there were two aediculas in my own little house in Orinda, and more in larger houses later. After that, there were variations: houses built, like the Bonham cabin, with mechanical spaces hung onto a high central space like saddlebags on a horse, and houses, like the Jenkins House project in Saint Helena, California, where the house is a quartet of sheds spiraled around a middle space open to the sky. The Otus House project, too, on a steep hill is built around a center, here a stair.

There are two houses for Fred and Dottie Rudolph. One is in Florida on a Gulf Coast beach where a central court is divided by a walk that leads to the Gulf, one side a jungle, the other side open and sunny, but protected from the winter breezes. The other house is in Massachusetts, and more formal, a mini Villa Rotonda on a side hill. Here a dome very literally marks a center, which in the more casual Florida house is indicated by the diagonal walkway to the open waters of the gulf.

The Burns House in Santa Monica Canyon is meant to accommodate two different worlds, built on the one hand around a fine organ, and on the other around a sybaritic swimming pool. In between is a twisting stair up to the third floor, dark and lined with books, in contrast with the bright and cheerful space around it. The exterior colors were developed by Tina Beebe, dozens of them, to make ambiguous the volumes of the house, to entice the soft light of the coastal canyon into playing around the stucco planes, and to camouflage the three-story box so it might better fit among its one-story neighbors.

The Miglio House, at the Sea Ranch, finished in 1986, is not so much at the center of the world as at the edge of it, its rooms lined up along a slope to share a view of the sea. A slight curve in the phalanx under a continuous roof gets extra height and more light and life in the living room.

The Hoffman House in Dallas, to be built in 1986, spreads relaxedly around a central plaza. Its chief gesture inside is a stepped ceiling which forms, with the two adjacent sloping roofs, a tray ceiling.

Groups of dwellings also need to make their several inhabitants feel at the center of the world (this is harder than in houses, since the inhabitants may not be known in advance). At Church Street South, in New Haven, a diverse set of public spaces—greens and streets and plazas—give at least a memorable address to each of the identical apartments. At Whitman Village in Huntington, Long Island, town houses all have their own front doors and fourplex buildings match in scale the big old houses across the street, to avoid the isolated look of a housing project. At Kresge College, at the University of California at Santa Cruz, student dwellings each claim a position along a street between faculty offices and a dining room, with a set of offhand monuments (telephone booths a laundromat) to help mark the way.

Buildings, I have insisted for a long time, can and must speak to us, which requires that we grant them freedom of speech, the chance to say things that are unimportant, even silly, so when they are grave or portentous we can tell the difference. I have taken it as my particular mission to emphasize the light and sunny moments. I'm calling some of the projects *Frivolous and Serious Play*; I think the two are not inimical, and that both can be joyous. These are all places where people are meant to have a good time. The Faculty Club at the University of California at Santa Barbara was meant to evoke the brio of the Santa Barbara of the twenties and thirties, especially its County Courthouse, alternatively exploding with joyous leaps of scale and beguiling with romantic shadows, like nothing that the past had ever created.

Lovejoy Fountain in Portland, Oregon, made in Lawrence Halprin's office in 1964, is a waterfall in the High Sierra abstracted into 5½-inch steps, brought alive with water falling and enticing people to come closer. We started on the next fountain in 1974, in a piazza for the Italian community in New Orleans, Louisiana. This time we weren't so shy about abstracting our spaces, and straightforwardly employed the map of Italy, made in steps with water running down the Po and the Arno and the Tiber, with more water forming details of the classical orders of architecture. Working on the piazza took me onto a board for the 1984 New Orleans Fair; when an issue arose about burying one-half mile of unsightly high-tension lines along the main boulevard of the fair site for 11 million dollars, I offered to stage an architectural tantrum vivid enough to take attention away from the lines for a third the amount. The gauntlet was picked up and Bill Turnbull and I architected the one-half-mile-long Wonderwall, with Leonard Salvato and Arthur Andersson, with lighting by Richard C. Peters and color by Tina Beebe, with program and "tree domes" by Kent Bloomer. The Wonderwall did seem to bring an otherwise dreary street alive. It worked, I think, because it was so complex, the record of so many overlaid agendas, that it was able to transform its part of the fair. Its antecedents from a Piranesi etching to Bernard Maybeck's Palace of Fine Arts were not necessarily recognized by anybody, nor did they need to be; people carry around images of their own, and if lots of things are present, the chances of their connecting with something are much improved.

Next to the Wonderwall we made a lagoon, with a walk alongside suggested by the Dowager Empress's walk at her summer palace near Beijing. On the lake were seven pavilions, unrelated until you stood at the Kodak point, whereupon they snapped together to resemble the main building at the 1884 New Orleans Fair. Like history, we figured, you need a point of view to make any sense of it.

Indiana Landing, in Indianapolis, was to be a place like Tivoli Gardens in Copenhagen, full of fun, and beautiful things as well. In honor of the universal grid in Indiana, we made a grid expanding from a single point—the point of entrance—so everything else grew larger and, as you proceed, was to have the eerie sensation that you were growing smaller, like Alice in Wonderland. The expanding grid is meant to open as well from urban to rural, and from the everyday to the fantastic.

A continuing theme in all our works involves being a good neighbor to what lies around, whether it be the natural world or existing buildings or peoples' memories or (especially) peoples' energies. I'm calling the buildings in this section *Fitting*. At the Sea Ranch, in 1964, our concern was to harmonize with the magnificent landscape, not to dominate it nor to hide in it, but to appear as a congenial partner. We were delighted when someone said it looked like a large wooden rock at home on its bluff.

Jones Lab at Cold Springs Harbor Laboratories on Long Island is in a great old building of the 1890s, next to Long Island Sound. Faced with the need for sensitively controlled laboratories for study of minute organisms, we made hi-tech metal containers and set them about in the large wooden hall. Outside the capsules is plenty of room to sit with other people, by a stone fireplace or near the open windows, as the season indicates.

A new art gallery and space for the art department at Williams College is in an addition to a beautiful nineteenth-century building with an octagonal rotunda. A triangle between the new galleries and the old allowed us to find new space of mysterious dimensions to connect the rectangular galleries. At Dartmouth, a new art museum, the Hood, was squeezed between Hopkins Center, a giant barrel-vaulted building which was the predecessor of the Metropolitan Opera House at Lincoln Center, and Wilson Hall, a handsome Romanesque structure of the 1880s.

Beverly Hills has a beautiful Spanish Colonial/Depression Churrigueresque city hall of the 1930s. Our Civic Center, which was selected in a competition, builds onto the old building, extending the bay spacing, the heights, and the general sense onto an axial string of elliptical open spaces, to continue into the outdoors, among some new buildings, the sense of what was already there.

In another competition, in Berlin, in the neighborhood of Karl Friedrich Schinkel's Tegel castle we adopted a cross between Schinkel's fine classical forms and the crisp warehouses of Berlin for a civic center (the library is soon to be built), a recreational center on a pleasure island, and housing by various architects; we are building some and coordinating the scheme of six others.

At the University of California at Irvine, for the first time, we took almost literally a scheme for which I have a strong fondness—three little chapels close together in front of San Gregorio Magno in Rome, designed by Flaminio Ponzio and built in 1607. The chapels have become the prototypes for three

Keep the myth up off the floor!

places where the extension department meets the public, on a little plaza across from an alumni house, also one-story high at the edge of a campus otherwise composed of big buildings. People tell me they feel much at home in the two buildings, though no one yet has ever heard of the Roman chapels.

Most important, I believe, for what may come in the future, is the enlistment of the energies and images of the people who are going to use the buildings. St. Matthew's Episcopal Church, in Pacific Palisades, California, was designed by about 150 members of the parish, with the architects in the background until we became needed to compose the extensive directions and vivid images that the members of the parish had developed. Our contract called for 67 percent acceptance of a scheme; we got an 83 percent vote and the sense, clearer than ever, that enlisting human energy is the key (or *a* key, anyhow) to making buildings in which people feel they belong.

Form, Shape, and Order in the Work of Charles Moore

Kent Bloomer

When Charles Moore referred to the word *form* in his early lectures at Yale, he often referred to Louis Kahn's particular definition. Kahn said that a form represented the most basic organizing principle in a structure, like the wheel in which something revolves around a stationary axis. The *shape* of a wheel is a particular configuration of its form, such as a water wheel with its paddles or a bicycle wheel with its treads or the mythic wheel-of-life.

Most designers who have investigated that definition agree that there are only a few truly basic spatial forms in which to organize the rooms and principal passageways within the boundaries of a building. For example, rooms can be strung out along a passageway like a railroad flat or they can encircle an open hall or they can be stacked, one upon another, like a Saxon keep in medieval England. Each of those basic forms may be shaped differently by bending the walls, employing different systems of construction, or by accommodating different conditions of light. In terms of spatial form, versus actual shape, one would describe a hemispheric dome and a shed as being alike if both were organized with rooms facing inward and surrounding a central skylit atrium.

It is important to note that some designers do not make this distinction between form and shape and prefer to use the words interchangeably. For them, the domed house would have a different "form" than the gabled house because, I suspect, they give to the word *form* a sculptural or at least "outline" character rather than a "topological" or "spatial" character. To understand Charles Moore's work, it seems essential to treat the sculptural properties in his buildings as shapes which he subordinates to the organization of a particular species of spatial form.

In addition to *shaping* form in a particular way, he also *orders* form in a particular way; which is to say that he gives certain values, meanings, or metaphors to certain parts of his architecture. Charles Moore has often quoted Kahn's preference for "served" and "servant" spaces as a strategy for ordering his architecture, and he often implies that certain spaces are less sacred and others more spectacular or more absolute. I dare say that the desire to order space by dramatizing differences of importance, by resisting homogeneity, by freely moving from the miniature to the magnificent is Moore's greatest compulsion. Indeed, it is by examining the orchestration of Charles Moore's choice of *form*, mastery of *shape*, and assignment of *order* that we are allowed a glimpse of the methods of composition and the virtuoso underpinnings of his work and style.

An examination of the formal and the methodic in Charles Moore's work cannot dismiss the mysterious, romantic, charming, and quirkish attributes that so many recognize. Charles Moore is an individual full of surprises and in possession of seemingly infinite resources and talents. Often his colleagues and students have had to exert persuasion before he would lecture about his formal strategies, because he almost always prefers to talk about the joyful and memorable responses that architecture allows.

To talk about joyfulness in an architectural school of 1965 was probably about as offbeat as discussing sex in a middle-class parlor in 1865. Joy, for many, was simply not a serious property of architecture, if a property at all! Yet for Charles Moore joy performs a principal function, which is to proclaim life. He never suggested that joy should displace the practical or the ecological requirements of building, but simply proposed that it was one of architecture's agendas.

I believe that Charles Moore has also found joy in much of the architecture he has visited over the years and instinctively wants to re-create or re-present those moments in his own work. It is well known that he has an extraordinary memory, which combined with his inexhaustible touring of the

Fig. 1

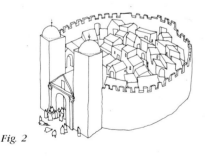

Fig. 2

world establishes a formidable body of knowledge. I can recall more than once announcing with enthusiasm that I had "discovered" a wonderful chapel in some relatively obscure corner of Mexico, only to hear him respond that he also liked it but preferred another church, around the corner, two and a half blocks up the hill, particularly because of its ornamented ceiling. He has never attempted to disguise his sources of inspiration, and many critics of his work have cited architects like Kahn, Jefferson, and Schinkel; or places in Rome, Mexico (*fig. 1*), and rural America; or buildings like Soane's house in London and a shrine in Ise as special influences. While I have heard these and other specific references many times, I have been most impressed by his freedom from dependency upon any one source, period, culture, or style. His knowledge is encyclopedic, his recollection of that knowledge immediate, and his utilization of specific recollections has always revealed a curiously uninhibited or hybrid character. Some critics and historians have suggested that his work is primarily influenced by a Roman "classicism," but how do they explain his lack of commitment to facades, monumental entries, or to the specific ornaments, harmonic ratios, and homologous geometries, which many would require as essential ingredients to that unique tradition? He may design a courtyard that recalls the Mediterranean in its qualities of light and enclosure but that may very well be overshadowed by a chimney curiously English in profile. Perhaps it is because he understands so much about architecture throughout the ages that he recognizes the hybrid (*fig. 2*) elements of so many great structures: Hawksmoor's steeples atop Greek temples, Michelangelo's Roman dome atop a Gothic nave, or Jefferson's agora-cum-Pantheon functioning as a residential complex along the greensward of a college campus.

He has taught many of us the principle that great architectural traditions and styles, like the tenets of Christianity and democracy, are not pure, immutable systems; instead they are modified and wed over time with the customs of the local population, descendants, or subsequent invaders. This mutability signifies the secret strength, not the theoretical weakness, of a living tradition. Indeed, it is one of Charles Moore's most important messages that architecture is a living tradition, very dependent upon renewal, and that the pantheon of memories resulting from pilgrimages to magnificent and humble buildings everywhere is a prerequisite that must precede any claim of invention.

Form

Many have declared that Charles Moore was among the very first to denounce modernism in post–World War II America; but any visitor to one of his buildings must be struck by the kaleidoscopic wonder of its spaces and feel the pulse of today's world in an architectural ambience that modern painting and music promise but only occasionally deliver. Yet it is true that he has opposed particular doctrines that have dominated modern architectural academics in the middle of this century, particularly those that reject the past or try to explain the great works of the past with an ideological, self-serving, and sparse vocabulary. He has also opposed the overacceptance of certain forms or formal systems that plagued the drafting rooms of the fifties and sixties, particularly the authority of gridded Cartesian coordinates and the linear regulation of form.

René Descartes himself would probably have rejected the Cartesian grid as an appropriate form to dominate the design of an actual building, because he never intended infinitely extendable coordinates to perform any more than a mathematical function suitable for deducing relationships or measuring space. He considered the coordinates to be absolutely immaterial. The grid for Descartes was a property of the brain's rational apparatus, which, in his seventeenth-century viewpoint, was separated entirely from the physical body and from any of its experiential or sensual apparatus, including sight.

Infinite extendability is never an abstract presence in the work of Charles Moore unless it is a reflection of shapes already manifested in some material context such as a street or a network of streets in a town or landscape. Recent work such as the one-half-mile-long and eleven-foot-wide Wonderwall (*37*) or the footprint of the Angel's Flight urban housing proposal for Upper Bunker Hill dramatically conform to hills. If the surrounding streets were angular or

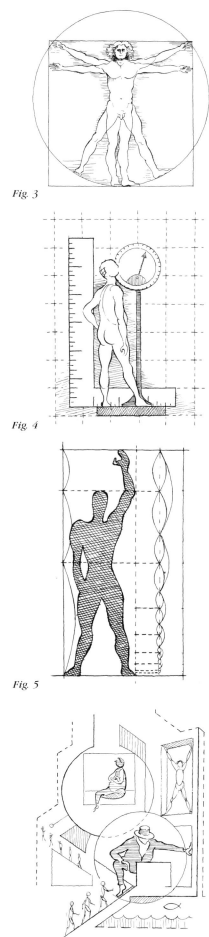

Fig. 3

Fig. 4

Fig. 5

Fig. 6

curvilinear, as they were in his Church Street South Housing (*26.2*), the buildings would probably be oriented to those configurations as well, for obvious practical or visual reasons. In no case, however, do his buildings presume to extend an arm or imaginary coordinates beyond the civilized boundaries, a gesture of infinite or aggressive extendability.

Another species of form, less loudly rejected but as visibly omitted, is the fashionable cubes, spheres, and cylinders curiously considered by designers to be the so-called "primary" geometries. While those forms do not claim an extendability, they do tend to establish a tyranny of their own. Pythagoras and his followers might be said to have regarded the cube and sphere as absolute and eternal forms capable of pervading architecture with a divine and harmonic rightness, while Charles Moore seems to regard them as somewhat impotent but not particularly evil nuisances to be carved up and served to higher callings.

The architectural form that Charles Moore values above all others may be described topologically as one dependent upon a series of concentric boundaries denoting inside-outside and establishing a centerplace or centerplaces. The centers may "geographically" be inside or outside the building. They may be focused about a point or a path and may expand or contract upward or outward, but in all cases the centers are the most powerful organizing events. His enclosing forms are rarely intruded by a strong axis of approach, and while his entrances are legible, they are visually subordinate to the continuity of the outer boundary.

Another way of describing form in the work of Charles Moore would be to illustrate its relation to the human body. The cultural historian Anthony Vidler once compared the Pythagorean form to the Cartesian form by showing a picture of the Vitruvian man (*fig. 3*), nude and heroic with limbs outstretched neatly inside concentric circle and square, next to a picture of a twentieth-century Cartesian man (*fig. 4*), naked and neurotic, standing on a doctor's scale which registered on "Cartesian" rulers his height and weight. We could add to those two illustrations the outstretched abstract silhouette of the Modular Man (*fig. 5*) by Le Corbusier who is expanding and gesturing upward next to an exponential scale.

The Pythagorean man is centered or noncentered within boundaries which are far too singular, static, and idealized for Charles Moore. The Cartesian man is ignoble and pathetic; the modular man is too abstract, a little scary and even cartesianized by the mathematical formulation of his body. Moore's man (*fig. 6*), if he were to be illustrated in a similar cosmic diagram, might be expanding, turning, or contracting, and there might be two or more men functioning in a multiconcentric grouping with some standing still and others walking, ascending, or descending. Such an illustration might suggest that his architecture simply dramatizes the conventional functions of the people who are expected to inhabit a building by identifying spaces derived basically from a functional diagram and igniting them with unusual energy. That suggestion, however, does not adequately explain the persistence of the concentric boundaries and the shifts in scale from spaces which are smaller than life to those which are larger than life. Neither does it explain the shift from the physically uninhabitable, to the conventionally inhabitable, to the apparently supernatural habitations often found at the centers. Indeed, if we are to characterize Charles Moore as a member of the humanist tradition, we might understand that his body-centered architecture forms a collective "body-spirit" with characteristics ranging from the divine and devilish to the commonplace, and derived from an architect's mind as rich in human spirit as it is in recalling architectural places.

Important architectural theorists in the nineteenth and twentieth centuries argued that architectural form should be determined by the geometries essential to engineering, expressed by the tectonic details of physical structure. After the First World War some of those theories, such as those proclaimed by the authors of the International Style, were to be "modernized" to include an expression of the regularities and economies of mass production. Those theorists argued that the machine was liberating man from the social tyrannies of the past and was therefore a more benevolent image in architecture than the expression of man's figural self. Charles Moore has always been sympathetic with the pragmatics of construction, although for him the dramatic or exclusive expressions of construction or structural

systems do not necessarily provide better economy or superior expressions of our age than conventional construction. He recognized that the two-by-four, a sheet of plywood, and a nail are not only extremely economic units of production but constitute a remarkably strong system that is practical in the hands of the ordinary builder and capable of adopting many shapes. Given a choice of engineer, he usually selects one with the greatest understanding of conventional construction and the most common sense. Although his principal concerns in architecture have been inclined toward human choreography and expressions of the natural environment, he is probably more responsible than any other architectural educator during the sixties and seventies for promoting a measure of craftsmanship and a love of building among his students by requiring that they collectively design and build a small public building in their first year of architecture school. For many of these students those experiences in basic technology marked the beginning of their careers and the beginning of their style as architects. His own expressions of construction and technology have not been limited to walls, posts, and brackets, but also include the designs of solar-heating equipment, low-voltage and neon lighting systems, and water devices suitable for bathing, washing, meditating, or cooling down. A look at the tentlike beamed ceiling in the Jobson House (**11.11**) or the Slater House (*fig. 7*), or at the hot-water tank and belvedere commanding the interior of the Barber House, reveals a relaxed and skillful expression of technological realities, which he honors as helpful and economic codeterminants of his architectural form.

Shape

Although Charles Moore rejected certain prevailing doctrines associated with modernism, his mastery at shape-making reflects a strikingly modern sensibility. His shapes are taut, spatially graphic, and abstract. They are abstract at least in the sense in which his figures subliminally represent certain human gestures, natural forces, or very basic shapes traditionally found in architecture, as well as shapes commonly perceived in the landscape.

The landscape is the most powerful determinant in the shaping of the edges and profiles of his buildings. Early works like the Sea Ranch (**48.13,14**) and the Lovejoy fountain (**33.2**) correspond figuratively to the contours of hills and waterfalls. The embanked profile of the St. Simons Island condominium, Xanadune, echoes the shapes of surrounding dunes (**29.2**). The House Near New York embodies the romantic and more complex, picturesque massing of the mythical English country house, which itself evolved over time from responses to multiple views and the cragginess of hillsides and real or imagined rock outcroppings.

Viewed from a distance, his smallest buildings are perceived as simple solid shapes basically rectangular in plan with pyramidal roofs like the Moore House in Orinda (**2.2**) or central sheds surrounded by "saddlebags" or buttressing subsidiary sheds like those in the Johnson (*fig. 8*), Jobson (**11.4**), Bonham (**12.1**), and Karas houses. As the buildings increase in size and programmatic complexity, the basic shapes do not inflate in the Roman manner but instead divide into a larger number of the discrete solid shapes visible in the Sea Ranch and Burns House (**18.1**). They are often roofed with single sheds, loosely oriented and increasing in size toward the center of a composition, punctuated at the highest points by ridges or smokestacks or belvederes. The wooden textures and colors of the siding and roofing are similar and joined by eaves elements in which both the fascia and soffit are minimal (*fig. 9*). The result is the perception of solid prismatic shapes rather than planar walls capped by overhanging roof shapes. With the exception of the very largest of structures, like the Turtle Creek Condominiums, neither horizontal bandcourses nor vertical mouldings are employed as compositional elements to divide the surface continuity from grade to eaves. Conspicuously absent is the rigorous bilateral symmetry, the boxiness, the gable ends, and the wind of the classical Eastern American house. Clustered, asymmetric, explicitly nonfrontal, and rarely pretentious in the sizing of the individual shapes, the compositions seem more indebted to villages and farms than palaces.

Charles Moore's employment of purely defined prismatic shapes is typically modern, but his manipulation of them is unique. The purity of the

Fig. 10. MLTW
Tempchin House
Bethesda, Maryland
1968, exterior
(Photograph courtesy Centerbrook)

solid shapes is reiterated in the taut, geometrically simple and minimally trimmed openings in the walls. The window glass in most of his work is set as nearly as possible in the plane of the exterior wall surface. Mullions are minimal and apparently installed as concessions to the practical requirement of the moveable sash, rather than as important compositional elements. In the many instances in which the openings are voids without glass, the framing members virtually disappear and the shapes of the voids correspond in size and proportion to the windows and doors. Although the openings are generally regarded as abstractions of "conventional" shapes, such as window, door, balcony, and gate, Moore's method of abstracting them delivers ambivalent readings. That ambivalence is particularly visible in the openings in the terrace side of the long gallery (*fig. 10*) connecting the two ends of the Tempchin House. Do those openings represent a row of doorways cut out of a wall, or are they an arcade of flattened columns? Why do the two rows have different rhythms of spacing? Clearly Moore is a master at striking the balance between figure and ground in which at one moment the dominant shapes are windows and doors on a wall and at another the dominant figure is a continuous wall with the openings serving as cutouts. That tendency to compose multiple readings explains the positioning of the glass on the surface plane of the wall from which the opening is cut, where at one moment the window is a hole in the wall and at another, a continuation of the opaque wall expressing a wall virtually without openings. This strategy recognizes both the transparency and the solidity of glass.

Figure-ground and solid-void manipulations may conjure alternate images over time and provide the designer with the power to make multiple references, instead of subordinating the composition once and for all to a dominating visual shape. If, for example, the windows, doors, walls, and columns were subordinated to the shape of a regular grid, the grid might prevail to the extent that the subordinate shapes would become compositionally impotent. Moore's compositional strategies provide more choices for the viewer; thus on one level of perception his cutout shapes represent architectural elements taken from the grammar of construction. On another level, they represent conventional windows and doors. On still another, they are autonomous graphic shapes serving the total composition. In the Moore, Rogger, Hofflander Condominium (*6.4*) some of the readings are less conventional: the rotating cutouts seem to represent windows, half-arches, buttresses, and the spokes of a giant wheel, at different moments of perception.

The outer boundaries of his buildings are generally the lowest in height as well as the "hardest" in shape, like the crusty surface of a geode. Because his buildings are rarely set within formal or "walled" yards, the building boundary represents the first transiton from the landscape to a civilized interior space. If a piece of the outer boundary is chipped away, as it is on the terrace side of the Faculty Club (*34.5*) or the front of the Larson House, a second boundary may be revealed and often those secondary boundaries are tautly articulated. Further within, additional walled boundaries may be established to encircle the center. At the Faculty Club, the innermost boundary is a high-stepped arcade facing inward to an open court.

In the Tempchin House, the culminating centerplace is not a courtyard but a stairwell dramatically extending the long exterior gallery connecting the residence to the garage. Like a courtyard, the stairwell is enclosed by side walls composed with rectangular voids. The voids signify windows, but more significantly, they suggest walls larger than the section of the house they occupy, by incorporating openings which seem to extend through the ceiling. The apparent extension through the ceiling does more than proclaim that there is space and a bay above the body of the house. It provides a presence which is larger than life or at least the habitable "life" of the house and which begins to merge in size and shape with the trees outside.

Almost all of the shapes in the plans, sections, surfaces, and voids of Charles Moore's architecture seem to respond to a motion striving at once to contain the multiple forces of the landscape and the activities of the program and ascertain a firm and tranquil centerplace like the eye of a storm. Although they produce a sensation of encirclement and helical ascent, forces also found in storms, curved lines or curved surfaces are seldom employed. There are spectacular exceptions, like the pool and peristyle of the Piazza d'Italia (*35.9*),

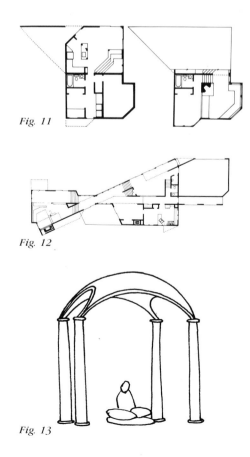

Fig. 11

Fig. 12

Fig. 13

the convex facade of the Rodes House, and the sequence of elliptical courtyards in the Beverly Hills Civic Center (**55**). But more often, the buildings are shaped from fundamentally rectangular plans, the corners of which are often carved away with diagonals. In the extreme case of the Klotz House, the pervading diagonals (**15.5,6,7**) form enclosures which are more cylindrical than square. In the plan of the Burns House, the diagonals are incorporated more sparingly, with several inflections at the key points of entry, alcove, and pool wall. In the Shinefield House (*fig. 11*), the simple rotation of the fireplace and the entry steps and the parallel 45-degree cutting of the two diagonally opposite corners act in unison to confirm the center. In the Larson House, where the virtual center is in front of the building, there are two wings projecting at 45-degree angles from either side of the entrance, revealing an interior space which doubles as a grand facade. The plan for the St. Simons Island condominium (**29.1**), by rotating the principal passageways of the entrance and diagonal walk, a strategy more classically developed in the Beverly Hills Civic Center, dynamically centers the entire composition with streetscapes rather than wallshapes.

The Stern House (*fig. 12*) is probably the most extreme instance of two passageways intersecting to establish a horizontally dynamic and volumetrically low centerplace. Movement from the center upwards toward the edges is a reversal of Moore's convention. It is dramatized by a sequence of windows stepping upwards toward the outside, unlike stepped windows rising toward the center. An example of the latter is found in the House near New York or the south wing of the cancer research facility in Cold Spring Harbor (**49.1,2**).

The many-faceted, three-dimensional manipulations of shape reveal the deft hand of a virtuoso of space, who spins a web and endows it at one moment with altogether ordinary spaces, and at another with towering enclosures bathed in a dazzling world of light and shadow that both animates the ordinary with, and lends the spectacular, extraordinary moments of repose.

Order

The least ordered spatial arrangement in a house would be one in which all the rooms were identical. A slightly more ordered condition might develop from a large single room like a loft in which the inhabitants could at least shuffle themselves and their furniture around as they wished. A higher order could be achieved if the inhabitants unanimously agreed that they wanted three bedrooms, bath, a kitchen, a parlor, and a dining room and all of those rooms were efficiently related in a plan. None of these schemes, however, is constituted to provide an architectural order between the inhabitants' house and the world at large.

An order which includes the world must have a public dimension as well as a sacred dimension, like a shrine (*fig. 13*) located inside a grove of trees on a respected hillside facing east. If a shrine could be invested with an appropriate amount of privacy, community, comfort, and utility, it would probably deliver the greatest amount of architectural order.

Some architects believe that the sacred order in building is articulated by incorporating certain geometries which they claim are eternal and immutable. Charles Moore, I suspect, is far too earthbound for that, honoring instead the temporal world with its seasons and particular places. His icons are neither mystical nor esoteric. If I were to name at least four of them, they would be Earth, Water, Fire, and Air. No other architect in recent times has given more architectural order to these elements by expressing them within the realm of ordinary, domestic, and public buildings.

His homage to the elements of earth is evident in the shaped and crystalline responses to the landscape both inside and outside his buildings. The geodetic and naturally textured materials of his buildings at once engage the profiles and colors of nature and brace against the environment, by turning inward to contain and civilize portions of earth, water, fire, and air.

Charles Moore used to tell his students about a Japanese principle in which it was supposed that one could more clearly see and comprehend a body of water in the distant landscape if there were a bowl of water on a table facing the view. The architectural act of possessing and claiming the element of water is completed with magnificence in his Orinda House by placing a

Fig. 14

Fig. 15

Fig. 16

Fig. 17

bathtub (*2.4*) literally within a shrine. Water served subsequently as the architectural centerplace in the swimming pools of the Burns House (*18.1*) and the St. Simons Island project (*29.1*), and was proposed as the content of one of the three grand elliptical courtyards in the Beverly Hills Civic Center (*55.9,10*). At Kresge College a mere draincover (*fig. 14*) becomes the focal point within the central courtyard, while in the forty-acre urban design for Tegel Harbor in West Berlin, water dominates by invading the landscape with lakes and canals, leaving behind an island in the shape of a riverboat. The Piazza d'Italia is a water extravaganza representing in microcosm the Po, the Arno, and the Tiber pouring into the Mediterranean Sea. In the New Orleans World's Fair, the Wonderwall (*37*) was to include a half-mile-long chain of fountains, while nearby the Theme Building emerged from an artificial lake which provided a spectacular and immense center to a cramped fairground.

The element of fire is the most conservatively treated of the four elements, as illustrated by the treelike hearth standing tentatively outside the center of the treelike peristyle within the Johnson House (*fig. 15*). In his earliest buildings, chimneys barely appeared; but over time, the fireplace became more monumental, with dominant chimneys like the one at the Faculty Club (*34.3*) or multiple chimneys like those of the House near New York (*fig. 16*) and the Licht House, all derived from Stratford, the Lee house in Virginia.

It is significant that Charles Moore does not design empty space, a condition that he often referred to as representing "no place." If he is not using space to choreograph human movement and settlement, he is using it to choreograph light and air. His colleague Donlyn Lyndon is often quoted for having proposed that "myths belong on the ceiling," and in many of Charles Moore's centerplaces, a mythic body of air hovers above and expands through the windowed inner boundaries as though the world had turned inside out. This containment of the "sky" may be sensed in the interior towers of his house in New Haven, or the windowed walls in the stairwells of the Tempchin House. It is similarly found in the hall (*fig. 17*) of the Psychoanalytic Associates Building, and the Airslie House at Cold Spring Harbor. Whether it is night or day, the bouncing and reflected light in the inverted cascades of space seem to illuminate an elemental presence.

Charles Moore seldom used the word *space* in the sixties and seventies. Today he refers to space more frequently, and that word is used by most architects when they describe the particular strengths of his work. *Space*, however, has many meanings; to me the tall, white, overhead "places" are pieces of the world captured and animated. They are the sky, imaginary clearings in the forest, or small streets in Mexico with earth underfoot and air above.

The presence of the environment inside Charles Moore's architecture distinguishes his work from a hard-core humanism in which nature is walled out, in order to pay man the greatest possible attention. This presence, therefore, dismisses the faith of the rationalists who argue that architecture should become a geometric or machinelike substitute for an otherwise unsettling and, at best, romantic vision of nature. It is precisely the act of representing the environment in the order of his architecture, rather than treating the "outside" as an entity to be stared at through a picture window, that endows his work with visions of an American legend. Indeed, the work can be unsettling because it harbors the restless, exploratory nature of the American psyche with a choreography in which the elements, vistas, and enclosures are often surprise encounters to be discovered after walking up, down, and around a potential centerplace. His paths ultimately lead to clear places of repose, but the journey is along loosely prescribed routes with uncertain edges. Choices of path, dramatic arrivals, and the onward motion record both the passage of American life and the ambiguity between the inside-outside or town-country character of the places in which Americans choose to settle or camp. Although he has been generously informed by his memories of world architecture, he has been more powerfully informed by his own culture, particularly the more mythologically Western American sensibility of his childhood.

I believe he has created a style as vivid and recognizable as that of Frank Lloyd Wright or H. H. Richardson before him. Even more than those of his antecedents, however, his may be a style that is very difficult to mimic or perpetuate intact unless we understand and grant the content and strategy of its order. It is an order that is essentially responsive and only secondarily formal. His knowledge of the architectural forms and shapes from history is immense, but recollections are employed only in an episodic, abstract, and hybrid manner, as the necessary ornaments and grammar in the ordering of specific places. The minimum requirements for working within his style would include a thorough knowledge of architectural history, the experiences gained from touring distinguished and vernacular sites, the love of specific places, a practical sense of construction, a knowledge of contemporary conventions of design, a dislike of frozen or assertive conventions, close collaboration with colleagues, wonderful clients, a brilliant imagination, and the talent to coherently distill so large an agenda. That combination necessarily establishes a profoundly modern style of process always dependent upon influences and destined to change over time.

Spirit Play

Donlyn Lyndon

The secret of Charles W. Moore's success, fame, influence, and notoriety is very simple. He's smarter than most everybody else. And more energetic. His energy is not displayed in biceps or spartan abstentions from leisure or uncommon feats of endurance (unless you count his tolerance for airplanes). It is much more subtle than that, difficult to discern without close attention, and related to his smarts. His mind never idles, never moves aside into aimless stalling for time. He's always there—scheming, comparing, remembering, countering, and second-guessing, imagining what if... and testing the results.

All this would not lead to significant architecture, or to any architecture at all, if it were not encased in images. But it is. Charles Moore's mind works its way through a wide array of stunningly specific forms, weaving them into the fabric of his conversation, casting them like catalysts into a brew of uncertain aspirations in order to precipitate design possibilities.

One of the by-products of such incessant imagining is an extraordinary form of self-confidence, self-confidence that is based in the certainty that another scheme is always possible, or that circumstances and adversities can always be circumvented, if not subsumed.

It is this which makes him, by all accounts, a good listener. He can afford to be, because he is certain that whatever he hears he can deal with. He differs from most of his peers and predecessors in his willingness to accommodate diverse motivations and interests, to wander into unfamiliar territory and make it his own. This is the self-confidence at work: if the presumptions going into a situation don't fit, then he fully expects that a new set will be called forth and that everyone will come out smiling.

It's hard today, I suppose, to recognize that this freely exploratory mode was once a radical position, hard to call forth the temper of the late fifties when dogma was the central concern of many architects. At that time Alcoa released a long-playing record of the words of the great masters of architecture and Ludwig Mies van der Rohe's deep guttural voice intoned the summarizing phrase, "I do not want to be interesting, I want to be good."

The sound of that phrase still rolls around in the brain. In Charles Moore's brain too. It was not coincidental that a few years ago he declaimed to an ACSA Teacher's Seminar at Cranbrook that the architect has a *responsibility* to be interesting. His phrasing was more insistent than normal, and though the sound of it was not memorable, the shock of it remains so. Interesting? We had raised our banners to answer to more serious endeavors than architects who simply tried to be "interesting." Was Moore falling prey to the celebrity hype that surrounds him? Was he, after all, becoming a purveyor of sideshows just as his detractors have often maintained? More recently, when he was queried regarding the carefully detailed planning in the Oceanside Civic Center competition scheme, he replied, albeit winsomely, "I guess we're neo-Functionalists."

How does it go together? What binds the disparate witticisms and the varied images into a body of work? Many things, obviously, but for my purposes it is an insistent desire to see evidenced in his surroundings the presence of an indwelling spirit. He wishes ever to bring things to life—to make not only his own sensibilities but the things around him follow Walter Pater's injunction "to burn always with this hard gemlike flame." The dull, the stupid, the inert are Charles Moore's nemeses.

Throughout his professional career Moore has shown a predilection toward images and forms that convey at once the operation of a set of rules and the dynamics of forces almost out of control, that are teetering on the edge of dissolution. Take a dripping ice-cream cone, for instance—bizarre food for the architectural imagination, surely, but there it all is: the cone, certainly legitimate fodder for architects, the gleaming dome of its top likewise, and both owe their incarnation in ice cream and waffled dough to the exigencies

Fig. 1. Oceanside Civic Center
Oceanside, California
1986, auto court entry
Urban Innovations Group

Fig. 2. Oceanside Civic Center
1986, plan, ground floor

Fig. 3. Oceanside Civic Center
1986, perspective, view from Third and Hill
streets

Fig. 1

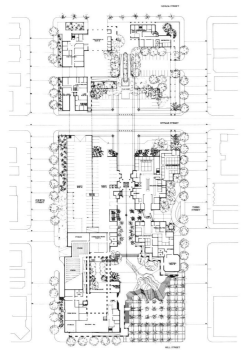

Fig. 2

Fig. 3

of industrial process. But it's melting . . . the ice cream is breaking its bonds to the imposed imagination of industrial geometry and seeking a form of its own, one that requires adroit juggling by the hand of the holder. It is a moment when reason, industry, natural process, and manual dexterity are in tenuous balance—the moment in which Charles Moore likes to dwell. An overextended interpretation, you say? Perhaps. Nevertheless, it was an oft-repeated simile in the old days, and it takes just a little looking among Moore's work to find forms "dripping" from the roof—usually bay windows.

The erosion motif has similar attributes; that is to say, it simulates the physical evidence of interacting forces to create a pattern so complex and so sensitive to the nuances of the specific situation that each is a unique instance. The pattern serves both as a model and as a source of form to be literally represented in fountains and paving (see Copley Square [39.1,2] and Oceanside [figs. 1–3], both "graced" as in musical composition by the overlay of rivulets that trace a continuity between one segment of the composition and another). Water itself, which looms so large in the Charles Moore legend, is both of the moment and of eternity, ephemeral and enduring; water deforms and changes things through time. It evaporates, condenses, splatters, and collects. So too, it would seem, does the playful spirit, leaving its trace in inert matter, despite the odds.

Not only natural systems and whimsical formulations but geometric rules as well are adopted for the guidance of spirited form. The rules may vary from project to project, but there is bound to be a set that is imposed on the situation in order to let the operations of the design game be traced (and, incidentally, to facilitate collaboration). Various rule makers have been pressed into service: Kahn and Palladio mostly, the classical more generally, the baroque more specifically, Wright vaguely, and Gill fleetingly. Note, however, that in *Ah Mediterranean!*, a publication of the Center for the Study of American Architecture at the University of Texas at Austin, there is a string of articles, many of which Moore coauthored. These go off in search of the true significance and usefulness of classical forms, while Charles Moore's editorial ends with the suggestion that "So far, the only sure bets are the plants of the garden, which can confirm linguistic redress—full of memories and associations, even classical ones—with realness (how could a living thing not be real?) . . . if we could only get our architecture to do that." This is not just an artful dodge away from the present fetishistic concern with classicism, but an entirely consistent shift of attention from the confines of dogma (linguistic now, but no less guttural) to the lived reality of flickering shadows, aromatic breezes, and trickling water. These are the romantic emblems of energies that flow around all built works, classical or otherwise. Architecture exists in a world that can be apprehended by the senses and Moore would have us remember that, when others would bid us forget.

Gill's rule making, simple as it was, and embedded in his work, was adopted by Moore and his collaborators for the Oceanside Civic Center competition. The choice was not arbitrary, since the competition terms made much of the existence on the site of a fire station by Irving Gill (much renovated) that formed one part of an intended civic center that Gill had planned in the 1930s. Most of the competitors were mesmerized by the problem of the fire station itself—the problem being to accede either to the wishes of the Fire Department or to those of the preservationists. Most teams found some way or other to punt; they left the building but relocated the Fire Department or they moved the building or they divorced it from their scheme so that citizens' groups could battle it out. Only Moore's group went beyond the relic to what it might presage—an entire civic center complex enclosing a garden, with white walls articulated by arched shadows and modest windows, an interweaving of room-sized masses and long terraced courtyards, a flat-roofed, lumpy, foliage-enlivened quadrangle. Actually, a drawing by Gill of the intended scheme was included in the material given the competitors.

Moore's scheme works within these parameters, but extends them, not only in size but in scope. The buildings are bigger as they were required to be; the courts are perhaps harder on the whole than those of Gill's, but then Gill hadn't grasped the havoc the automobile would bring to Oceanside. Moore's great entry court, embellished with ceremonial arrival motifs, absorbs the fact of the automobile within the heart of the complex. Operationally the scheme

*Fig. 4. Beverly Hills Civic Center
Beverly Hills, California
1982–, model from northwest
Urban Innovations Group*

brings Gill's vision into the present. And then, naturally, Moore does it one better, creating a great open-air hierarchical center that is to this complex what the great open arch of the Santa Barbara Courthouse is to that favored Moore reference. Except that here, for giddy emphasis the inside of this center is treated to a dripping pattern of hotly colored tiles descending in layers from the square, open crown at the top. He creates an outdoor room surrounded by raspberry, tangerine, and lemon ice-cream cones, if you will, marked at its center by four gilded palmlike *torchères*.

Significantly, the jury, while enthusiastic about the scheme (as were the majority of "citizen input" statements), had some real difficulty deciding whether the scheme was "Gillish" or "Moore-ish." A local newspaper editorial, on the other hand, unhesitatingly, declared it to be neoclassical.

The Oceanside competition entry was, like so many of Charles Moore's efforts, a collaboration. Who knows who had what hand in what? As always, it is unclear. Obviously many people worked on it, including a number of former students and Edgardo Contini, who introduced a sense of serene factuality into the project, as he had in the earlier Beverly Hills City Hall complex. Here, as elsewhere, the traces of all those hands meld into the common fabric and Charles Moore's willful signature strokes characterize the place. Why? Because they're uncommonly vivid and usually just sufficiently distorted, enough outside the bounds of the commonplace, that they stand alone, and defy emulation.

One much admired feature of the Oceanside scheme, for instance, is a square palm grove set in a pond at the most important corner of the complex. Did Charles Moore place the trees there? Or did they simply escape from his drawing *The Spaniards Introduce Palm Trees to Santa Catalina Island*, in which clusters of palms descend from the sky in great saucers suspended from what appear to be flying turtles. This "exotica ex machina" is a fantasy all too real to be discarded: the trees are also like the black helicopters of the Hunter Liggett Military Reservation hovering over the hills that shape the approach to Mission San Antonio de Padua; they are also like the breezy can-do of six-story palm trees being set into place on the blank side wall of a Marina condominium in Venice, California. Did Charles place those palms on the corner in Oceanside or did the turtles? Does it matter? Look carefully at the drawing. Mountains become temples which become waterfalls which become reflections which become barges which become pavilions which become stairs. Each part melts into the next; all burn with an energy that renders their distinctness less pronounced than their relationships. I'll wager that in the next scheme for Oceanside, the palms, once landed, will have spread.

It has often been observed that Charles is an incessant collaborator, and that yet, paradoxically, the results always bear his mark. Once again, it is the intensity of attention that brings it off, and the commitment to getting it right. He listens well: he generously absorbs ideas, giving credits and remonstrances where they are due (or effective). What is singular about working with Charles is that he never demurs. He either adopts, one-ups, or fights with whimsical bitterness each design move ventured, in a swirling cloud of proposals and counterproposals that surround the drafting table. But it's totally serious play, and he does not defer—tantrums maybe, rueful abdication, no. Only some years later may his collaborators notice that it was Charles who usually drew the plan, who retained the most generative drawing at his fingertips. He has an uncanny tolerance for kibitzers, drawing, erasing, and redrawing before their blinking eyes. Where others are distracted, Charles is stimulated. Why? Because this moment, too, will pass, and somewhere down the line a different place will be built and it will be one bit more careful, one bit more tested than had the kibitzer simply been ignored.

Perhaps it would be pertinent to recount my most recent collaborative venture with Charles Moore, the Copley Square competition entry. Charles and I have thought together about Copley Square off and on since the early 1960s, when MLTW was young. We were jointly teaching a course on the History of Oriental Architecture at U.C. Berkeley and wondering how one might best teach American Architecture. Copley Square, with Trinity Church on one side and the Boston Public Library on the other and lesser lights all around, could constitute all by itself, we speculated, a marvelous basis for a course on American Architecture, if we were ever to give one. As it happens, we never did (though I have written about the Square in *The City Observed: Boston*, and in an issue of the *Journal of Architectural Education*, edited by Charles Moore and Wayne Attoe, in the essay "How Not to Teach Architectural History"). It seemed necessary, then, that we should try our hand at the recent competition to redesign once again Copley Square's problematic middle.

Scheduling being what it was, we decided to do it mostly by telephone and to ask Bill Turnbull and Bill Hersey to join us. In the end, we four and Marvin Buchanan, Alice Wingwall, and Chris Noll each had a significant finger in the pie. The work proceeded fitfully, in my office, with a gradual build-up of historical and geometric overlays modified by phone calls to discuss the bases for an approach and the relative advantages of certain notions. Some of these were borrowing for one corner of the site a Colossal Foot fountain that Charles and Alice Wingwall once schemed for a plaza in Urbino, Italy; or constructing a "Cairn of the Unaccomplished," suggested by an eloquent phrase I read in turn-of-the-century proceedings of a scientific society publication sitting on the bookshelves of a bar in the Copley Plaza Hotel; or creating a great Swan Boat sculpture instead. Meanwhile, the plan shapes were simplified and made more elegant through penciled exchanges with William Turnbull during critique sessions at unspeakably early hours in the morning. As the deadline neared, the project outlines were made firm, Bill Hersey's wonderful perspective drawings were laid out, and the stage was set for a final charette. Charles joined us for an intense day of modifications and reconstruction.

The events of that day are too complex to remember, but the final presentation became bolder in configuration. A great summer awning appeared that partially blocks views of Trinity Church. Rivulets of water that faintly recall the original mud flats of the area escaped their contained channels to one side of the square and trickled picturesquely through the paving. The sculpted mythological figures anticipated as a marker on one corner moved to the center and proliferated into a clutch of fauna from the vanished mud flats, sporting about beneath a gigantic plume of water spouting from the exact spot once proposed by Charles McKim for a similar fountain—sans fauna. Our mythological fauna (including, in truth, swans from the Boston Public Garden and turtles that arrived by airplane) never got quite right in the scheme, arriving, as they did, a bit late. As they emerged in the discussion, it was intended that they be larger than finally depicted and less literal, fused into aedicular pavilions to shelter them from the descending splash.

All this was taking place in an office a few blocks down the street from the little defunct railroad station in which the firm of Moore, Lyndon, Turnbull, Whitaker had been lodged some twenty-odd years ago. Then was not so very much different, but it was then every day, not just one day, and Whitaker was here, not in Chicago. There was more Kahn-based geometry on the drawing boards we gathered around, more Chinese landscape painting in the back of our minds, less space, and somewhat less furniture; there were more straight laces in my response, and a repartee more biting, with mock jibes cutting so close to the bone that they would set uninitiated observers fleeing from the room. The laying on of many hands, however, the whirling, pointed fantasies, the disciplined, supple lines flowing from Turnbull's fingers, and the easy, subtly directed, "let's try this next" flow of ideas across the table were the same.

The language of these collaborative discussions—full of puns, allusions, and playful similes—is puzzling to outsiders. There is an abundance of action language: forms "slip" and "slide," "wiggle," "wind," "drift," "hover," "melt," even "schlurp" into one another. (During one unfortunate period, they were said to "collide" a lot.) Roofs, passages, and stairs are the elements that most often are called upon to perform these operations. Passages and stairs are surrogates for, and directors of, the human inhabitants' kinesthetic experience of the place. Roofs because they are the characterizing form for many small buildings. They determine silhouette, which forms the first ideogram of the building from a distance. They also lend themselves to rules; roof slope can be a stern taskmaster, determining the width and disposition of spaces and dictating proximities and orientation. The sloping roof is already in action and the length and reach of its slope can become a means for absorbing disparate elements under a single form, or for accommodating and highlighting the particulars. In the Jobson and Johnson houses (*11.3,4,5,6; Bloomer, fig. 8*),

Xanadune (*29.2,7,8*), or the complex in Kuhio Shores, Hawaii, a simple memorable roof form is stretched out or eroded to accommodate particulars while retaining the suggestive clarity and familiarity of the basic volume.

With a very broad brush architecture can be swept into two piles, one characterized by roofs and one by walls. The architecture of roofs (mostly medieval or domestic) is approached as something to imagine being inside of; the architecture of walls (for the most part of urban or institutional derivation and large) is meant to be looked at, to be admired or suffered as an outsider. Most of Moore's work is of the former ilk, naturally so, since much of it is residential; the house is seen as a realm of private exploration and memory made alive by its inhabitants. The major works to be found in the wall pile are projects that create their own public realm: Kresge College (*27.4,5,7*), Church Street South (*26.3*) and a few public buildings, including Oceanside, Beverly Hills (*55*), and, most significantly, Piazza d'Italia (*35.7,8*). In all these, the walls are penetrable; they have porches and recesses and places to dwell, outside as well as inside. They too are places where the imagination and the body may jointly explore. They are never made of simple seals separating outside from in, with a lavish display on the surface. Even the Wonderwall in New Orleans was not a dividing screen on which to see a dispassionately proportioned series of shapes, but a lodging for innumerable fantasies of inhabitation... opportunities to imagine and enjoy being there.

Architecture in which Moore has played a part is lived in, walked through, climbed over, squeezed between, and nestled under; it is not simply looked at and argued over, or tested for ideological purity.

Too little attention has been paid to the very great role that Charles has played as educator. Most of his collaborators are former students, Turnbull and myself among them, Ruble, Yudell, Grover, Harper, Simon, Floyd, Oliver, Buchanan, and Allen as well. Many of us have also made major commitments to architectural education: Robert Harris, William Mitchell, Ron Filson, and Richard Whitaker, to name a few who currently hold influential positions. At Princeton, while working on his Ph.D., Charles was mentor to student and peers alike and played a dominant role in the ethos that developed there in the late fifties. At Berkeley he was quickly made chairman and presided over what many still consider to have been its golden age, a period when Berkeley led the way in opening the doors of architecture to a wider range of interests, techniques, and skills than had yet found their way into academic drafting rooms. At Yale, as chairman, then dean, he was confronted and surrounded by the turmoil of the late sixties and through it all kept students engaged in reality while ameliorating their conflicts with the administration. He would don mud boots to lead students in the actual construction of community structures in Appalachia and pin stripes for dinner with Kingman Brewster. When the excitement was over and a subsequent generation of students settled into more routine concerns for job prospects, Charles moved back to California, this time without administrative responsibility but with enormous influence at U.C.L.A.

More recently still, as a new generation of dogmatists struggles for center stage in academia, Charles has moved on to the University of Texas, where an endowed professorship allows him to exercise freely his favored role of conspirator in the opening of minds and eyes to the richness of a world where form, action, and aspiration are linked, but not frozen, where the spirit dwells in tangible, often unexpected, places. At Texas, with a selected group of advanced graduate students and extensive opportunity for field trips, Charles can engage in his most effective form of teaching—being on the site, in place, pointing, enthusing, chuckling and sneering; hosting an investigation of the experiences provided by all manner of works that escape official discussion. Such teaching, it should be noted, does not fit well in lecture slots and syllabi. It requires an altogether different level of personal commitment and involvement than is asked of or given by those who parcel their efforts conventionally.

There are, in my observation, two essential strategies in Charles Moore's teaching of studio design: blessing and extending. Charles has a keen eye for talent and is a great and generous encourager. He is so constantly on the alert, so persistently involved in making judgments, expressing likes and dislikes with considered abandon, that one believes in his encouragement. He nevertheless gives his encouragement for what might be, not for what is. The characteristic mode of critique is to extend the reach of some design move already taken; often to take some segment of an idea already spawned and caricature it, leap with it to a position so far beyond the students' initial grasp, so apparently absurd, that the student following later and with more prudent steps can find ground of his own to claim, ground that was previously unattainable.

All this is aided by an extraordinary memory. A man whose mind has stored, for the fun of it, Latin conjugations and popular songs from the forties has little trouble conjuring up from his wide-ranging travel and study likenesses or similes for what a place might become—these likenesses that feed the imagination with direction even as the specifics of the problem are being enumerated and digested; likenesses that, once their purpose has been served, are likely to be submerged or dropped when new insights prevail.

A number of years spent studying and teaching the History of Architecture established Moore's basic store of images, which have been supplemented in almost every case by visits to the places in question. An even greater energy, however, has been spent in seeking out and bringing to attention a wide array of vernacular forms and neglected genres, Andalusian and Japanese farmhouses, town houses in Cairo, ghost towns in Colorado, the sturdy porched houses of Michigan and the Midwest, superbly eccentric courthouses in Texas, the simple spare structures to be found in California fields, and half-mad nineteenth-century exuberances wherever they are to be found, even the Madonna Inn, and Disneyland. These and more redolent places such as the Alhambra and Hadrian's Villa inhabit his articles, lectures, and conversation, not as simple talismans, but as active possibilities to be explored, along with melting ice-cream cones, Russian Easter eggs, the economies of compact utility layouts and windows so placed that they can be easily washed. The vernacular bears a special place in this lexicon for several reasons, not the least of them being that it is the architecture with which he grew up in Michigan, Florida, and California. The vernacular architecture that captures our attention under Moore's tutelage tends to be especially spirited, either in defiance or in ignorance of established design conventions. More commonly still, it is possessed of a vision that outreaches the materials at hand and requires some judicious improvisation. In all three cases, the indefatigable spirit triumphs. What's needed and wished for is built no matter what; and fit to the specific situation at hand.

Charles Moore's commitment to the particular and the specific, to the uniquely formed, is a part of his search for the spirited. That which is alive adjusts and responds. A tree, for instance, adopts a specific configuration which is uniquely a function of the forces and situations to which it has been subjected, by which its growth has been informed. Collaboration is for Charles a way of being more fully informed, of adding to the mix of ingredients that will give rise to particularized shape. Then the forms that result are fused and controlled by the unmentioned willfulness of his vision, by the unmitigated drive to achieve that carries him from one encounter to the next.

Or is it, after all, the obligation to achieve? Authors and friends, prone to lay psychology, refer endlessly to his "inability to say no" when asked to take on a new commitment—a drawing, a lecture, a commission, a dinner—and are wont to intimate weakness of will or an obsessive need for admiration. Unraveling deep-seated psychic motivations is dangerous territory for me, as for them, but I would venture that there's more of a sense of obligation burning inside that ambling, oversized Koala bear than his good-humored witticisms and sly modesty would ever let one suspect: an obligation to emulate Pater's "hard gemlike flame" and to use and to share to the utmost that ample allotment of spirit with which he is endowed.

Charles Moore:
The Architect Running in Place

Robert A.M. Stern with Raymond Gastil

Among the leaders of America's architectural revival in the 1960s, Charles Moore had the clearest understanding of what had gone wrong with modernism—the God that Failed: it had never offered the public the fundamental gift of architecture—a sense of place.

To Moore, the architect's most important role was as a maker of places, not as an elaborator of forms, although he has from the first been a brilliant shape maker. In his 1967 essay "Plug It in, Rameses, and See If It Lights Up, Because We Aren't Going to Keep It Unless It Works" Moore defined architectural responsibility. and, by implication, the irresponsibility of architects of the immediately preceding generation.

If architects are to continue to do useful work on this planet, then surely their proper concern must be the creation of *place*—the ordered imposition of man's self on specific locations across the face of the earth. To make a place is to make a domain that helps people know where they are, and by extension, know who they are. (Moore and Allen, *Dimensions*, 1976, p. 51)

As a writer, architect, and teacher, Moore has discovered, designed, and taught an architecture of American places. He taught that the creation of American places is an arduous and ironic task. The arduousness comes from the newness of the continent, the difficulty of creating a place from scratch. The irony comes from the embarrassing recognition of how contrived such a place must necessarily be, especially in a nation of nomads. A further irony is Moore's own life, in which he rarely stays in place but as a professor and architect is constantly traveling—to California, Texas, New York, Connecticut, Berlin, in short, the world. In his essay "The Temple, the Cabin and the Trailer" (*Home Sweet Home*, 1983, pp. 133–134), Moore brought the concept of hyphenated Americanism up to date:

Almost all of us are new-comers in the place where we are, wanderers bringing what used to be called a Yankee ingenious responsiveness to our dealings with a new place but we also bring dreams and maybe even homesick fantasies about some place far away from which we've come or some place far away in both time and space about which perhaps we've read (some generations of Americans have been far more bookish than others).

Moore inspired a generation of architects, a generation to which I belong, to practice architecture as an inclusive art. He showed us that we could put in as much as an earlier generation had taken out. The modernist movement had declared its greatest ambition the public good but had never shown much interest in the reality of the public's world as it was and openly despised the public's dreams and fantasies—bookish or otherwise—of the world as it had been or might be. All that had to be excluded in favor of pure form. Moore welcomed it all, albeit critically. He condemned the American scene as it was: "I think that the environment is lousy, and there is hardly any place in North America that the hand of man has touched that it hasn't ruined" (John W. Cook and Heinrich Klotz, *Conversations with Architects,* 1973). Moore had no illusions that the solution was sociological. "I get very upset at the standard student approach now which supposes that, if you interview enough housewives in a housing project, and write down what they like best about where they live, you'll know what the solution ought to be" (Cook and Klotz, p. 235). Yet at the same time, Moore believed that the best architecture, an inclusive architecture, required listening to those housewives, including their dreams and homesick fantasies. In one of his most direct experiments in participatory architecture, he led the first-year students of Yale's architecture school to Appalachia in 1967. In eight weeks, New Zion, Kentucky, had a new community center, designed and built by the Yale students and professors in accordance with the local wishes and dreams of what a building should be. The building wasn't bad as a work of architecture, either.

For young architects, the first lesson of New Zion, which Moore had really begun to teach in the early 1960s, was one of exhilarating power. They didn't have to be old and hoary to build; they could make things now. The second lesson was that each time an architect undertook a design, he didn't necessarily have to begin a heroic quest for "original" or even "significant" form, the latter of which had been the approach of one of Moore's most important mentors, Louis Kahn. Architects could use what was available from the past and present: good and even bad buildings could stimulate new production; ornate Victorian details and contemporary advertising graphics could be served up with classical columns and subtle compositional moves from mainstream modernism to result in buildings that were pleasure-giving and life-enhancing. Moore showed that the familiar and the ordinary could be raised to the level of the extraordinary. America's built environment, however "lousy," was an inevitable and appropriate sourcebook for Moore.

My particular interest is in using familiar pieces, mostly cheap pieces, putting them together in ways that they have never been before, so as to get something that's strange and revolutionary and mindboggling and often uncomfortable, but only using the ordinary pieces. I think that it's a better way of making a revolution than just inventing a whole new crazy set of shapes. (Cook and Klotz, p. 235)

In a sense, the revolution had already occurred—in Disneyland, in Las Vegas, in Solvang, a Danish village in Southern California, and in the movies—but the most successful American places were outside of the architectural canon. It was up to teachers like Moore and Robert Venturi to bring them in.

In 1964 Moore went in search of monumental architecture as part of the urban scene in California. He came back with startling news. The private realm of the air-conditioned house and the air-conditioned car had triumphed over any traditional notion of monumental, urban architecture in California, but the public realm, the place where civilization had traditionally flourished, was somehow surviving in an animator's amusement park.

In as unlikely a place as could be conceived, just off the Santa Ana Freeway, a little over an hour from Los Angeles City Hall, in an unchartable sea of suburbia, Disney has created a place, indeed a whole public world, full of sequential occurrences, of big and little drama, of hierarchies of importance and excitement...("You Have to Pay for the Public Life," *Perspecta* 9/10, p. 65).

Moore was percipient enough not to underestimate Disney. Disney had not only marketed a place, he had marked a place. As Moore wrote, "This process, the establishing of cities and the marking of important places, consititutes most of the physical part of establishing civilization. Charles Eames has made the point that the crux of this civilizing process is the giving up by individuals of something in order that the public realm may be enhanced" ("You Have to Pay," p. 58).

In 1964, in California, the crux of the civilizing process, the notion of sacrifice to the common good, had come down to buying a ticket at the gate of Disneyland. As Moore put it, with and without irony, "You have to pay for the public life."

In America, the proprietors of the private realm, like Disney, have most often paid for the manifestation in brick and mortar of something resembling a public realm. The putative representative of the public realm, the government, has had to be dragged kicking and screaming toward that "physical part of establishing civilization"—making places. Witness the stingy public subsidy for Moore's own Church Street South Housing in New Haven (*26.3*). Although the project was ultimately unsuccessful, Moore made a heroic effort to raise ordinary building materials and uniform facades to extraordinary levels by using siting and surface color as sufficient stimuli to make the residents feel at home. What a remarkable idea in 1966, building housing for the poor that wasn't designed to discipline them to the cruel geometries of some brave new world. For Moore, "The place that you live should allow for the everyday to become the exceptional. It should lead your mind to multiple associations" (Moore, Allen, and Lyndon, *The Place of Houses*, 1974, p. 140).

Given sufficient budget and freedom, Moore has built exceptional places that are rich in multiple associations. The year before he began Church Street

South, Moore and his associates designed Sea Ranch. It was fundamentally vernacular, a shack style assemblage of shed roofs and walls sheathed in the traditional local building material—rough redwood boards (*48.13, 14*). The architects responded to the specific coastline site and, more generally, to northern California. Yet more than merely acknowledging the place where they were to build, they managed to make Sea Ranch itself a place. The architects were able to compose—not merely cluster or group—condominium units into a single building, bold enough in its overall shape to command its site. Yet they were able to compose them diversely enough to satisfy the need for individual identification.

Moore took on that characteristically American place, the campus, beginning in 1966. For Kresge College, at the University of California at Santa Cruz (*27*), Moore set out to provide a stage for what he called "an urgently important four-year-long operetta" (quoted in Littlejohn, *Architect, The Life and Work of Charles W. Moore*, 1984, p. 230). The college turns an earth-colored wall to the exterior to blend its architecture with the surrounding forests and create an enclosure and a suggestion of remarkable secrets for those permitted to enter. Inside, an eclectic array of building forms are disposed to create as richly articulated a stage set for human action as any ever offered by Hollywood. Kresge is a self-contained village within a larger university, lacking only a chapel, a major library, and a gym to achieve complete independence. Without these symbolic and functional foci, Moore aggrandized the laundry and canteen, which later became a Chinese restaurant, to provide moments of architectural grandeur. An amphitheater, a red-white-and-blue rostrum, two-story dormitories that vaguely resemble roadside motels, administrative offices, shops, and a mailroom—all decorated with strips of neon—and freestanding walls with rectangular openings that visually frame the sky complete the assembly. The buildings are arranged along a grand thousand-foot-long street—the thoroughfare of the college, intended to serve as its symbolic and functional nexus, the sort of linear quadrangle guaranteed liveliness by the movement of students along it.

The use of highly abstract forms robs the scheme of much of its power. The sense of street and shelter were derived from a careful study and evocation of historic precedent—a more literal translation would have been wildly daring at the time. Moore displayed that kind of daring in a later project, the Piazza d'Italia in New Orleans (*35.7,11*). It is perhaps the fullest expression of his inclusivist philosphy to date, combining architectural allusion of the highest level with kitsch. The reason for the piazza was to symbolize New Orleans's Italian-American community. Moore and his associates provided a dream of Italy (perhaps what he would call a "homesick fantasy") made of both cheap, ordinary materials and expensive, inherently luxurious ones: steel frame and stucco, slate, marble, granite paving stones, stainless steel, tile, water, and neon. The overt staginess and deliberate mockery of architectural tradition seem enough to appall even Morris Lapidus's sensibilities. As Lapidus often did, Moore created a sensual, exciting place to be, as close to the stagey Trevi Fountain as anyone was willing to go in 1975. The classical architecture, the earth-colored walls, the Latin inscriptions, and the eighty-foot long relief-map pool of Italy are explicit references to the collective past of the piazza's sponsors. To place the project even more specifically, Moore put Sicily, the original homeland of most of New Orleans's Italian-Americans, in the bull's-eye center of the project (*35.6*).

The Piazza d'Italia is representative of Moore's aggressive playfulness, an attitude that has occasionally put this status as a serious architect in question among architectural pundits. But it is Moore's capacity for finding the serious meaning in play, whether at Disneyland or in his own work, that marks his place in the history of architecture. Moore, Ruble, Yudell won the competition for Tegel Harbor in Berlin because it offered one of the few proposals that looked as though anyone could have fun at the recreation center, a barge resembling a huge toy boat (*54.2*).

Moore's best humor is subtly instructive as well. At Cold Spring Harbor Laboratory, Moore, Grover, Harper was commissioned to renovate and design several buildings for the 100-acre campus on Long Island Sound, which had a score of nineteenth-and early-twentieth-century structures. The new waste-water treatment plant could have been the most banal building at the laboratory, but Moore and his associates designed it as a focal point. The main concrete structure, invisibly tucked into the hillside when seen from above, but visible from the harbor side, is sheathed in shingles and scrollwork. The shingles continue upwards onto a gazebo that sits atop the plant. On the campus side, the gazebo is set at the edge of a landscaped terrace. A typically Moore-ish witty extra, this shingled architectural folly, with its spire topped by a model of adenovirus, has come to symbolize the laboratory and its dedication to research in molecular biology.

Moore is a very modern, very American architect, a maker of places that correspond to the very American fluidity and restlessness of his mind. He transformed a profession by reintroducing the reality of architectural experience into the ideality of the Academy. Traditional materials and the craft to use them began to be taken seriously by a generation of architects weaned on steel and glass. Architecture could once again give pleasure, whether in a theatrical composition of staircases, balconies, cutouts, and skylights or in a sensual use of colors and materials. Architecture could also give the pleasure of memory, informed by an awareness of context, and of history. The radical pluralism of Moore's art can push it to the outer reaches of coherent design, but is is always held in place by Moore's sly serenade of communality.

Charles Moore in Miniatures

Heinrich Klotz
translated by Charlotte Melin

Fig. 1. Charles Moore at work

Fig. 2. Charles Moore in Marburg, West Germany, working on a house project, 1977

When I first saw the Piazza d'Italia in New Orleans, I was delighted by one detail that added a human touch to its scenery, though I could not believe that Charles Moore had made a monument to himself in this fashion. It was the small portrait medallion in the spandrel of the "wetopes" of the lower series. From the midst of the architectural ornaments, Moore's face laughed down at me.

Later I learned through Allen Eskew, who had taken over supervision of the Piazza's construction, that he and Moore's collaborators had, without the architect's knowledge, placed the relief portrait in the arcade (Moore had wanted to install a windshield wiper there that was supposed to wipe the falling water away from the "wetopes").

This charming addition evoked the presence of the architect with subtle irony and accorded him a subordinate place within the scenery as a whole. It also reconfirmed my impression (one corroborated time and again since the beginning of my friendship with Charles Moore) that the numerous people who deal with and work together with him admire him not only as an architect, but as a person in whose presence they themselves can often amicably blossom and become more human.

During the course of my studies, I often heard from my art history professors that works of art and architecture should be judged irrespective of the artists. Not the person, but the result of his artistic labor should be examined and interpreted. Very early I understood that this demand was a methodological check against letting oneself be impressed by the artist and projecting the psychological qualities of the man onto his work—against rediscovering the characteristics of the person in the art. As a historian one can remain true to this maxim; as soon as we turn to architecture of the present, however, and stand before the architect as a living person, it becomes difficult to be puritanical in this respect. It is all the more difficult with Charles Moore because one hardly ever finds an architect whose character, whose attitudes and predilections, are so directly reflected in his buildings. His houses are just as friendly and people-oriented as he himself is. No one would ever imagine that he could have built Bofill's "Abraxas" or even a monumental building like the Pentagon. An air of freedom—the informal attitude—is the mark of his architecture.

One can best become acquainted with Charles Moore when he is surrounded by students (*fig. 1*) or by patrons who are communicating their ideas to him and urging that these proposals be transposed into form. There he stands with crossed legs, holding a pencil curiously entwined in his hand (*fig. 2*), draws tiny sketches and miniature views, marks first loose then more and more solid lines on the paper, and reacts within seconds to this or that objection. I have never met an architect who has made such beautiful things from the awful ideas of his clients. Moore never rejects a suggestion from his students or patrons. He investigates everything, yet the final result is unexpected and startling. Words metamorphose themselves mysteriously into a form; thoughts become a line on the paper—a highly animated construction of lines that always surpasses the bare needs, the utilitarian notions of his patrons—and ultimately become a poetic image of quite purposeful statements.

What distinguishes Moore are, above all, three characteristics: unique imaginative power, vast tolerance, and humor. I could as little envision a combative, dogmatic Charles Moore as a deathly serious one. In a certain way he shares a kinship with children.

Visiting him at home, one comes across toys and fantastic objects everywhere, mementos from trips and crazy souvenirs. Large and small, they stand in apparently random disarray on every ledge, cupboard, and windowsill. Yet on closer observation these juxtapositions reveal an ulterior and uniquely

appropriate logic. A small Mexican church stands next to a Japanese geisha, a giraffe beside Hansel and Gretel. With wit Moore reorders the world and combines things that in reality never come together.

I have become familiar with some of his houses, first of all that small, inconspicuous bungalow in New Haven that he made into a humorous Pop-world inside. Fantastic, colorful towers extend through the small space running from the basement up to the attic and transform Moore's house into a little private stage. Here each division of space has a bizarre name and the eye constantly encounters new surprises—a unique declaration of war against the sobriety of sixties architecture. But he did not put forward his argument in the dogmatic tone of a preacher; rather he mounted resistance in his own good-humored and ingenious manner. Here moderation united with understatement, yielding a sensibleness manifested in unusual forms sawed out of plywood walls for the trick of making something out of nothing. That was Charles Moore's world of play and theater, where he could stretch himself out in a hammock or rest up on a star-spangled bed.

On Selby Avenue in Los Angeles he then built a more imposing house. Actually, though, it consists of only a single stairway to which adjoining rooms are attached. The stairway, which narrows and expands, connects to an alcove and thus dominates the entire apartment. The goal of this ascent from far below is Charles Moore's library, where, at the midpoint of the production, he has fixed a richly profiled Victorian arch to the shelves. One looks up to the arch, which stands in the line of view like a quotation from a past world. And again there are the toys and souvenirs that accompany the ascent. On corbels and cornices with mirror profiles that have been expressly attached to the wall for this purpose, these things stand about and enliven the architecture with all their small existences. Improvisation's lack of seriousness reigns, that liberal attitude of the loose arrangement, where apparently nothing wants to fit with anything else and yet in a marvelous way everything does go together.

In the meantime, sober parties have fallen upon Moore's inner worlds and eviscerated that most beautiful environment of Pop art—Moore's house in New Haven; have changed back into normality the hammock room called "Howard" (after Moore's dog in New Orleans) and the attic room called "Berengaria" (after the wife of Richard the Lion-Hearted). Likewise the restaurant of the Faculty Club in Santa Barbara, bisected with neon signs, has in the meantime turned serious and now goes against the freedom of its rooms with old velvet and plush, as if it were an issue of recouping the seriousness of the United States of America.

The difficulties that have risen in the minds of public patrons in accepting Moore's humor and irony are further demonstrated by those bank directors for whom Moore wanted to place an oversized five-dollar bill on the facade of their concern. Although money was their business, they nonetheless found such a sign all too frivolous.

Moore has taken a stand on this dichotomy in no uncertain terms: "One of the great paradoxes is that art appears to be, by its very nature, revolutionary, but architecture, at the same time, is also establishmentarian art" (Cook and Klotz, *Conversations with Architects/Architektur im Widerspruch*, Zürich, 1974, p. 309).

The entrenched stance of patrons also tries to shackle the child in Charles Moore, all too quickly fettering the play and wit. And thus Moore again and again runs up against good taste, which as the servant of the serious governs art. Defiantly Moore claims "bad taste" for himself and gains freedom from it.

"Bad taste" also includes those marvelous Christmas cards Moore sends to his friends (*fig. 3*)—fantasy landscapes he draws depicting carnivallike castles standing on steep cliffs. Long pennants wave in the wind from the cupola tops, and rope ladders ascend to air castles from the terrace steps. This is how Moore defends his dream and play worlds, much of which—contrary to all the expectations of sober minds—overflows into the architecture he builds.

Pop art, with its irritating monuments to the consumer world, shaped Charles Moore, as well as Robert Venturi. He found in its approaches the welcome occasion to let subculture be incorporated into the banks and "faculty clubs" and to taint with the impermissible those reserves of propriety that had been unsullied by popular taste. When we talked about the famous flag pictures by Jasper Johns, Moore immediately picked up a pencil and drew

Fig. 3

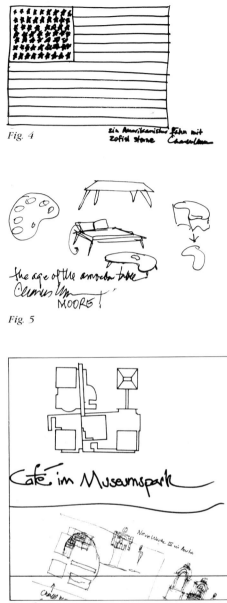

Fig. 4

Fig. 5

Café im Museumspark

Fig. 6

his version of the American flag, "An American flag with too many stars" (*fig. 4*). He crammed the upper left field with a plethora of stars. This simple idea, however, carried the ironic comment that one could imagine the United States with each newly acquired state and each added star as gripped by endless growth until a superabundance of states and stars pressed together....

I frequently took advantage of the opportunity to push a sheet of paper over to Charles Moore when he wanted to communicate something. Often he set down his explanatory miniatures on a napkin or coaster. Once, in 1977, we spoke about the fifties, about the age of kidney-shaped tables and amoeba forms. With great rapidity he drew all the typical objects: a table with slanted legs, Aalto's vase, an eminently typical sofa, and a kidney-shaped table (*fig. 5*). What was incongruous was the kidney-shaped palette he finally added. With this he wanted to say that there have always been forms like these kidney-shaped tables—just not made absolute! He made this comment playfully, giving into an association.

A few months ago when I was sitting with Charles Moore in the café of the Museum of Arts and Crafts in Frankfurt, designed by Richard Meïer, Moore drew the floor plan of his own house (which he had just begun to build in Austin, Texas) in irreverently oblique style on one of the table napkins stamped with Meïer's plan of the museum (*fig. 6*). What was important for him was the colonnade running through the individual structures that was intended to link the entire arrangement, also the floor tiles that would cover the floor of the house in a circular pattern, and the detail of a pilaster resembling a human figure from the rear elevation of Schinkel's original plan for the Neue Wache in Berlin. Details, narrative details, matters of apparently secondary importance, which pictorially enrich the architecture, a decorative thought, play as important a role in Charles Moore's conceptions as the larger whole.

Finally, we talked about the exhibition we were preparing. When I suggested putting some of the drawings in colored frames, he was immediately gung ho. He urged that the frames be designed with profiles and that mirror shards be added so the viewer could see himself in the frame, not just Moore's drawings or plans. Then he began to talk about what was crucial for him in the exhibition: little "memory palaces," historical baldachins beneath which he wanted to place his toys and arranged souvenirs, that is, the personal things to which he linked his memories (*fig. 7*). We could construct these baldachins so that they could be folded up and sent as "cultural baggage" to Frankfurt. "The colored frames and the 'memory palaces' will be really beautiful in white rooms," he said and began to imagine to himself how the strict architecture of Ungers would be subverted by his colorful exoticism. At this moment I again saw that almost imperceptible grin on his lips, and at the same time his eyes grew large as if he had just concocted a daring prank.

On Being Clients of Charles Moore: Not Once, But Twice

Dorothy and Frederick Rudolph

How did we come to choose Charles Moore as the architect for the first house that we were to build? Why did we stop renting? Why didn't we buy a house that has what every house has—"great potentiality"? Only the first of these questions is relevant here. The others are of interest only to our bankers and children. We chose Charles Moore neither scientifically nor intellectually but purely by fluke and a great amount of luck.

In 1969, after two visits to the island of Captiva on the Gulf Coast of Florida, as guests of an alumnus and his family, we bought a parcel of property. Even then, life in Florida was simple enough for a $50.00 deposit to hold for us, until we arranged for the financing, a 100-foot frontage on the Gulf of Mexico that stretched 1,400 feet deep to the other side of the island.

The property had once been homesteaded but by 1969 it was covered with tropical growth, difficult if not impossible to penetrate on foot, and was populated by a nesting pair of bald eagles and some burrowing tortoises. One hundred feet to the north and right next door to the south were resort residences too close to the water. For us there was no rush about building. Fred was not yet fifty. The house we had in mind therefore was not a retirement home nor exactly the second home that somewhat later dominated the real estate market. We liked Captiva and someday it would be nice to be there. So, while there was no rush, we decided in the spring of 1970 that we had to build as soon as possible. It was there, the children would get more pleasure out of it the sooner it was built, books could be written to the sound of waves and rustling palms.

We first heard of Charles Moore from a friend in New Haven. She knew of an architect whose work she thought that we would like. It so happened that on the Sunday after her remark the *New York Times Magazine* featured a house that Charles Moore had designed for clients in Westerly, Rhode Island. Dottie was in Florida at the time; one look at that *Times* article assured her that she liked that house. But she also decided that it looked too grand and expensive for us. She reported her enthusiasm and her hesitation to Fred in Williamstown; he more or less ignored her, as Dottie would put it, or he was otherwise engaged in preparing classes, as he would put it.

A few weeks later, reunited in Williamstown, we asked Whitney Stoddard of the Williams Art Department if he knew of any Williams graduate or, indeed, anyone else who was a practicing architect in Florida who might design a house for us. Whit said that he didn't know anyone of that description, suggesting at the same time that our innocence in architectural matters had led us to believe we needed a Florida architect. Actually, he said, there was an architect whose work we would like, he was sure. The architect had, as a Princeton professor, once served as a critic of architectural projects dreamed up by Williams undergraduates majoring in art history and yearning for some architectural guidance. His name was Charles Moore.

Fred asked Whit to call Moore, and the very next day, Sunday, Whit called and found him at home, on his way, in minutes, to Portugal. Only as we came to know Charlie Moore did we realize that it was always thus with him and that it was our great good fortune to find the peripatetic Moore in one of his few moments at home. He was home and he would love to design a house in Florida. This would be a first for him in the state where his predecessor as dean of the School of Architecture at Yale, Paul Rudolph (no relation to us), had begun his career, in a stark modernist style that was the antithesis of the eclecticism and joyful exuberance that charcterized the work that had helped to draw Moore to our attention. The message that Whit Stoddard conveyed to us that Sunday assured us that Charles Moore would call us when he returned. That is how Charles Moore happened to become the architect of our Captiva house (*17*).

Charles Moore did call us. He went to Florida to look over the site and, with his apprentice Jim Righter, now a prominent Boston architect, he visited us in Williamstown on June 27, 1970. They were late in arriving (there are always transportation connection problems with Moore, but he appears not to be aware of them); they had been expected to stay the night, but when they learned that Fred's father had died that day in Pennsylvania, Charlie Moore insisted that their presence not be allowed to impede our early departure in the morning. We made the most of that evening, getting to know one another a bit, falling into the use of first names. Dottie elected to call him Charlie, although later we learned that most people call him Chuck.

We had prepared a long list of things, both large and small, that we wanted to have in the house—a master bedroom facing the Gulf of Mexico, two guestrooms with baths a bit apart from the main living area and our own quarters, a study for Fred, a convenient but unobtrusive bar area, a place for trays. We also had a few pieces of antique furniture that we thought would give warmth to a beach house. We did not discuss matters of design, either big questions of architectural style or such particulars as types of doors and windows. Our view was and is that it was up to the artist to present us with a design that met our needs and desires: his responsibility was design, ours was to make sure that what we wanted to happen inside that design did really happen.

Of course all this occurred in 1970 and it is difficult to remember all the details of our conversation that evening, but we do remember Charlie remarking, "You seem to have a lot of sitting areas in your present home." It was true, for besides a living area, there was a library that had once been a playroom, a porch, a study, and a sitting area in the kitchen. Charlie's question meant that our Captiva home would also be hospitable to life's sedentary pleasures.

Later that summer Charlie and Jim reappeared with an exciting model and blueprints. We recall making few suggestions. The design thrilled us, but our builder, the most experienced and reputable builder then practicing on the island, would have to decide whether he could build it and at what price. Karl Wightman, who was surely a barefoot boy with cheek, was not daunted by the great Moore's design, although we all knew that he was not a master builder with any great degree of sophistication. He was, however, honest, he knew the ropes, he was the one who built the houses on Captiva, and he concluded that it could not be done within our budget.

Moore and Righter returned to the drawing boards and came up with another plan so unlike the original that surely they knew we would reject it. It was then that Fred asked what would have happened to all the design ideas of the first plan if the lot had been somewhat narrower. Zoning regulations required a ten-foot setback from the property line, so the house could not be wider than eighty feet. Suppose the lot had been ninety-nine, not a hundred, feet. That in the end was the supposition with which the final design was shaped. Charlie gave the house a width of seventy-nine feet, lowered the ceilings, reduced correspondingly the depth of the house, squeezed bathrooms and bedrooms (those essential spaces that only sybarites require to be of luxurious dimensions), added a covered porch off the guest area which gave an illusion of a larger area but was less costly. Of course, the master bedroom/ bathroom suffered the same diminution, frustrating Dottie's not necessarily sybaritic but certainly romantic desire for something large and glamorous.

Although final plans were essentially in order by early winter, not until spring was the lot bulldozed to make way for our house. We often met with Charlie and Jim during the spring and summer, sometimes in New York, while picking out furniture. We also went down to Captiva with Charlie several times during the summer. There were many on-the-spot decisions. One of Dottie's more brilliant suggestions was adding two windows to the kitchen and dining areas because these rooms seemed dark. Charlie's response was immediate and approving.

Building our house in Florida, working with Charlie as it was in the process of creation, watching him making decisions, observing his mind at work, sharing the fun he was having, was one of the most enjoyable experiences of our lives. Charlie has one of the most secure of egos. Both of us have some definite ideas about color and interior design ourselves. With Charlie, if Dottie didn't like the color proposed for the rafters in the main body of the house—and she didn't (Charlie wanted them an elephant gray, Dottie suggested terra-cotta)—his response was quick and cheerful: "Great! I like that even better." That secure ego must elicit the best from his partners, the builders of his houses, and his clients. We felt very much a part of the house that Charles Moore had designed for us. Maybe here, too, is where we should add that our Captiva house came in *under* the estimate, even as we acknowledge that some of the reasons have nothing to do with the skills and efforts of architect, builder, and clients.

We moved into our house on December 29, 1971, not on Thankgiving as we had expected. The house was not exactly finished nor would it be during January when four Williams College students lived with us as participants in a Winter Study project that Fred offered and that was made legitimate by the presence of either Charlie or Jim or both during most of the period. It was a fascinating experience in teaching, learning, and design. We listened as he escorted our group through an early Paul Rudolph house, visited a house in progress that Karl Wightman was building for himself, and beamed with friendly satisfaction as he shared a reception one Sunday with the fifty or so men and women who in some way or other had worked on the house. One of them was the president of a Fort Myers lumber company who had asked if he might be invited. He wanted to meet the architect who was responsible for the most lumber he had ever delivered for one house (Charlie had been unhappy with the acoustics of one of his recent houses; he doubled the number of rafters in ours).

Ten years passed. Our children were married or about to be and we felt that the largish house that we owned in Williamstown needed a lot of work to make it right for us. The alternative was either to buy another house or build one. We had built once. Why not again? Would we use the same architect? We didn't contemplate looking for another architect for more than two minutes.

Charlie came up to Williamstown, this time with a partner, Robert Harper. Dottie had investigated two possible building sites, property that the college had for sale. Then there was also the possibility of dividing our own property, slicing off two acres or so as a building lot for ourselves. The lower part of our property had a special appeal to Dottie because of its vistas into New York and Vermont. It turned out also to be the preference of Fred, Charlie, and Bob. The meadow site recommended itself to Fred, who was resolved to dispense with every piece of lawn equipment along with the old house.

A setting with low maintenance costs was one of the requests we made of Charlie this time around. We also asked him to give us a combination kitchen/ sitting area/dining arrangement, something open but intimate. We wanted a separate living room. In addition to a master bedroom, each of us asked for a room and a bath of our own. There must be guestrooms, somewhat distant from our own quarters, for visiting children, spouses, and an undetermined number of grandchildren. We needed well-organized storage space, and because we were moving from a larger to a smaller house, the new house would have to be designed to place specific pieces of furniture and paintings in particular rooms. Since we were starting from scratch, we asked for a swimming pool that was an organic part of the house. Fred also wondered if somehow the garage might be put out of sight, perhaps right into the sloping side of the hill.

Charlie was now much more famous, busier, even more peripatetic. He was living in Los Angeles. This house was coming out of his Essex, Connecticut, partnership; clearly he was not going to play the same role in our second house as he had in our first. One day at lunch in New York, he drew on the back of the envelope that held his airline tickets (he was on his way to Ireland) a quick sketch of the Palladian inspired design that would become our Ide Road house. The design inspiration was his, he was consulted throughout the design and building process, but it was certainly Bob Harper who worked out particulars of the design and who carried the burden of translating an idea into a house.

Our Williamstown house (*19*) is full of marvelous detail, whimsical and dramatic. We love it as much as our Florida house. It must have been difficult for Bob Harper to achieve in Williamstown a house that we could like as well as the Captiva house, but he most certainly did. He was not as easy to work with, nor as open to suggestion as Charlie; nor in some sense was the design—the Palladian point of departure argued for a symmetry that cautioned against tinkering.

This second house cost about twice as much as we wanted it to. We could never get a clear idea of what each decision—mouldings, roof, quality of brick—was adding to the ultimate cost. Moore and his partners design with exuberance and that can be expensive for their clients. Our builder, Gordon Oakes, was considerably more sophisticated and knowledgeable than our Captiva builder, but our Williamstown house is a far more complicated affair and a more challenging building. It took time to build. Also, our own attitude toward this house differed: this was our permanent house, the last one we would build. It was in the North; heating, cooling, and security considerations were paramount. The ruling mood among all of us seemed to be, "Let's make it the best we can." There is no better formula for doubling the cost of a house. One happy result is that we are proud that Bob Harper and Gordon Oakes think of our house on Ide Road as their house.

As with Charlie, Bob was helpful with matters of interior design; Charlie played a role here too, but the placement of furniture, the choice of fabrics and colors, were ours. We realize that there are architects who mistrust their clients and insist on creating the total environment and even clients who mistrust themselves. We were delighted that both Charlie and Bob were happy to leave us to our own devices but ready to help us when we asked.

We moved into 234 Ide Road on February 19, 1981. Of course the house was not finished, but for a second time we had experienced the exhilaration of building not just a house, but a Charles Moore house, this second time more accurately a Robert Harper-with-Charles Moore house.

We have sometimes been asked why anyone and ourselves in particular would want to live in a house designed by an eminent architect. The question had not occurred to us when we became clients of Charles Moore, but we suppose that because we had been collecting paintings since the first year of our marriage, calling in an architect to design a house for us seemed the most natural thing in the world to do. We suspect that implicit in the question is a degree of wonderment that anyone would have the guts or the audacity to want a house that draws attention to itself. A Charles Moore house certainly does that, but we did not give any thought to how the house would look to others. What was important was how the house would be to live in.

Our Captiva house is a shelter, as every house must be, but it is also an unending series of experiences—with color, light, space. It is a house that is bathed in light during a full moon and that invites the out-of-doors unobtrusively indoors. It hugs the ground and it soars. Two people do not rattle around in it, nor do a hundred people at a party crowd it. We enjoyed watching Charles Moore have fun as he watched the house take shape. The house that he designed captured some of that spirit. Every year we see something new, another surpise that Charles Moore put there, whether he knew it or not. Our Williamstown house is much the same; it is both cozy and dramatic, and we are forever seeing or experiencing something new.

It is said that an architect protects the client from the builder, but it is also true that the builder protects the client from the architect. How did these bits of building wisdom work for us? We didn't need any protection from Charles Moore. He was as flexible as his designs; he quickly earned the respect of our builders, he respected them. There was a remarkable absence of tension in our architect-builder-client relationships. This was attributable certainly to some degree to our own withdrawal from design matters, even while being determined to get the amenities and spaces we desired (we did not always get them because they were not always possible to have; we all compromised at one time or another).

Moore is a genius who wears his genius lightly. Both builders had secure reputations for reliability; they built good houses and they knew it. Both builders were accustomed to dealing with architects and confronted with a Moore design would not have been willing to build to a contract price. We were thus saved from the bargaining, dealing, and haggling that sometimes becomes a part of the process when a contract between builder and owner is subjected to changes or refinements in plans. At no time were we or the others distrustful of one another. We never felt embattled. We believe that the cost-plus arrangement was one source of harmony, even though it may be argued that a contract price arrangement is financially safer.

In engaging Charles Moore and his partners to design our houses, we were not simply hiring someone to do a job. We were involved in a trusting relationship with professionals, similar to that which occurs with one's lawyer, doctor, or clergyman

In the end, in both cases, did we feel that we spent more than anticipated? Gordon Oakes was properly baffled by a Williamstown resident who asked him what the cost per square foot was for the Moore house on Ide Road. It's not quite the same question that the man asked J. P. Morgan about the cost of running his yacht, but it doesn't make sense to ask conventional questions about unconventional houses.

No one transgressed the trust on which all relied. The architect had a known body of work which, by fluke or taste or both, had drawn the clients to him. The builders, barefoot Karl Wightman in Florida and Yankee Gordon Oakes in Williamstown, had a reputation for integrity and reliablity. We made clear to everyone at the beginning what we wanted and—in most cases— accepted the responsibility for paying for (or rejecting) changes and refinements and surprises as they came along. Houses can be built in other ways, but participating as clients in the creative process of a house being born, we found working with Charles Moore a privilege.

It's strange, but he and we never argued about what is beautiful. We knew. Robert Rauschenberg, who lives on Captiva, was openly negative about our house there: "too much hard geometry," he said. We were, if not bothered, at least intrigued by his remark, until we realized that he did not see beyond the windows and doors, where soft geometry and nongeometry were moving out and in to us. We think both our houses are "beautiful." So does Charles Moore. We suspect that even though the pursuit of beauty is an adventure beyond ending, that may be one of the reasons that bland simplicity and nondescriptness in a house were not our goal. If we opted for elegance and drama and difference, we were probably making psychologically autobiographical statements. How fortunate that Charles Moore was there to hold our hands!

An essay that begins as an exercise in throwing some light on how two clients experienced the design and building of two Charles Moore houses ends up inevitably as grist for some psychologist's mill. So let it. We'll make it easy. We are two people probably excessively sensitive to the beauty of things. There is a certain thrill in looking at something that responds to our taste. Charles Moore has a sensitivity, a taste, an essential lack of arrogance on matters of taste and style that allowed him to say "Why not?" to industrial overhead lights, to the windows Dottie suggested that he punch into the north wall of our Captiva house, and to the elimination of thousands of dollars of refinements in both houses.

Charles Moore has slept in both our houses. He snored and left his pyjamas. The memory of his snores remains, but we forwarded his pyjamas. We doubt if they ever caught up with him. We are looking forward to his next visit.

Charles Moore and His Clients: Designing St. Matthew's

Richard Song

The church of St. Matthew's, Pacific Palisades, California consecrated on March 20, 1983, grew out of a most intriguing design process, because of the design workshops in which the parishioners participated. The series of three "Take Part" workshops was an innovative alternative to some of the traditional architect-client relationships.

Background on "Take Part" Workshop

The St. Matthew's workshops were coordinated by Jim Burns, who invented the "Take Part" workshop process with Lawrence Halprin and Charles Moore in 1968. Although Charles Moore held workshops for "Where the River Meets the Sea Park," Seal Beach, California, and the Riverdesign project, Dayton, Ohio, they were both urban planning projects. The St. Matthew's workshops were the first to be focused on a single building. In all these examples, however, the ideas are the same: development of users' environmental awareness, user participation in design processes, cooperative decisions between users and designers, "responsive rather than reactive" attitudes on the part of the designers toward the desires of the users, getting the users "psyched" about their new environment (J. Burns).

When Moore was asked how he felt about the St. Matthew's workshops, he said it was not one of those "groovy get-togethers" between economically poor users and inexperienced students of the late 1960s. The St. Matthew's workshops, in the late seventies, had educated and caring clients, an able coordinator, and experienced and sensitive architects.

History of St. Matthew's

St. Matthew's Episcopal Church is situated off Sunset Boulevard after it passes through Hollywood, Beverly Hills, and Westwood on its way to meet the Pacific Coast Highway near Malibu Beach. Its parish is a wealthy, suburban, conservative, fashion conscious, elegant, proud, educated, and professional community which wanted a church that "showed good taste" (Card). One of the problems for Moore, Ruble, Yudell was that every decision, after the workshops, needed approval from committees composed of "all chiefs and no Indians" (Kreitler). Although committee members respected the professional specialists, they were strong-minded and determined people.

The old St. Matthew's, designed by Quincy Jones in the 1930s, was a small A-frame chapel which seated about 150 people. The first rector served the "very stable parish" (Curtis) for nearly fifty years, and during that time the parishioners grew fond of their church and community. To many parishioners, especially the older generations, St. Matthew's had long been an important part of their lives; "people grow up and live with the parish" (Curtis). Some members, out of nostalgia, may still prefer the old chapel, in which their children were baptized or married, or from which their parents had been buried. A new church could not possibly be the same to these people.

When the old church was destroyed by the Santa Monica Mountain fire on October 23, 1978, the parishioners decided to rebuild. Although this desire was unanimous, the parish simultaneously experienced an internal dispute over the selection of a new rector. With the retirement of its first rector, the parish found it difficult to choose between the younger assistant rector and a rector chosen from outside the community. Soon after the selection of the new rector—Father Arnold Fenton from Tacoma, Washington—the parish had to select its new architect during "an acrimonious period" (Card). Because some parishioners felt the popular voice was ignored by the vestry in the selection of a rector, they decided that the schematic design of the new church had to be approved by two-thirds of the parish—enough to scare away many architects.

Architect Selection and Moore, Ruble, Yudell's Proposal

Moore, Ruble, Yudell's proposal to the Selection Committee was written by Moore himself; he wanted this commission, which would be the first major commission for the new partnership of Moore, Ruble, Yudell (MRY) and his first opportunity to design a church. He wrote, "the most important act of the architect is listening, and the successful building grows out of an intimate and continued relation with the clients." In describing his earlier "Design Through Participation" projects, Moore stated that "the energies of individuals and the community as a whole have enlivened and strengthened the designs that developed. In each situation, individuals grew closer to one another, developing a stronger sense of community as a result of meeting, exploring their needs, and sharing ideas. . . . The occasion of building a new church is an opportunity for the members of that community to come together, explore ideas, and celebrate the process of synthesizing ideas toward a common goal." He proposed a series of workshops "which will allow interested parishioners to participate as individuals . . . and would bring young people together with older members of the parish to exchange ideas and learn."

The Selection Committee eagerly responded to the proposed workshops, which it viewed as a possible way to "heal those wounds" (Card) caused by the controversy over its rector selection. Moreover, the parishioners "wanted to be educated" by their new architects and the Selection Committee knew Moore both as educator—Professor of Architecture at UCLA—and architect. According to John Davis, a real estate developer who served on the Selection Committee, Moore, Ruble, Yudell's proposal was the "thickest" in terms of quantity and quality. Although Davis "did not know about Moore before," he was "impressed MRY's initial proposal." However, the selection of Moore, Ruble, Yudell as the architects could not have been hurt by the fact that it took place in the first house in Southern California designed by Moore (constructed in 1974), whose owner, Leland Burns, was on the Selection Committee. Through Regula Campbell, the landscape architect who had grown up in the St. Matthew's community, and Leland Burns, MRY was at least aware of St. Matthew's internal politics and sympathized with the general parish.

By volunteering to hold the workshops, MRY managed to get the commission, implement a program involving direct user input, educate the clients, present the design, and receive approval for the design. The general parish involvement in this design process benefited from many intangibles, such as enthusiasm, pride, religious fervor, community spirit, and "greater user care" (L. Burns). Practically, the workshops helped a tremendous amount in raising funds—the most important ingredient in getting a design built.

For the participating parishioners, the design workshops were a chance to express "creative interest and artistic taste" (Card), "diffuse the tension that had been suppressed" (L. Burns), create "a tremendous common bond" (Jensen), vote on the design of the new church, and leave something behind for future generations. Many parishioners attended the workshops purely out of curiosity and eagerness to be involved and educated. Furthermore, it was "a lifetime opportunity" (Jensen) to build a monument to "glorify God" (Mann)—a church that enhances the beautiful, God-created environment.

Workshop I

From 4:00 P.M. to 9:00 P.M. on Sunday, August 5, 1979, more than 120 parishioners attended the first design workshop for an "exploration of site planning and design concepts." After short introductions by Moore and Jim Burns, the participants took an "Awareness Walk" (a California nature walk) to explore the thirty-seven-acre property. During the walk, they stopped at various stations and were asked to record observations, thoughts, images, visions, impressions, emotions, and desires for their new church, using the senses of sight, sound, and smell. They were also asked to comment on the old chapel, the major source of their preconceptions.

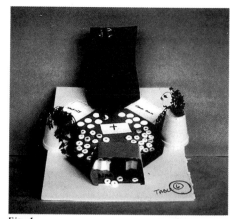
Fig. 1

Fig. 2

Fig. 3

Fig. 4

Fig. 5

After a picnic dinner, the participants worked on "programming and design priorities." While the parishioners were divided into nine groups to discuss the issues and develop ideas, "the consulting team *performed* as a catalyst to listen, make suggestions, answer questions, and provide working materials (such as Fruit-Loops, parsley, cellophone) for models and drawings" (*figs. 2, 3*). Some of the expressed desires were: "an intimate atmosphere for worship yet embodying a sense of importance and majesty..., full of natural light, with unobstructed sight and sound of the pulpit and altar..., a wide and shallow seating pattern to bring people closer to one another and to the altar ..., more ample and accessible ancillary spaces..., preserve and complement the great natural beauty of the site," and lots of natural wood for the interior.

Workshop II

The second workshop, held between 11:00 A.M. and 3:30 P.M. on Sunday, September 16, 1979, with participation by seventy parishioners (according to the workshop report, a smaller number because of the unusually hot and smoggy weather), began with MRY's presentation of a series of alternatives, with emphasis on the endless possibilities, for spatial arrangements based on the data gathered in the first workshop (*figs. 4, 5*). During lunch, MRY gave a slide presentation (according to Moore, "a kind of Rorschach test") of churches from various places and times and asked the parishioners to vote "like" and "dislike" for each of the eighty images, ranging from St. Peter's to Le Corbusier's Ronchamp. In this taste test, Aalto's Vuoksenniska Church at Imatra and Maybeck's Christian Science Church in Berkeley were the most preferred for St. Matthew's; MRY had included four images of the Aalto and two of the Maybeck. Nobody liked Guarini's SS. Sindone, Hawksmoor's St. Mary Woolnoth, Wright's Unity Temple, St. Peter's, or the Hagia Sophia. After seeking the clients' desires and preconceptions for the program of the new church in the first workshop, MRY showed the parishioners other possibilities and deprogrammed some of their preconceptions ("began to break away from the old chapel" [Davis]) in the second workshop. If MRY's main purpose was to learn the client's architectural taste, another purpose was to educate the clients, or perhaps to manipulate their tastes.

After lunch, the participants were divided into six groups to work on the form of the plan for their new church. The drawings, sketches, and crude but informative models from this design session showed a unanimous choice for the semicircular seating arrangement. Although this seems unusual and even miraculous ("God had a hand in designing the chuch" [Kreitler]), the congregation had enjoyed "the intimacy of the old church" (Romig), and had used portable chairs arranged in a semicircular pattern during services held in Briggs Hall, the gym, after the old church had burned.

Workshop III

The final workshop was held from 11:00 A.M. to 3:00 P.M. on Sunday, October 14, 1979, with apparently "the largest group assembled during the three-part series." After reviewing the first two workshops, MRY presented "three alternative design directions . . . using plan variations derived from Workshop II." The presentation included scale models for "an opportunity to look inside, to 'feel' the space created by different plans" (*fig. 6*). The participants "also studied the different site layouts at the location of the prayer garden and former church building ruins."

After breaking down into seven groups to discuss the three alternatives, six out of seven groups agreed on the second alternative—"a symmetrical layout with semicircular seating area housed under a navelike roof, crossed by transepts over the altar." The participants also expressed a desire for "more connection between inside and outside," with the understanding of the "acoustical and liturgical advantages of a solid wall immediately behind the altar and organ." The final workshop closed with Charles Moore's summary of the parishioners' desires, as understood by MRY.

The schematic design was further developed by MRY following the workshop guidelines and was presented on December 16, 1979, to the general parish. On January 13, 1980, 83 percent (well over the required two-thirds) of the congregation approved the schematic design.

Moore Workshops

For Moore, the workshops are an experiential design process for his clients, a performance, and an extension of his design sessions. As a proponent of experiential architecture, Moore allows accidents to happen in his designs for visual excitement and for experiential surpise or discovery. Such a surprise is presented by the structural piers and arch that confront the visitor upon entering St. Matthew's. As the viewer explores Moore's spaces, the space appears to be in constant motion; in St. Matthew's the lofty interior is only gradually revealed to the viewer. In many of Moore's buildings, Moore is involved in a dialogue with his users. Similarly, in the workshops, MRY provided an opportunity for the users to "discover and realize" (J. Burns) the design process through observation and exploration; the parishioners were excited in their participation and "delighted by surprises" (Davis) in their discovery of the design process. The workshops were a "shared experience for strength of design through collaboration" (Campbell), and the participants found Moore to be "a great listener" (Davis).

With a busy architect like Moore, who never stays in one place for long, the clients wanted to see him as much as possible. After all, they had hired Moore, Ruble, Yudell in order to get Charles Moore. In the workshops, Moore was presented to a large number of clients—a showcase or a performance, starring Charles Moore, architect. What could be more fitting for an architect who so much enjoys designing stagelike, dramatic architecture? Recently, in his speech at the opening of the Hood Museum, Dartmouth College, 1985, Moore even said architecture is a performance art. A masterful architect needs to be a masterful performer during his presentations. With the performances in St. Matthew's, Moore was able to train his young, stage-shy, inexperienced partners through their appearances in supporting roles. Like all successful performances, St. Matthew's workshops had an experienced director who organized the show for "a sophisticated audience" (J. Burns) and brought out the best qualilties from his stars. The successful presentation/performances increased the clients' confidence in the archtiects; confidence from clients meant greater design freedom and more readily approved design.

Some writers have called Moore's design sessions jam sessions, comparing them to Duke Ellington's jazz sessions. Moore seems to be most comfortable when he designs with a group of poeple; he never designs alone. Not only do the gigging cats admire Moore, they also encourage him with ideas, reactions, observations, and contradictions. All designers desire positive reinforcement for their self-confidence and ego, but, fearing input overload, not all designers can tolerate distractions. Moore can easily organize, digest, and produce with input from others (in St. Matthew's as many as 150 people); "the workshop process can be a disaster under a less able architect but under Moore a wonderful process" (Davis). This quality of Moore's mind is a crucial ingredient in his creations of magic that seem to put the participants in awe. In order to design an exciting building, the designer must get excited, and Moore gets excited when others get excited by his designs. Such performances and gatherings are supported by Moore's writings on "gathering places," "stage-set architecture," "people watching people." A letter headed "Welcome to the St. Matthew's Take Part Workshop" and signed by Moore begins with "We are *gathered* to begin the evolution of a new environment for St. Matthew's that will *serve* your needs and *respond* to your hopes for your new church."

Result/Analysis/Conclusion

As one approaches St. Matthew's (usually in a car, since it is in Southern California), the bell tower and the cross configuration of expansion joints on the street facade announce the church. After parking the car, one can see the entrance facade screened by large trees preserved from the old church (*53.12*). The steps leading to the entrance porch and the arcade connecting the bell tower to the building direct the visitor toward the entrance. After ascending the steps, the visitor is funneled toward the narthex by decreasing enclosures of the entrance porch; the octagonal narthex is detached from the building, and reaches out to receive the visitor. By entering the narthex, the visitor is further compressed by a floating octagonal halo, in anticipation of the grand interior. The visitor entering the main sanctuary first encounters the structural pier and arch because the narthex is off the main axis of the nave (*53.14*). Progressing through the space, the viewer is surprised and emotionally moved by the revelation of the altar and the soaring height of the ceiling. The floating cross, triumphal arches, semicircular light rings, and the back-lighted cross webbing work in ensemble to call the viewer's attention to the architectural action above (*53.13,15*). The two arches that support the nave truss which in turn supports the cross-shaped roof and off which the floating cross is hung form an aedicula frequently used by Moore to mark a special place with structural elements, not unlike the two aediculas that support the truss in Moore's house in Orinda. If the earlier aediculas are Sir John Summerson's miniature temples, the St. Matthew's aedicula is the architectural symbol of a church.

If the visitor desires to walk around the building before entering the sanctuary, it is possible to walk under the covered arcade to a courtyard surrounded by trees—a protected outdoor space for gathering. Through a narrow alley that suggests tall, dark, monastic passages lined by rooms, one reaches the prayer garden, preseved from the old church, that is completely enclosed on three sides and partially enclosed by a screen wall with Moore arches on the fourth side. The old prayer garden has become a cloister, even provided with a cross formed by the expansion joints on the exterior wall of the altar. In comparison to the courtyard, the prayer garden is more private, intimate, and protected, to create a space of retreat, meditation, and solitude. Along the winding path through the seasonal flowers, the visitor once again arrives at the entrance porch after circumventing the main sanctuary through a series of passages and rooms (entrance porch, courtyard, and prayer garden) that are outside the main sanctuary but within the outer perimeter. These enclosed outdoor spaces satisfy the clients' desire for "more connection between inside and outside" (Workshop Report III).

In the introduction to Moore's article, "Working Together to Make Something," *Architectural Record*, February, 1984, Charles K. Gandy wrote, "Moore would have us believe that he and his partners . . . did not design St. Matthew's Parish Church. Although we may be suspicious of the claim . . . we are nonetheless intrigued by the argument." Who did design the church, then?

St. Matthew's is the result of the collaboration between clients and architects. In discussing his clients, Moore wrote, "the parish of St. Matthew's . . . embraces a particularly wide variety of views about theology (and every other subject). . . . There were a great many opinion about what the new church should be like." Often these opinions and desires conflicted with each other, and the architects had to satisfy both parties for the two-thirds approval.

Although the architects and the clients compromised on some design details, the main architectural idea of a cross-shaped roof over a semicircular seating arrangement provided a solution to the age-long dilemma of the longitudinal vs. the centralized church. The symbolic architectural action of the cross is kept out of the way of the the functional activity of worship. Moore, Ruble, Yudell, however, did not develop this idea all by themselves; the clients' desire for a circular pew pattern was a crucial catalyst in the evolution of the design, and "the cross-shaped nave and transept are similar in shape and size to the foundation of the former church." Geometrically, the semicircles of the altar and the pews, the octagon of the walls, and the square of the base of the hip roof are all concentric with their centers on the head of the cross-shape roof (*53.8*). Furthermore, all the centers of the crosses in St. Matthew's are on a single axial plane passed down the center of the nave: the two expansion-joint crosses on the east and west exterior walls, the cross of the nave-transept roof, the cross of the intersecting trusses, and the floating cross that hangs from them.

Three of the contradictions in the parishioners' desires were: lots of wood and glass (like the old chapel) versus good acoustics (wood and glass are both poor materials for acoustics); a view of the outdoors (especially the prayer garden) versus undistracted attention on the altar; and small ("intimate . . . cozy") versus big ("important . . . majestic . . . grand"). All the above oxymorons and tensions are manifested in St. Matthew's. Moore, Ruble, Yudell created order from chaos, but the old chaos is still visible in the new order. The tension between order and chaos gives life and creates the excitement of St. Matthew's church.

When one first enters the sanctuary, there seems to be a lot of wood and glass, but at a closer inspection, there really is much less than there appears to be at first sight. The two end walls of the nave are both solid plaster walls, without glass or wood (the reredos is only a wooden backdrop) for sound acoustics. The secrets behind the visual trick are the vast wooden ceiling to which the eye is first attracted upon entry; the two-inch-deep wood battens on the plaster walls that appear more pronounced from acute angles; and the wooden furniture and decorations (pews, altar furniture, floating cross, reredos). A similar illusion is created with glass. The Aalto-esque windows flanking the altar, with their vertical windows of varying heights, create an appearance of more glass. The south wall with its appendages exposed to natural sun contains more glass than the north. The chapel under the south transept is like a breakfast room surrounded by a bay window (the chapel is most often used for early morning services). The narthex is essentially an octagonal glass telephone booth. Although there seems to be lots of glass, from most seats one can see out only into the peaceful prayer garden during a service.

The "cozy and intimate" place for worship is provided by the semicircular pews, only seven rows deep, that bring the congregation close together. While the seats themselves are intimately arranged, the space above them is lofty and majestic; it rises to thirty-eight feet. To fit modestly into its environment, the giant interior had to be clothed in a suit fit for a dwarf. Thus, all four elevations of the building are cleverly massed into a low-key exterior at the residential scale of the neighborhood, not unlike Maybeck's Christian Science Church. On the north and west elevations, the ancillary spaces are placed into the hill and covered by a shed roof with low eaves to give the perimeters of the building a human scale. On the west street elevation, the arcade and trees intervene between the street and the building to mask the large facade and provide a gradual increase of height. On the south entrance elevation, the large volume of the main sanctuary is once again dissolved by various appendages. The chapel grows out of the large transept; the baptistry and the narthex are fused into the nave.

Although the clients clearly participated in the design process, how democratic was it? The design of St. Matthew's was democratic only up to the approval of the schematic design. Later decisions were made by the representative governing body of various committees, similar to the vestry that makes most decisions for the parish. When asked, "Were the workshops democratic? and "Was every participant able to express his thoughts?", the replies varied from "definitely" (Flynn) and "only the dissatisfied bitch" (L. Burns) to "democratic in expressed ideas and desires but not in the actual design" (Curtis) and "expressed ideas at the beginning but became more difficult and lost later" (Mann; "later" refers to the committees). But there seemed to be a general consensus of satisfaction with the workshops, and some even felt "any other process would have been unacceptable" (Jensen). According to Moore, "people creating something, working together to make something, have a much easier time working with each other and find the experience far more exciting and positive than people on committees, who are cast automatically into a kind of critical role of wondering whether what's already in front of them is all right or not." The general contractor of St. Matthew's said, "I had meetings to death! ... In twenty years experience as a contractor, I never attended so many meetings with the clients." Although some parishioners tried to blame the archtiects' lack of business sense for the slow process of building, the reason for the latter was, if anything, the overinvolvment of the clients. "The workshops were great, but the committees did not bring out Moore's full artistic potential ... They said 'no' to Moore too many times. ... St. Matthew's does not contain 100 percent magic of Moore. ... With Moore, the client should allow him the artistic freedom, speaking from experience ... " (L. Burns).

If a normal attention span in today's society is about two hours (as demonstrated by movies, shows, lectures), how did the design team keep the attention of the participants for four to five hours on Sundays, the day of rest? The design team kept the participants occupied with a variety of activities. The agenda included a picnic as a diversion and a communionlike ritual; MRY used the necessary act of eating as a way to bring the participants closer together. The parishioners were willing to sacrifice their valuable rest time for a worthy cause because "it was our work and our process" (Davis). The architects were successful in exciting the participants, but the parishioners also had strong interest and care for their new church, and longed for the close community they once had. The parish is "thrilled about the new church . . . [and] has grown since the new church" (Card); the new church has "at minimum, doubled attendance" (Jensen). "The building reflects the unity of two rectors working together in harmony" (Kreitler). For Father Arnold Fenton "the church is only a building that encloses action" and "the emphasis [should be] on the action of worship and community." Indeed, by designing St. Matthew's together in the workshops, the parish was once again politically reunited.

This essay is based on a series of interviews with twenty people who were involved in the building of St. Matthew's.

Leland Burns, Selection Committee and Organ Committee, professor of urban planning, UCLA
David Card, Building Committee, lawyer
Sue Curtis, Senior Warden of the Vestry
John Davis, Building Committee Vice Chair, real estate developer
Arnold Fenton, Rector
Jill Flynn, Interior Committee, writer for *Home* magazine
John Ingram, Building Committee Chair, contractor
David Jensen, General Chairman, business executive

Peter Kreitler, Assistant Rector
Fredrick Lee, Treasurer, insurance
Tita Mann, workshop participant
Jean Romig, Organ Committee Chair, realtor
Adams, workshop participant
Corky, secretary of St. Matthew's
McVey, workshop participant
Jim Burns, workshop coordinator
Regula Campbell, landscape architect
Tim Felchlin, assistant project manager
Russ Meskell, contractor
Charles Moore, architect

These people were interviewed in January 1985. The questions concentrated on the three workshops held on August 5, September 16, and October 14, 1979.

The following documents in the Moore, Ruble, Yudell files were consulted:

Proposal for St. Matthew's by Moore, Ruble, Yudell
Introductory letter signed by Charles Moore

St. Matthew's Design Workshop Report(s) Numbers I, II, and III
Handout for the schematic design presentation

Performing Architecture:
The Work of Charles Moore

Eugene J. Johnson

Opposite. Fantasy with fish, 1971
Pencil, colored pencil, and ink on paper
16.5" x 19.5"
Drawing by Charles W. Moore

Fig. 1. Marcel Breuer
Preston Robinson House
Williamstown, Massachusetts
1946, exterior

Charles Moore says that architecture is a performing art. Typically, this is a definition that tends to hide the intellect of the speaker behind an image that suggests entertainment rather than thought, but he takes his definition seriously. He understands that it takes brains to be a good performer, even if many of the rest of us do not. His buildings are complex creatures that simultaneously take their inspiration from more sources than one can easily keep in mind: architectural history, local traditions, client needs and personalities, climate, character of site, an impulse to joke, the chance appearance of a photograph on the table at which he is designing, or almost any other factor one can possibly imagine having an effect on a building. To continue the performance metaphor, one might think of Moore as a juggler of architectural ideas, whose buildings show those ideas all tossed into the air at once to form an original shape. Or one can see the buildings as records of the collision of all those ideas that have informed their design, a collision that avoids chaos because Moore has strictly grounded the design in geometry.

Moore is a man who responds to all kinds of buildings, from the grand to the seemingly worthless. No architectural impression is discarded without its having been subjected to at least a brief, but always searching analysis. He has said that he reacts to sources in two ways, either with "the soaking action of a sponge, or with the gulps of a piranha fish." His intelligent absorption of what was around him we see from the very first of his buildings, a cabin at Torch Lake, Michigan, of 1947, which Moore says has a strong resemblance to the Goetsch-Winkler House of Frank Lloyd Wright at Okemos, Michigan, which he knew as a child.

For his second design, of 1949, only two pages of blueprints that give us plan and elevations are preserved (*9.1,2*). The Jones House, designed for a site in Oregon, reflected some of the most recent developments of its day, particularly the butterfly roof that Marcel Breuer was using in houses such as that for Preston Robinson in Williamstown, Massachusetts, of 1946 (*fig. 1*). Moore's elevations are pure late 1940s International Style, popular in advanced architectural circles in this country at the end of World War II particularly because of the arrival of Breuer, Gropius, and Mies van der Rohe on these shores in the years just before the war. Moore's clearly organized plan shows a taste for clean, open spaces arranged in neat rectangles and a desire to give the interior spaces a close relationship to the outside. This last he could have learned from Wright's houses directly, rather than from the Breuer designs he had only seen in architectural magazines. There is also a sense that the house fits the land, particularly in the way the steps of the south elevation follow the slope of the site. The house was not built. If it had been, it would not have been particularly remarkable, save for the fact that its designer was only twenty-four when he affixed his signature and the word *architect* to its plans.

The precocious age signals the fact that we are in the presence of a rather precocious person, who had graduated from college in 1945, when he was twenty, and had completed an advanced degree in architecture at the University of Michigan, his home state. He had set up practice in California, the preferred winter home of his parents during his childhood. They, loathing the Michigan winters, annually abandoned the Midwest for Florida or California, taking young Charles with them. Free of the drudgeries of school from late September to early May, Charles was also free even of the ministrations of tutors. Each June, back in Michigan, he took the examinations for his classes, and each year he got all A's. Thus Charles Moore bypassed the American school system. Remarkably, he has come to play a role of some significance in that very system, at the university level.

The year 1954 found Moore serving in the the army in Korea, with what delight one can well imagine, given his abhorrence of regimentation. At least he was in the Corps of Engineers rather than the trenches. Thus he had the chance to design at least two buildings, of which prints, once again, are the sole remaining evidence. His proposed A-frame Yun Chon Chapel, which looks in some ways more like a ski lodge than a religious structure (*42.1,2*), is not one of his happiest works, particularly in the awkward way it juts out from its sloping site. Some passages in the design, however, deserve our attention. Atop the chapel's stone foundation platform is a splayed stone terrace with plantings that suggest fruitful observations of Japanese gardens, as well as some of Moore's later attempts to integrate stairs and landscape. Above and behind the terrace an Asian tempietto, in which Bible classes were to be held, rises alongside the very Western-style chapel. In his later works, as we shall see, he continues this kind of confrontation between elements of disparate origin, but in his mature works the disparate elements coexist in one whole rather than stand side by side. The elevation of the altar wall of the Yun Chon Chapel, on a second sheet of plans, shows a window set diagonally into the left side of the altar wall, to produce a single light source for the east end of the building. This same motif reappears more than twenty years later in St. Matthew's Church in Pacific Palisades, California, albeit in a more sophisticated way.

In Korea he also produced a design for the Chung Wha Girls' Middle and High School (*43*) that is, in many ways, more satisfying than the chapel. At the core is a rectangular court partly surrounded by rooms and corridors. The whole may be seen as a rectangle with fragmented edges. The theme of fragmentation is one to watch in later works, as is the long, axial path that leads from the entrance pavilion to the inner parts of the complex. Such long paths, some straight, some angled, will appear again and again in Moore's work. The International Style glass walls of the Jones House project of 1949 reappear, but with a more Miesian flavor, especially in the rhythms of the courtyard elevation. The closeness of Moore's windows to those of Mies at the Illinois Institute of Technology probably results from the fact that both Moore and Mies looked back to Asian prototypes, particularly Japanese, rather than to the fact that Moore was drawing directly on Mies's designs. It is fair to say that both of Moore's Korean designs show an interest in giving his buildings a sense of belonging to the place in which they were intended to be built.

Back from Korea in 1954, Moore designed a house for his mother and himself—his father was dead—in Pebble Beach, California, on a small lot on a sloping site overlooking the Pacific far below to the south. (The house still belongs to Moore and his sister, and they now rent it to the widow of Roger Bailey, the man who had taught Moore architecture at Michigan.) Although Moore's mother's house predates the one designed by his equally famous contemporary, Robert Venturi, for *his* mother, Moore's is less well known, because, one suspects, it is not a radical statement of new purposes.

In plan, the house is simplicity itself (*1.5*), a long rectangle containing two bedrooms at one end and a living room at the other. The center is occupied by the kitchen and bath, the rooms that need plumbing. The long hall contains ample closets, at the client's request, but the form, according to Moore, once again goes back to Wright's Usonian houses that he knew in Michigan. Particularly clever is the positioning of the two outside doors; back and front are side by side, separated only by a short screen wall that hides the rear entrance, and the garbage cans, from visitors.

The most arresting visual details occur in the rhythmic changes Moore wrings from the basic modular unit of the 16-inch centers between the vertical members of the balloon frame. In the plan and in the south perspective (*1.1*) these rhythmic patterns are clearly visible in the varying widths of the windows of the bedrooms, bath, and kitchen. The regularly, and thus serenely, spaced verticals of the living room, on the other hand, held Japanese shoji screens (these now cover up the back hall closet shelves). What Moore sought to achieve here was an inexpensive house graced by visual variety, one that had attained rhythmic complexity without complicating the budget.

The construction drawings for this house, all in Moore's own hand, show his keen but often unnoticed interest in structural details (*1.4*). His focus here on wood joinery, of course, had much to do with his direct experience of the wooden architecture of Korea and Japan. It also reflects the interest he has seemingly always had in the architecture of the San Francisco Bay area, as well as in the work of Greene and Greene around Los Angeles. The Moore House has some remarkably complex wooden decorative details that Moore not only designed, but also built.

Moore's perspective drawing of the house from the entrance (*1.2*) shows once again one of those long paths leading into the complex, a wooden walkway that stretches out almost to become a road. Alongside this path is a small, quiet, Japaneselike garden that Moore also built himself, more or less as it is shown in this perspective view. Only after passing through the serene garden, pulled along by the wooden walk, does one understand how to enter the house. Once inside, one finds a rather cramped entrance hall—the house is, after all, quite small. In contrast, the living room takes on an appearance of grandeur that in actuality it lacks. Its apparent size is further augmented by the view out through the shoji screens and the Monterey pines to the ocean far below. Through these screens one emerges onto a narrow walk that leads to a deck which provides a view of the ocean, without blocking that same view from the living room. (The deck has now been replaced with an extra room.) In other words, this inexpensive little house, with its knowing play of rhythms, contains an architectural promenade of some sophistication as well as a sense of spatial expansion and even serene grandeur that is quite unexpected.

In hindsight, it is clear that several major themes of Moore's future work appear here, even though the house looks little like the work for which he has become famous. One theme is sensitivity to the lay of the land. The house is sited to make best use of its splendid ocean view from all the rooms. Another is Moore's lack of great concern about the view the house presents to the street or even to the visitor initially. One encounters the rather large garage first, which is made even more forbidding by the fact that it rises above land that slopes down toward the street. Even granting that this is a California house, where the automobile always gets its fair share of the architecture, this garage is hardly splendid to look upon. A third theme is the use of complex rhythms to enliven a simple, inexpensive design. Finally, the roof, here clearly based on Japanese prototypes, is given the prominent and psychologically crucial role of making clear that the house is a shelter. This last is to be a principal element in almost all of Moore's designs.

Before going to Korea, Moore had taught for a year in the architecture school at the University of Utah, brought there by his old teacher from Michigan, Roger Bailey. In Utah he had begun to think of the study of architectural history as an important part of the curriculum of an architecture school, but he had also come to realize that his knowledge of that history was inadequate. After the year in Utah, he received a grant to travel in Europe, before he was urged to travel to Asia by the army. In Korea, he determined to prepare himself in those areas in which he felt his education had been lacking. Once back in the states, he wrote to Yale, Harvard, and Princeton, suggesting a course of study of his own devising that would lead to a Ph.D. in architecture. Princeton was the only school to answer his letter, and it did so with enthusiasm. To Princeton he went.

In 1956, when Moore arrived, Princeton was one of the most interesting places to study architecture in this country, if not in the Western world. The school was run by Jean Labatut, a Frenchman who had gone through the Ecole des Beaux Arts, but had not been turned into a knee-jerk classicist by the experience. Indeed, Labatut was never a knee-jerk anything. In his teaching, he tended to dwell on architectural fundamentals, such as scale, site, materials, and plan. What the building ultimately looked like, in stylistic terms, was a matter of some indifference to him. Labatut designed few buildings himself. They have a modest lack of style, although they make use of standard twentieth-century devices, such as large glass walls. Thus there was much in Labatut's teachings to make Moore think about fundamentals, and few personal stylistic gimmicks that might have forced Moore's vision into a particular mold.

Also on the faculty was the Milanese architect Enrico Peressutti, who, according to Moore, was more important to him than Labatut. Peressutti's firm, Banfi, Belgiojoso, Peressutti, and Rogers (BBPR), was deeply committed to what it saw as the great achievements of modern architecture in the decades before World War II. Like many of the most influential and innovative architects of the fifties, however, they found that the architecture invented by the great masters of the modern movement in the twenties did not suit present needs. Particularly, the new architecture, deliberately ahistorical, was

difficult to fit into the context of the old Italian cities in which BBPR found itself working. During Moore's years at Princeton, BBPR designed and built what may be its most important work, the Torre Velasca in Milan, a skyscraper with a deliberately historical top (*fig. 2*), rather than the flat roof that had become the norm for most tall buildings in the years following the war. Its upper floors projected out over those below, in imitation of the late Gothic and early Renaissance fortress towers of Lombardy. BBPR here deliberately attempted to seek in the local history of tall structures a formal solution to the problem of the modern tall building. Peressutti was never afraid to use modern materials in old contexts—to mix the two to the advantage of both. His design for the installation of works of art in the fifteenth-century Castello Sforzesco in Milan, in which brutal steel I-beams act as pedestals for works of medieval stone sculpture, all inside spacious Renaissance rooms, is one of the glories of modern museum installation. This brave desire to accommodate old and new Peressutti passed on to his students.

As Peressutti's student, Moore produced one of his most ambitious Princeton projects—a cultural center for Chichén Itzá, one of Mexico's great archaeological sites, which Peressutti's whole class visited. Moore's project looks nothing like the ruins alongside of which it was to rise. Rather, it envisioned a light, modern structure of bent concrete canopies set into a grid which he then broke to create open space within the whole (**44**). The thesis here seems to have been that new concrete forms, derived from the work of Pier Luigi Nervi (one thinks of Nervi's contributions to Breuer's UNESCO Building in Paris, for instance), could somehow be made to look suitable alongside forms with which they had little in common. The desire to accommodate old and new here may have outstripped the means, but the important point to remember is that the desire, already evident in the designs Moore did in Korea, had been made to grow by Peressutti in the mind of the pupil.

The grid of the roof is superimposed on a pavement grid that runs diagonally against the one of the roof. On a conceptual scale, this collision sets up an interplay of forms that would have been hard to understand on the site, unless one could observe it from the bird's-eye view of Moore's drawing. In 1982, in the margin of a sketch for the Beverly Hills Civic Center, Moore produced precisely this same clash of grids.

The third important teacher for Moore at Princeton was Louis I. Kahn. In the middle years of the fifties Kahn developed an architectural space that set itself deliberately in opposition to the "universal" space championed by Mies and other modernists. The first examples of Kahn's new spaces, completed in the year Moore arrived at Princeton, are found at the nearby Trenton Jewish Community Center Bathhouse (*fig. 3*). The square changing rooms of the bathhouse, covered with truncated pyramidal roofs, form discrete, continuous units from floor to ceiling (*fig. 4*), rather than the open spaces of Mies. These latter could be manipulated with freely hung planes, but they could never define the discrete enclosures, complete unto themselves, that Kahn made at Trenton.

The changing rooms, which Kahn designated as served spaces, are entered by smaller units, also square in plan, that are among the earliest examples of what Kahn called servant spaces. This notion of a main space that is a discrete geometric form, served by smaller units, also of pure geometric units, was taken up by Moore during his Princeton period in an unrealized project for the Inn at Cannery Row, a hotel complex in Monterey, California. This design of 1958 employed a pattern of large octagons—the served spaces—and small squares, which would have "served" the octagons as entrance halls, balconies, or bathrooms (**23.1,2**). The plan, clearly derived from a common tile pattern of interlocked octagons and squares, is an important document of the impact of Kahn's ideas on Moore's work at just the moment Moore was working in Kahn's office in Philadelphia. Indeed, the whole structure of the Inn at Cannery Row would have been supported by an open concrete or steel frame (**23.3,4**) that recalls the concrete structural frames of the laboratories of Kahn's Richards Medical Research Building at the University of Pennsylvania. Kahn was working on these labs the very year Moore designed the inn.

Also from the years when Moore was heavily under Kahn's influence comes Moore's only design of a tall office building, the addition to the Citizens

Fig. 5. Clark and Beuttler (Charles W. Moore and Alan Morgan)
Citizens Savings and Loan Building
San Francisco, California
1960–1961, exterior
(Photograph © Morley Baer)

Fig. 6. MLTW/Moore-Turnbull
Sea Ranch Athletic Club II
Sea Ranch, California
1969–1971, interior, showers, men's locker room

Savings and Loan Building on Market Street in San Francisco, 1960–61 (*fig. 5*). Designed in collaboration with Alan Morgan, when both were employed by the San Francisco firm of Clark and Beuttler, the addition consists essentially of one of the brick servant towers from Richards attached by glazed corridors to the side of the old structure. The floor levels of the tower are marked by concrete string courses that derive their inspiration from Kahn's Yale Art Gallery of the early fifties. The new tower was topped by a pyramidal roof that both recalls the Kahn roofs at Trenton and the mansard roof of the building to which it is attached. (Moore disclaims parentage of the dormer windows in the roof of the addition.) Although the details can almost all be traced to the work of Kahn, the remarkable thing about this addition is the way the severe Kahn vocabulary was made to make sense alongside a building that indulged itself in Second Empire details with a Western (Mae, that is) exuberance. Moore's desire to make new buildings that lived happily with old ones seems no longer to have outstripped the means.

The Inn at Cannery Row and the addition to the Citizens Savings and Loan are not the only works from these years that recall Kahn. In an undated project for the Retail Milk Products Drive-in, Pacific Grove, California, 1960 (*46*), Moore, with a wit that seems gradually to emerge in these years, plays with Trenton Bathhouse roofs to the point of absurdity. One grows much too tall, so that it in essence becomes a sign board, while another offers a kind of triumphal entrance to a parking lot in front of a restaurant that was to be built later. This four-columned canopy presents us with one of the first examples in Moore's work of a theme of absolutely crucial importance: that of the aedicule. It also shows him using a form of great purport and antiquity with something less than all-consuming seriousness.

In 1948 John Summerson, the distinguished British architectural historian, published a group of essays under the title *Heavenly Mansions*. In the title piece, "Heavenly Mansions, An Interpretation of Gothic," Summerson introduces the notion of the little house, which he relates to the desires of children to play under tables, where they feel secure. For Summerson these little houses, in Latin *aedicula*, have both a cozy character—the one that appeals to children—and a ceremonial character. He suspects that the aedicula, or "miniature temple used for a ceremonial, symbolic purpose, may even enshrine one of man's first purely architectural discoveries, a discovery re-enacted by every child who establishes his momentary dominion under the table."

Summerson's concept of the aedicula recurs with an astounding frequency in Moore's work. It is fitting that one of the first times Moore should have used so formidable an idea was in jest. But the jest was made, as always, with an architectural point in mind, an architectural point that Moore, no matter how outrageously funny he is being, never neglects. As Moore often put the notion in his writings a few years later, he feels that the prime duty of the architect is to give his client a sense of place, of a spot on this globe the client can call his own. For Moore, the aedicula provides that sense of place with particular power. The customer under Moore's drive-through aedicula, then, would have known that he had arrived at a place of some importance on an otherwise placeless strip. For a similarly tongue-in-cheek use of the same motif, one may turn to the showers in the mens' locker room of the second Athletic Club at Sea Ranch, California, 1969. There, yellow aediculas are painted around openings in a wall that holds the shower heads on its opposite face (*fig. 6*). As one descends the stairs from the changing room to the showers, one sees the bathers as if they were classical nudes in niches.

For his Princeton dissertation, submitted in the fall of 1957, Moore chose to write on the rather broad theme of water in architecture. The text shows that Moore's view of architecture had become as broad as the theme he had chosen. The text skips around over centuries and moves easily from Europe and America to China and Japan, in an attempt to understand some of the principal reasons people have used water in their buildings. It is a gently scholarly piece, not overloaded with the weighty paraphernalia of learning that one might expect to find in a dissertation produced in a great university— Moore is hardly the man for that. But the dissertation shows breadth of study and depth of understanding, as well as an ability to think in surprising juxtapositions.

Fig. 7. Charles W. Moore
Martin Studio
San Francisco, California
1958, perspective of exterior, blueprint

Fig. 8. MLTW/Moore-Turnbull
Johnson House
Sea Ranch, California
1965–1966, plan and schematic plans
Drawings by Richard Song

The dissertation also includes design projects, in which Moore uses his historical study of water in architecture to inform his designs for fountains in his time. Part of the dissertation deals with the area of the Glen Canyon Dam in Arizona. A series of watercolors (*32.1*) shows the approach to the dam—the architectural promenade again—that is timed by the clocks below the drawings. Part of the approach is decorated with water spouts over the road, a very early example of environmental sculpture, one suspects. Of particular interest for his later work, however, is the little floating community of water-borne aediculas and platforms that were the ultimate goal of this promenade by car, foot, and boat.

The dissertation also includes a group of three fountains designed for New York's Park Avenue. The most interesting for our purposes were those intended for Lever House and the Seagram Building, the latter opened only the summer after the dissertation was submitted. These widely heralded steel and glass triumphs of the International Style in previously hostile New York were, for Moore, two alien intruders into the solid masonry walls of buildings that had once defined the sides, and thus the axis of the avenue. With his fountains, Moore hoped to return a sense of density to the boundaries of the street and thereby to restore the axis. For Lever House, headquarters of a giant international soap corporation, he created a somewhat surreal set of stone washtubs raised on short legs (*32.2*). In plan, some of the troughs formed a disjointed versions of Le Corbusier's Modular Man, through whose waist passed the glass curtain wall of the lobby (*32.3*). This being Lever House, one of the fountains would have blown soap bubbles. Simultaneously, then, the fountains would have suggested soap and the destruction (washing away?) of one of the sacred images of modern architecture.

The plaza in front of the Seagram Building, diagonally across the street from Lever House, would have lost the two rectangular pools of water that Mies had planned for it. Instead, a rectangularized stream would have meandered through a gently but irregularly contoured plaza that Moore called "the beach." Moore wanted beach and stream to form a continuous visual surface that would have suggested that the building could only be approached over water, perhaps as if it were a pavilion in a Japanese garden (*32.4*). This contour map plan of the plaza (*32.5*), which introduces a carefully designed but seemingly random natural form into a relentlessly geometric urban context, seems the earliest instance in Moore's work of a very important but often overlooked tendency of his to insert natural forms into architectural situations where one might not expect to find them. It is also the first instance in his work of the artificial stream, probably derived from those in Japanese gardens, introduced into an urban context, an idea to which he will return with some frequency.

The Princeton years produced a host of remarkable designs that do not quite seem to fit with what we have come to know as Moore's style, but which, nevertheless, announce ideas that will be taken up at various points in his career. One such design is the undated project for a Jewish Community Center in Seaside, California, the drawings for which are in Moore's own hand (*45.1,2*). From the rather gloomy sky (dare one think here of nineteenth-century German romanticism?), formed by closely spaced parallel lines of black ink, emerges the white mass of the structure, which is approached up a long flight of steps flanked by curved walls. In plan, the main building is a simple and rather uninteresting rectangle, but the stairs and their flanking walls are far from ordinary. The stairs narrow as they approach the main building—just as Bernini's Scala Regia in the Vatican Palace narrows—to create visually a greater sense of depth than actually exists. For Moore, apparently the promenade offered by the rather shallow lot was inadequate for the effect he wanted; he used perspective to remedy the situation. Here one sees the direct result of the study of the history of architecture that Moore undertook at Princeton. Such quotations from Baroque architecture one does not find in his pre-Princeton days, but they will now reappear with some frequency. (The formal language of the courts that flank the staircase may suggest the curvaciousness of the work of the great Finnish architect, Alvar Aalto, whose considerable influence on Moore we will take up later.)

In 1958 Moore, again while working with Alan Morgan in the offices of Clark and Beuttler, designed the Martin Studio (*fig. 7*) on Leavenworth Street in San

Fig. 7

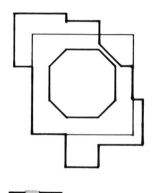

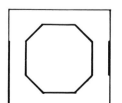

Fig. 8

Francisco. The drawings for this, not in Moore's hand, are preserved only in prints. They show a curiously deformed cube, raised on a Nervilike umbrella, such as Nervi had designed for the Gatti Wool Factory in Rome in 1957. As built, the studio lacks the umbrella structure, which was probably too costly to construct. The studio is reached by means of a flight of winding stairs that pass beneath it into a garden, designed by Lawrence Halprin, and to a house beyond. The studio thus also serves as gatehouse. The square plan of the studio is twisted—Moore would say "massaged"—so that the window at the left corner can be angled toward the street and, particularly, to the view north to San Francisco Bay. Pure geometry, of the type used by Kahn, gives way here to the pleasures provided by the site. One will find, over and over in Moore's work, the same kind of "massaged," compromised geometry, in which two seemingly opposite elements that complement each other are joined to form a whole. Invariably, however, if one looks hard enough, the original geometry of the individual parts can be reconstructed from the evidence of the mishapen object at hand.

With the Ph.D. at Princeton completed, Moore took a job as a teaching assistant there, while he also worked in Kahn's office in Philadelphia. Moore's admiration for Kahn is immense. Once, in 1977, visiting Kahn's Yale Center for British Art, he said that he used to think that Kahn could do no wrong. (The wrong he thought Kahn had done at Yale was hardly major. Moore was talking about some rows of tiny light bulbs Kahn placed around rather grand openings in the walls of the entrance hall.) Clearly it was to the work of Kahn, more than that of any other architect, with the possible exception of Aalto, to which Moore turned in the next few years, when he left the Princeton ambience and went to Berkeley to head its architecture school, a prestigious post for one seemingly so untried in the profession.

The years before Berkeley, then, can be divided into two sections. Those before Princeton are characterized by a competent modernism enriched in 1954 by direct experience of the gardens and wooden architecture of Korea and Japan. Those at Princeton are marked by experiments with the vast variety of architectural forms to which his studies introduced him. One might call this his period of indigestion, given the fact that the banquet was so rich and the results so uneven. One would hardly suspect that the Jewish Community Center and the Martin Studio could have been produced by the same designer in almost the same years—much less that the Park Avenue fountains and the Chichén Itzá concrete shed were also the products of the same mind. In California, however, he seems to have set out to purify these ideas by subjecting his work to the formal geometry that characterized the work of the greatly admired Kahn.

The weekend house for Mr. and Mrs. Cyril Jobson in Palo Colorado Canyon, 1961, offers perhaps the clearest example of the work of Moore's first independent mature period. The Jobsons owned a piece of land in a canyon that runs inland from the Big Sur, south of Carmel. On weekends, they had camped on the land, but Mrs. Jobson had grown weary of holidays in a tent. Moore gave the couple, however, a memento of their former weekends, a kind of giant wooden tent, as Frei Otto put it, an open structure under a great shed roof (*11.11*). The roof is supported by four slender wooden posts that form the corners of a square. This square is the geometric core of the regular cubic volume with which the design of the house begins (*11.2*).

From this core, walls push outward as function dictates, to enclose the space required by living room, entrance, and dining area; the basic square is enlarged in an irregular way by attaching fragments of larger squares to it. It is perhaps easier to understand this design method if one compares the plan of the Jobson House with that of the Johnson House at Sea Ranch, California, of a few years later (*fig. 8*). The core of the Johnson House is an octagon formed by eight posts placed at its corners. In the earliest sketches for the Johnson House, the octagon is enclosed in a square, just as the central square of the Jobson House is enclosed in a larger square. The square of the Johnson House is then deformed to accommodate functional requirements (*fig. 8, top*). At the upper left corner, the walls are pushed out to make room for the bath and for a large closet. At the lower right, the walls are moved out a shorter distance to make the space needed for the kitchen, while the wall at the bottom is extended in the middle, just as the same wall is pushed out in the Jobson

House, to make an entrance hall. The upper right corner is cut away, however, in order to bring directly into the interior space the dramatic view of the Pacific coast the house enjoys. In the Johnson House, only the lower left corner, which contains the dining area, retains the shape of the original square that enclosed the octagon. Even the center of the top wall is pushed out just enough to make room for a double bed. The octagonal core, however, never loses its geometric clarity. The square at the center of the Jobson House persists in its purity as well (*11.1*). Moore's pushing out of the boundaries of a house to make room for functional requirements receives a slightly different treatment in taller houses of this early period, such as the Bonham (*12*) and Talbert houses. There, the projections, raised above ground level, become what he terms "saddlebags," a device that reappears later in the row of offices hung off the south wall of his addition to Lawrence Hall at Williams College (*51.14,15*). These saddlebags, one suspects, may also owe a certain debt to the squared-off bay window attached to the Small Bracketed Cottage published by Andrew Jackson Downing in his *Architecture of Country Houses* in 1859 (*fig. 9*). Of Downing's importance to Moore we will have more to say shortly.

Fig. 9

The exteriors of both the Jobson and Johnson houses have a characteristic irregularity of form. Both houses are covered by broad pyramidal roofs centered over the central square or octagon. The planes of the roof descend until they are cut off by the rising walls of the exterior. Thus, at some points the roof edge seems quite high off the ground, and at others, quite low. The rising walls carve away the roof, leaving only a fragment of the regular pyramid the roof started out to be. One might say that while the geometry of the plan is additive, the geometry of the roof is subtractive.

This kind of exterior massing, created by the collision between a regularly shaped roof and walls rising from an asymmetrical plan, Moore devised by fusing ideas culled from the work of Alvar Aalto and Louis Kahn. In Aalto's Villa Carré outside Paris, of 1956, the large single-pitch roof is cut off in a zigzag manner by walls that enclose interior spaces of different sizes (*fig. 10*). At the Jobson and Johnson houses, Moore's walls operate in the same manner. They intersect, however, not a single-pitch, shed roof, but a in pyramid, derived from Kahn's Trenton Bathhouse (*see fig. 3*). This fusion of two contradictory design approaches gives the Jobson and Johnson houses random appearances that conceal from the unwary the rigid geometry on which they are based.

Fig. 10

In the Jobson House, the four posts at the core control the three-dimensional development of the interior. The posts and the roof they support form an aedicula, lit by a hood glazed on its southwest face. The four posts define a square, but they are also turned out at 45-degree angles to conform to the diagonals of the sloping beams that support the roof. The posts work ambiguously, geometrically to define the center and structurally to support the roof and the light hood. At the same time they also define vertically a stacked double cube that encloses a staircase so broad that it occupies almost all of the space at the bottom of the tall, narrow volume (*11.9*). Such a spatially voracious staircase, placed at the bottom of a vertical space, one knows from only one earlier work, Michelangelo's entrance hall to the Laurentian Library in San Lorenzo in Florence (*fig. 11*). Moore's translation of Michelangelo's grand access to the Medici manuscript collection into flimsy wooden steps leading to a narrow sleeping loft represents Moore's wit at its most sardonic. Moore's deliberate domestication (or trivialization?) of a great moment in architectural history (more for his own delight than the clients', who probably knew nothing of the Laurenziana) represents an important break with the generation of architects that had preceded him. (He did this, incidentally, in the year that James Ackerman's great book, *The Architecture of Michelangelo*, appeared. Ackerman was on the faculty of Moore's architecture school at Berkeley when the book came out.) Such jokes at the expense of the past were not unique to Moore at this time. His fellow student at Princeton, Robert Venturi, who was born in the same year as Moore, was doing just the same kind of thing in Philadelphia. Venturi's acroterial anodyzed aluminum television antenna atop his Guild House, designed in 1960, descends from Baroque statues such as the Mercury who flies over the facade of Schloss Pommersfelden, an early eighteenth-century German country residence. Venturi, however, may have turned his source into an even more absurd and ironic object.

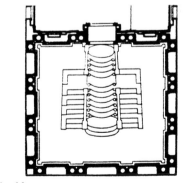

Fig. 11

Fig. 9. Andrew Jackson Downing
Small Bracketed Cottage
(From A. J. Downing, The Architecture of
Country Houses, *New York, 1859)*

Fig. 10. Alvar Aalto
Villa Carré
Bazoches-sur-Guyonne, France
1956–1958, exterior

Fig. 11. Michelangelo
Laurentian Library, entrance hall
San Lorenzo, Florence
1523 ff., plan

One is the wooden architecture of the San Francisco Bay Area, particularly the work of Bernard Maybeck, but also of such practitioners of the genre as William Wurster and Harwell Hamilton Harris, both of whom were producing in these very years less complex versions of the clean-lined wooden architecture that Moore offered the Jobsons. Moore, in his devotion to the use of local traditions here, was inserting himself into a tradition of American domestic architecture that goes back at least as far as the work of A. J. Downing, to which, of course, the domestic architecture of the Bay Area owes an enormous debt. Two remarks, excerpted from Downing's *Cottage Residences* of 1842, will perhaps suffice to demonstrate Moore's continuation of Downing's principles in houses such as the Jobsons'. On the issue of symmetry Downing wrote:

Now almost all persons, who have not cultivated a taste for architecture, or whose organizations are deficient in this faculty, would prefer a regular house to a symmetrically irregular one because with them the reason only demands to be satisfied, but with more cultivated minds the taste and imagination are active, and call for a more lively and varied kind of beauty, and the irregular building would be chosen, as affording more intense and enduring pleasure.

As for fitness of building to site, Downing believed that:

A great deal of the charm of architectural style, in all cases, will rise from the happy union between the locality or site, and the style chosen, and from the entireness with which the architect or amateur enters into the spirit and character of the style, and carries it through his whole work. This may be done in a small cottage, and at little cost, as well as in a mansion, at great expense; but it requires more taste and skill to achieve the former admirably, although the latter may involve ten times the magnitude.

It would almost seem that Downing in these lines had written a sensitive critique of the Jobson House.

Moore's complex use of sources, however, is always subservient to his own special gifts as a designer. The Jobson and Johnson houses do not look like Downing or Maybeck or Esherick, or even like Aalto or Kahn. One can return to the idea of Moore as a juggler of architectural ideas, as the designer of collisions that avoid chaos, because he controls all the disparate ideas by strictly grounding the whole in geometry. The difference between the Jobson and Johnson houses, on the one hand, and the earlier project for the Inn at Cannery Row (*23*) is that the latter is more a one-liner than a complex juggling act. The geometry of the Inn is not taxed by having to control a host of conflicting architectural ideas. It was only in Berkeley that Moore somehow found the freedom to create buildings of a complexity equal to that of his remarkably complex intellect.

To the richness of imagery, ideas, and sources in the Jobson and Johnson houses Moore added an openness of space that gives grandeur to their tiny interiors, just as he had done in his mother's house. Moore also displays in their design a startlingly original three-dimensional imagination. These buildings are not simply clever two-dimensional facades wrapped around an otherwise uninteresting space in which the client has to live. Rather, they are three-dimensional volumes that grow in intellectually and physically complex ways to ensnare the spaces the client needs. They are the product of an architectural imagination that surely has more in common with that of the sculptor than with that of the painter. Is not massaging, after all, what sculptors do to their materials, at least if they are working in clay or plaster?

Although the Jobson House had the distinction of being published in color in *Life Magazine*, the house that Moore designed for himself in Orinda, the next town east of Berkeley, was the one that got the most attention in the architectural press. (Moore, one should hasten to add, has always had a superb instinct for publicity.) Indeed, this was the first of his designs to win an award. At Orinda the geometry is far simpler than in the Jobson House, so much so that it even seems, at first glance, too easy. The Moore House is square in plan and cubic in volume, save for the fact that the roof is once again hipped and topped by a rectangular projection that runs along the ridge (*2.1,2*). The shape of the Orinda roof is not just a homage to Kahn's Bathhouse (*see fig. 3*), but also, in the projecting ridge, to Peressutti and the top of the Torre Velasca (*see fig. 2*). Like good Wright or Japanese buildings, both of which Moore also admires, the Moore House has a direct connection between interior and exterior, mediated by simple barn doors that slide open to reveal the fact that there are no supports at the corners. Here we are invited to reminisce about the world of Walter Gropius, whose Fagus Werk of 1911 first showed the possibilities inherent in modern materials for relieving the corner of its traditional responsibility of supporting a building. The modernness, then, of this detail and the openness between interior and exterior also make one think of another famous bachelor architect's house, Philip Johnson's glass house in New Canaan, Connecticut, of 1949. Like the Johnson House, the Moore House has no interior walls, save for the ones that enclose the bathroom. But at Moore's, the only plumbing actually behind closed doors is the toilet.

What, then, is going on structurally here? Inside the house are two sets of four columns, saved from a building under demolition. These columns support two skewed pyramidal hoods that hold up a horizontal wooden truss from which the hipped roof is hung (*2.1,4*). The fixed walls in the middles of the sides also play a role in this system, partly to help support the roof, partly to stabilize the house laterally. Thus the corners need no supports, and the piano can seem free to amble out into the yard, should it so choose (plate *2.2*). For an architect more famed for his puns and formal games than his structure, the Orinda truss, so well concealed up under the roof that almost no one seems to have noticed it, is remarkable, but, as we shall see, hardly unique in Moore's work. The great truss that supports the roof over the main gallery of the new Hood Museum at Dartmouth (*56.24*) is only the last in a series of some length.

As in the Jobson House, the aediculas at Orinda perform spatial and structural functions. They suggest the space of the living room—the larger square—and they enclose the open-air bathtub, while they support the roof. They also play a witty historical game by teaming up with an almost equally ancient form, the Mycenaean megaron. The megaron, the main room of the Mycenaean palace, was the kind of archetypal domestic space that architectural writers celebrated in the early sixties. Vincent Scully, for instance, in his *The Earth, The Temple and the Gods*, a book that Moore reviewed for the magazine *Landscape*, talked about one structure as a "megaron in a temenos enclosure." In a Mycenaean palace, however, the four columns of the megaron surrounded a circular fire pit. Moore, in an elemental shift, substitutes for fire the water of his combination tub and shower. Here, as in Japan, one bathes in public, or at least with whomever one has over.

Although the early sixties in Berkeley were the years in which Moore's style coalesced into something identifiably personal, these were also the years in which he completely ceased to work independently. In 1963 Moore, Donlyn Lyndon, William Turnbull, and Richard Whitaker formed MLTW (as in BBPR)—Moore, Lyndon, Turnbull, and Whitaker. It was this new partnership that was responsible for Moore's most successful building of the Berkeley phase of his career, Condominium I at Sea Ranch, a beautiful, semiwild coastal site about 100 miles north of San Francisco. Moore was drawn into the project by the landscape architect Lawrence Halprin, who had come to admire Moore's recent work. Halprin had been hired by the developers to do the site plan. He suggested Moore as the architect for one of the first buildings the developers planned to construct there, a condominium.

The original intention at Sea Ranch was to disturb the landscape as little as possible. The land meets the sea in high, jagged cliffs, back of which stretch open, gentle slopes crossed at wide intervals by hedgerows of Monterey cypress. Single-family units were to nestle into the hedgerows, to leave the meadows empty. One site on the meadows, and only one, was to receive intensive condominium development, to keep the large-scale structures in one place. Further development would take place on the steep, heavily wooded slopes that rose to the east of the meadows. There the houses or condos would be hidden in the forest.

Condominium I, on which MLTW began design work in the fall of 1963, was to be the first of several complexes that the firm would design for a rolling meadow directly above the cliffs. Early site plans from the MLTW files make clear that they were contemplating a cluster of irregularly shaped structures disposed sympathetically on the landscape. Of particular interest to the architects were three hillocks that appear on all the contour maps of the site; the building that was finally constructed was located athwart one of them. The partners had been reading Scully's *The Earth, The Temple and The Gods*,

Fig. 12. Sea Ranch Condominium I
Sea Ranch, California
1963–1965, west elevation
Pencil and colored pencil on yellow trace
Drawing by William Turnbull

Fig. 13. Sea Ranch Condominium I
1963–1965, roof planes
Pencil on white trace
Drawing by William Turnbull

Fig. 14. Alvar Aalto
Villa Carré
Bazoches-sur-Guyonne, France
1956–1958, exterior

Fig. 15. Sea Ranch Condominium I
1963–1965, south elevation
Pencil on yellow trace with two overlays
Drawing by Donlyn Lyndon

Fig. 12

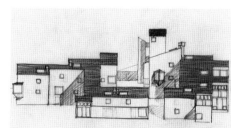

Fig. 13

Fig. 14

Fig. 15

which had intensified their already keen instincts for the relationship between building and nature. The little breast-shaped mounds that rose along the coast at Sea Ranch raised images of those grander breast-shaped peaks of ancient Greece that play a large role in Scully's book.

Sea Ranch is a complex building. The program called for ten essentially identical units of vacation housing organized into a single structure. Some preliminary sketches for the plans of individual units, from Moore's own hand, still survive. These are small drawings, no more than three or four inches across, that testify to Moore's penchant for drawing small in order to think big. In small drawings one doesn't have room to lose the main architectural idea in details (*48.3,4,5*). The units are square, and some are marked on the inside by the four columns of the Moore aedicula. Essentially, his thinking here follows that for his own house in Orinda. A cubic volume is punctuated by the four posts of an aedicula, called, at Sea Ranch, a "four poster." The main seating area is under the aedicula, facing the adjacent fireplace, while nearby one finds the rectangular enclosure for the kitchen, as well as the stairs that lead up to an open sleeping loft, poised atop the aedicula, and to an enclosed bath. Outside the aedicula and the kitchen is an all-purpose open space. Although this scheme went through numerous modifications during the designing of the complex, the basic idea of the four poster placed asymmetrically in a cube persisted (*48.1,2*).

As built, the individual units create a far more complex architectural experience than one might expect from Moore's quick sketch plans. The cubic volume is increased vertically by a shed roof that rises to a height of three stories on one side (*3.1*). Within, there is a complex, barnlike structural system. Large posts, placed toward or in the centers of the sides (again, no corner supports), rise to hold up a system of diagonal beams that soar upward to support the roof. Light is admitted through several small skylights that cap narrow, vertical spaces created in the interior by the aedicula and kitchen-bath units (*3.2*) and by a large skylight that lets light flood down onto the sleeping loft. The experience is one of several vertical tunnels with light at the end of them, surrounding the large skylight that is set above the four poster. More light comes in from the windows in the walls, some of which are hung out in saddlebag configuration. The saddlebags both expand the interior space and, most happily, provide a place outside the cubic volume from which the wonders of that volume can be seen. In short, here is a splendidly complex experience of light and dark and of narrow and wide—an experience hardly innocent of the Prisons of Piranesi—all within the confines of a simple cubic volume with a tilted roof. The kinetic experience of the interior is heightened by the clearly expressed areas of circulation. The staircase leads to a bridge that connects the sleeping loft with the bathroom. A balcony looks down on the living area, while a steep ladder gives access to an additional sleeping loft over the bathroom ceiling.

From the exterior of the condominium, there is absolutely no sense of the elaborate architectural game being played inside, much less that one is looking at a building made up of ten essentially identical units. In the early phases of the design, the units were arranged on a contour model of the site by placing sugar cubes on its cardboard planes. Fortuitously, sugar cubes happened to fit the scale of the model exactly; each cube could stand for the 24-foot cube of a single unit. By moving the cubes around on the model, the designers arrived at an irregular, U-shaped plan which was made into a single mass by a great sloping roof that follows the natural grade of the site (*48.12,14*). An elevation drawing (*fig. 12*) and a bird's-eye-view sketch of the roofscape (*fig. 13*), both by Turnbull, show how the great single roof plane that descends the slope is chewed away by the indentations created by the variations in the plans below. Here the design principles encountered at the Jobson House are brought to bear on a project of considerably larger scale.

From the south, on the other hand, the slope of the roof, punctuated by the tower to the east, makes a dramatic diagonal statement (*48.12*). The idea of the single shed roof that follows the slope of the site comes from a specific building by Aalto, the Villa Carré outside Paris (*fig. 14*). The office drawings that have been preserved make clear the importance of the hillock on which the building is set, the play of the roofs against the slope of the land, and the importance the architects set on getting the windows right. Lyndon's south

*Fig. 16. Alvar Aalto
Town Center
Säynatsälo, Finland
1950–1952, exterior*

*Fig. 17. Sea Ranch Condominium I
1963–1965, grading plan with contour lines
Colored pencils on paper
Drawing by William Turnbull*

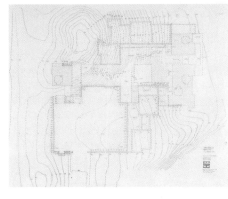

elevation, with its three overlays of yellow trace (*fig. 15*), is but one of many examples of the struggle to simplify the forms to give the whole design visual coherence, without, at the same time, lapsing into boredom.

That coherence, however, is made singularly clear by a very fine group of elevation drawings of all four sides of the complex, drawings that were worked on by the partners together (*48.8,9,10,11*). (In these drawings it is almost impossible to separate the hands of the various draftsmen. They cleverly hid their individual drawing styles to achieve a unified work.) The collaborative nature of these drawings reinforces the fact that the whole design was a collaborative one, not the product of a single genius, but rather the result of important contributions made by all.

The units surround an irregular courtyard that is dominated by a tower with a sloping roof at the upper end (*48.15*). The ensemble of courtyard and tower is strongly reminiscent of one of the most important buildings designed in the 1950s, Alvar Aalto's Town Center of Säynätsalo, Finland (*fig. 16*). There a similarly shaped tower rises above a more regular enclosure that opens to the town below through an irregular staircase that bears a striking resemblance to the winding staircase that flows down the slope toward the sea in the MLTW design. Aalto had also done the same kind of steps at the Villa Carré. These steps are actually laid out on the contour lines of the site plan (*fig. 17*). The green lines of the contours are broken by orange, where wooden risers were to be inserted into the ground. As one walks these steps, the meaning of a contour line is made palpable underfoot; an abstract concept is turned into a three-dimensional reality; a tool used in the design process, the site plan, has been permanently recorded on the site itself.

Aalto, however, is hardly the only source for this richly evocative design. MLTW was interested in producing a building that was appropriate to the landscape not only in a formal sense, but also in that it reflected indigenous architectural traditions. The woodenness of Sea Ranch obviously has to do with Bay Area customs that stretch back into the nineteenth century. The shed roofs and rough-hewn character of the redwood siding also make use of traditions established in the mining structures of California—the Sea Ranch tower is a particularly obvious reference to these, even if it also has to do with Aalto at Säynätsalo. Even more important, perhaps, is the fact that just a few miles south of Sea Ranch stands Fort Ross, built by the Russians in the nineteenth century as their southernmost point of penetration down the Pacific coast. Enclosed by tall wooden walls, Fort Ross sits on the sloping meadows that lead to the sea in the same way Sea Ranch occupies its similar site. An Italian publication that reported on Sea Ranch called it "Un fortino a piedi nudi," a recognition of the fortlike character of Sea Ranch (and of barefoot California life), without its being entirely clear in regard to local architectural sources. There are, in fact, wonderful old sheep barns still preserved on the Sea Ranch property. Their broad roofs and post-and-beam construction are exactly the forms taken up in the condo. In numerous ways, then, Sea Ranch partakes of the traditions of local buildings, without ever slavishly imitating any, because the local details, as it were, are subsumed in an overall form that owes its shape to Aalto, rather than to California designers and builders.

The instant success of Sea Ranch in the architectural press, and its almost instant adoption by a host of younger, and unfortunately often lesser architects, has tended to consign to obscurity two other interesting housing projects by MLTW from the same years, the unfortunately unrealized West Plaza Condominiums in Coronado, California, 1962, and the Monte Vista Apartments in Monterey, 1963. The partners largely responsible for West Plaza (*24*) seem to have been Moore and Lyndon, and perhaps some of the rough blockiness of particularly the last of the four projects is to be attributed to Lyndon's hand. The building was to be a large masonry structure with heavy towers and a meandering plan. In some ways, it suggested the neo-medievalism that one finds in much architecture of the late fifties and early sixties, when architects were particularly captivated by the irregular buildings of Italian medieval hill towns. One also detects here, however, a slight suggestion of the work of Paul Rudolph, whose designs for the Yale Art and Architecture Building were among the most widely touted of the period. There is in all the West Plaza projects a sense of what Gerhard Kahlmann, one of the architects of the new

Boston City Hall, called "Action Architecture," in an important article he published in *Architectural Forum* in 1959.

Although they are later than the West Plaza projects, the Monte Vista Apartments look back to advanced modern works of the twenties, particularly Mies's apartment block of 1926 for the Weissenhof Exhibition in Stuttgart. The long narrow site in Monterey, up on a slope overlooking a group of earlier apartment houses, is analogous to the one Mies had at Stuttgart, and perhaps that fact suggested the similar solution MLTW adopted. Perhaps also the International Style character of the Monte Vista design seemed to fit, in some way, with the local traditions of Spanish Colonial architecture, which also makes ample use of bare, stuccoed walls. The colors tried out in an elevation drawing that has been preserved, however, suggest more the primary colors used on the trim of Rietveld's Schroeder House in Utrecht than the dark wood of old Monterey. The Monte Vista Apartments demonstrate Lyndon's strong commitment to "modernism" in those years. Yet, the partners also gave the building a great shingled shed roof that hides from the view of apartment dwellers one of the key icons of the modern world—the automobile (*25.2*). This roof certainly foreshadows the shed roof at Sea Ranch.

What Coronado and Monte Vista make clear is that up until they actually designed Sea Ranch, MLTW had not yet hit upon something that worked for them, at least for large-scale buildings. Both earlier projects show a searching for solutions that involved investigating numerous possibilities, derived from equally numerous sources. Sea Ranch, reproduced in glamourous photographs in the international architectural press, caused a clamor that the architects could hardly ignore. It seemed to satisfy a need that was felt across the Western world in the mid-sixties for an architecture that did not abandon modern principles but could substitute for the universality advocated by modernists a sense that a building belonged to the particular place where it was built. The fusion of regional and international traditions at Sea Ranch was something many architects had been looking for, but it was something MLTW uniquely achieved in a building that had a memorable image. This image was seized on by legions of less talented architects, so that almost every woodsy resort or small town condominium development owes some debt, ultimately, to this potent building.

With the success of Sea Ranch, the career of Moore and his partners entered a new phase, partly brought about by the ever widening publicity their buildings were receiving, as well as by the prizes that they seemed able to pull off each year in the annual *Progressive Architecture* awards sweepstakes. These were won, of course, on the strength of the entries, but also on the basis of the skillful presentation orchestrated by MLTW, with Moore usually the director of publicity operations. Photographs of their buildings by Morley Baer, carefully staged with props imported by Moore for the occasion, played no small role in winning advocates to their way of designing (*2.2,4*; *11.11*).

In the fall of 1965 Moore moved to New Haven to take up the prestigious job of running the architecture school at Yale, succeeding Paul Rudolph. The move to New Haven caused the partial and then total collapse of MLTW— Lyndon soon went to the architecture school of the University of Oregon and Whitaker moved to Illinois—but Moore and Turnbull continued to function as a design team, even across the country, and the drawings that Moore produced for projects in the early years at New Haven all bear the MLTW stamp.

In what we can now see was to become a tradition, Moore made himself a new nest in New Haven. He bought an old house on Elm Street, gutted its insides, and produced a new interior that was a remarkable event in the architecture of the day, to say the least (*4.1*). As usual, Moore used the opportunity of designing his own house to try out some new ideas. One of the chief new ideas was the use of interior towers—rectangular voids of space enclosed by punctured plywood planes—rather than his former favorite aediculas. While the aediculas had been closed at the top and open on the sides, the towers were open at the top and closed on the sides. Their architectural functions may have been similar, but their visual effects were markedly different. The New Haven House had three towers, each with its own name: Ethel, Berengaria, and Howard. Howard formed an open central core, at the bottom of which the master had himself photographed at work

Fig. 18. A. L. T. Vaudoyer
House for a Cosmopolite (project)
1785, elevation

Fig. 19. Klotz House
Westerly, Rhode Island
Plan of three floors, dated January 6, 1967
Orange pencil and blue ink on blueprint

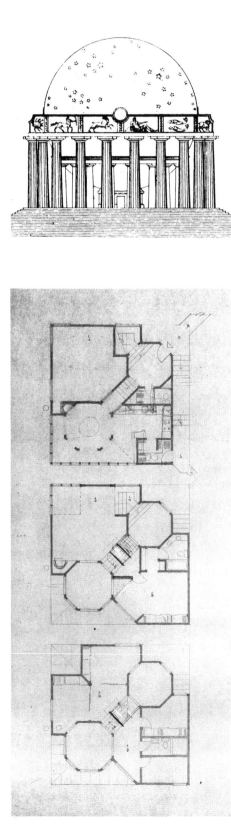

(*4.4*). No more calculatedly staged architectural photograph has appeared in recent memory. Intellectual calm reigns at the table, while all around is visual chaos. The towers, punctured by myriad holes of varied geometric forms, were covered in brilliant colors, overlaid by an abundance of supergraphics. The whole tiny interior took on the character of a Piranesi Prison—a favorite image of architects, no matter what their stylistic stamp, in those years—which had been turned into a stylish fun house. One can see Moore, seated at his table, as a satisfied mouse inside a gaudy and gigantic block of Swiss cheese, which he had designed as a set on which to act out his life.

Columns and aediculas do not completely disappear in New Haven, however. In the lower regions of Ethel a structural beam is saved from collapse by a pair of columns brought in from another building to hold it up (*see 4.1*). Upstairs in the bedroom, a ceiling, about to fall in, is shorn up by an aedicula, a four-poster bed canopy that marked the place to lay down a weary head, while saving that head from being crushed by falling timbers (*4.3*). The bed went through numerous decorative transformations. The hole in the center of the canopy was at first decorated by prints of flying, Berniniesque cupids, reproduced at larger than life size. Perhaps more appropriate to the owner, or at least more tongue in cheek, were the stars that replaced the cupids. They created a Pop-Art Dome of Heaven that slyly suggested a late-eighteenth-century French project that had received a certain play in architectural writings in the late sixties. This was A. L. T. Vaudoyer's House for a Cosmopolite, which featured a ring of columns supporting a dome that had the stars of the heavens painted on its exterior (*fig. 18*). The stars lead up to a reproduction of the false dome designed at the end of the seventeenth century by Andrea Pozzo for the crossing of the church of Sant' Ignazio in Rome. (One wonders if the perspective worked from the point of view of the pillow.) The staged photo of the cosmopolite's bed also adds a splendid note of coziness: the furry throw that appears in a number of photos of other Moore works. The bookcases, on the other hand, make clear that the cosmopolite is also a man of the mind. Normally, art historians do not dwell on artists' beds, but in this case, the bed speaks mightily of the architect's intentions: the learned, but jesting use of architectural history; the turning of an accidental need—in this case a structural necessity—into an architectural idea of more than passing interest; the stress on the parallel needs of the mind and the body for their own comforts.

The complex interior, marked by towers, of the New Haven House finds its counterpart in a much larger house Moore was asked to design in the late fall of 1966, the Klotz House in Westerly, Rhode Island. The Klotzes, a young couple inspired by Vincent Scully's lectures on modern architecture at Yale, at first wanted a house by Louis Kahn. Kahn's reputation for designing slowly and expensively, however, finally convinced them that they should look elsewhere. On the advice of Whitney Stoddard, Professor of Art at Williams College (Paul Klotz had been a Williams undergraduate), they sought out Moore in his Yale office, just as he was about to go off to give a talk at Harvard. So pleased was Moore at having his first clients on the East Coast walk into his office that he sat down for a long chat. He was quite late for his lecture.

The earliest preserved plans for the Klotz House, dated January 6, 1967, show a square containing two octagonal towers, the one to the north the entrance hall, the one to the south the dining room (*fig. 19*). In this set of plans, as in all subsequent ones, the corner of the square with the entrance porch points due north. The Klotz House, like the Jobson House, is sited so that its corners point in the four cardinal directions. These towers, connected by a rectangle containing the staircase, rise the full height of the house. There were to be five levels; the house was to take advantage of its sloping site to place the kitchen, on the east, four steps below the level of the living room on the west, and then to stack two levels of bedrooms above the kitchen and one above the living room. Even in this early and relatively simple state, the geometry of the square containing two octagons grows more compromised as the levels grow higher; the functional requirements of the house distort more and more the basic geometry of the design.

A beautiful plan in Moore's own hand, probably slightly later than the colored prints discussed above, shows the house beginning to grow appendages—a deck off the north corner and a garage to the east (*15.2*). The

Fig. 20.   Klotz House
First-floor plan, dated May 10, 1967
Black and orange pencil on white paper
Drawing by William Grover

Fig. 21.   Klotz House
First-floor plan, dated June 27, 1967
Black and orange pencil on paper

Fig. 22.   Klotz House
First-floor plan with elevations of three sides
of exterior
Black and orange pencil on yellow trace

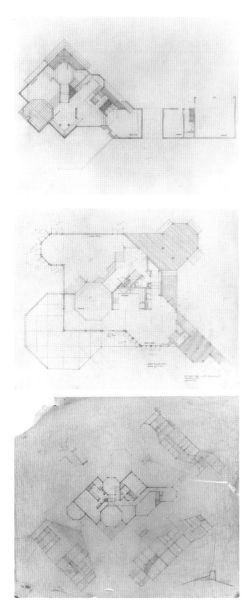

inscriptions on the sheet are also important, for they show Moore's interest in relating the house to the most important natural features of the area, features that would ultimately be incorporated into some of the views the house affords its owners.

The Klotz plan went through four significant revisions. Because drawings that show these changes in plan are still preserved (for many Moore projects the drawings leading up to the final design seem to have disappeared), we can see Moore at work with particular clarity here. Phase II, dated March 10, shows the basic square/octagon plan with major changes, as the needs of the house were redefined by the clients (*see 15.1*). On the southeast side a six-sided family room sidles up to the square, which in turn reaches out to the polygon. While expansion takes place at ground level, contraction takes place above. The number of levels is reduced to four.

The plan of May 10, Phase III, shows yet more activity to the east of the original square (*fig. 20*). A pottery studio for Mrs. Klotz and a garage now make their appearance, while the main house undergoes a second expansion through the addition of a rectangle on the southwest face that penetrates, in terms of its pavement, the square to become a second six-sided polygon (or, perhaps better stated, half an octagon attached to half a square). Upstairs, the master bedroom acquires a study, while the two childrens' rooms get somewhat more space. The fifth level reappears, now as a crow's-nest playroom.

In the next stages, which can be grouped under the heading Phase IV, the appendages growing off the basic square turn into octagons, to make the whole plan consistently a set of variations on the theme of octagon and square. A pair of undated sketches show this transformation with particular clarity. The earlier contains a single plan, drawn in black pencil (*15.4*). The family room has become an octagon fused to the east corner, while the entrance porch is an octagon of equal size, fused to the north point of the square. The octagonal porch bleeds into a walkway connecting the porch to the family room. A four-sided pyramidal roof, of the type we know from the Jobson House, is shown by the cross superimposed in orange pencil over the black lines of the plan. The use of the two colors is crucial here, to show two levels in one plan—to visualize graphically the complex three-dimensional play between the many volumes below and the broad sweep of the pyramidal roof above.

In the second of these two sheets of drawings (*see 15.3*), two plans appear, each showing the ground-floor level. The right drawing shows the possibility of a third octagon, a terrace, growing off the south point. But the most interesting part of this drawing is the set of orange lines superimposed over the right plan. They show a wholly new idea for the roof. The perfect geometry of the pyramidal roof has been twisted—"massaged" once again—so that the peak of the roof and the projection of the eccentrically placed chimney can coincide, as a quickly sketched elevation of the exterior on the same sheet suggests. Here one can see Moore's fertile three-dimensional imagination at work, in a drawing that gives us both the ambiguously slipping and sliding geometry of the plan under the skewed and twisted planes of the roof above. In these two side-by-side sketches one can see with particular clarity the way Moore manipulates geometric forms in space. In the Klotz House he adds the twisting we noted in the Martin Studio to the design principles announced in the Jobson design.

The plan of June 27 (*fig. 21*) shows a square with octagons at all four points; the whole has the force of one of Wright's centrifugal plans. To the north, the porch has ambled eastward, off the point, and also outward to become an outdoor aedicula supported on eight posts. The living room has grown five sides of an octagon off its corner, while the dining room has acquired a very ample patio centered on its point and connected by a brief walkway to the family room. This latter has become another octagon, penetrated by an almost rectangular kitchen. Outside the family room a back porch is developed. Like the extenstion of the living room at the opposite corner, it shows five sides, marked by six posts that recall the eight of the north porch. The interior of the house, as if overwhelmed by all of this activity at the corners, has given up the octagonal entrance hall all the previous plans had. The overall effect of this plan is one of a lopsided pinwheel about ready to rotate itself off the site. The centrifugal tendencies of the Jobson and Johnson house plans have become dominant.

Closely related to the plan of June 27 (it may be slightly later) is an undated sheet that shows a plan of the second floor together with three of the exterior elevations of the house (*fig. 22*). The master bedroom has moved to the west corner, over the living room, to take advantage of the splendid ocean view this side of the house affords. The children's rooms have lost their symmetry, and the playroom has become an odd, leftover space between a lozenge-shaped bedroom and the dining room octagon. There is no patio off the dining room, and the entrance octagon is once again in place. The elevations show the rather remarkable envelope that is to enclose all of this complexity. It is, if anything, even more difficult than the interior. The roof has regained its pyramidal symmetry, with the chimney placed slightly off-center. The planes of the roof slope down to meet the walls at whatever point they may rise to meet it—a device we know, once again, from the Jobson and Johnson houses. But the effect here is more elaborate, because the walls, enclosing the interior octagons, trace tortuous paths. The windows of the southeast and southwest sides show visual problems yet to be resolved, while the northeast facade comes close to the final version, which we will meet shortly in the drawings of July. The two octagonal porches bulge outward to form corner bastions under a continuous roof that slopes upward to its peak. The northeast elevation also shows the slope of the land. The main porch is higher and the back porch lower, but the larger mass of the former is balanced by the lateral extension of the latter. The house almost seems to reach out its stubby arms to embrace the visitor in its two airy porches. There is an amplitude and openness here that reminds one of the great Shingle Style houses built along the Rhode Island coast at the end of the nineteenth century. This was precisely the effect the Klotzes wanted. They were living in an old Shingle Style house on the water, to which Moore paid numerous weekend visits. He knew what his clients liked, and he was able to give them his own version of what they wanted.

A plan dated July 26, which is very close to the plan with the three elevations, shows a further development, the addition of a third bedroom. Mrs. Klotz had discovered, as the house was being planned, that she was to have twins. The house grew in response.

In the final version (*15.5,6,7*), there are really few changes from the plan of July 26. The partial octagon off the living room is moved around the corner, partly to provide a better view of the ocean from the terrace it carries on its roof above, but also just because it makes the plan look better. The sense of the rotation of a pinwheel is reinforced by this relativley simple change. (Wright's houses with polygonal elements may have played some role in the design here.) The irregular playroom on the second floor becomes a fourth bedroom, while the pottery studio in the garage turns into an octagon in its own right. The fifth level reappears as a study for Mr. Klotz.

During construction, a great stone fireplace was built between the living room and the hall that connects the entry with the dining room. The masons were some of Moore's students at Yale, getting hands-on experience. The students were unable to stay around long enough to finish the job, and the professional mason who completed the task found himself having to imitate amateur work, to make it seem of a piece. A typical bit of Moore-ish accommodation occurred in the upper reaches of the chimney. As it grew upward toward the peak of the roof, it became clear that the chimney was headed straight for a beam of structural importance. The chimney was rotated, with consummate skill, by the mason, to miss the beam. The resulting accident, which creates a splendid spiral sculptural effect inside the house (*15.8*), is just the kind of accident that Moore is able to prize for its happy visual effect. The necessity of turning the chimney during construction, however, also points to the fact that it is very difficult to calculate on paper all of the three-dimensional happenings that will go on in a Moore house.

The space of the Klotz House is constantly alive, even when there are no people moving about in it. Levels change, and walls shift directions. Openings present peek-a-boo views into almost all levels simultaneously. Light falls within from ample windows and a constellation of skylights; even on a dark day, it is bright inside. (The only other buildings I have experienced that have the same effect are some churches by J. B. Neumann, such as Neresheim and Vierzehnheiligen. Remarkably enough, the spatial effects of these churches are equally complex and impossible to capture in photographs.) The interior of

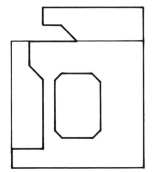

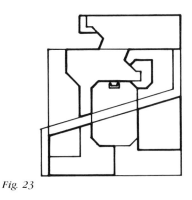

Fig. 23

the house is a jungle gym for adults and children, a larger scale Piranesian fun house than Moore's house on Elm Street, an even bigger chunk of Swiss cheese for the mice who own it to romp in. For the Klotz children, who sat on his knee and called him Uncle Chuck, Moore even made a sketch for an outdoor playhouse (*15.9*), complete with an aedicular sandbox. (One suspects that Uncle Chuck, who still collects electric trains and other toys, shares Brancusi's sentiment that once we have ceased to be children, we are already dead.) The playhouse inside, however, seems to have been enough. The Klotzes never built the one outside.

The play of octagon in square that dominates both the tiny Johnson House at Sea Ranch and the considerably larger Klotz House also underlies the fragmented, asymmetrical plan of the first Rudolph House at Captiva, Florida (Rudolph I). Early drawings for this house, including a rough sketch (*17.1*) and a more finished drawing dated "7/3/70" (*17.2*), show an octagon in the center of a square which is cut into two unequal halves by a broad, diagonal path through the house from the entrance to the beach it faces. The diagonal provides not only dramatic movement through the space but also gives guests their own access to the beach. At the top of the less finished sheet there is a remarkable plan with twin garages (shown by the entrance and exit lines of the cars) that form pylons through which one passes to enter the precinct of the house.

In a sheet of sketches dated July 9, 1970 (*17.3*), these same pylons reappear in a drawing on the left to form a gateway to a rectangular court cut from the center of the house, now a square placed on edge. This plan then gives way to a series of sketches in which Moore ruthlessly pulls the square apart to create a large, irregular central court dominated by a small, centrally planned gazebo. The sketch in the lower right-hand corner shows a particularly wild reuse of the Japanese motif of the wooden path, one he first used in the girls' school in Korea, and then in the house for his mother at Pebble Beach.

A fourth drawing, close to the plan as built, shows a diagonal walk that shoots through the house to terminate in an octagonal gazebo at the water's edge (*17.4*). (In the final version, the gazebo, no longer a pure octagon, returns to the inner court.) The plan of the house maintains its binuclear character, but now all the bedrooms are on one side of the walkway and the living areas on the other. In this drawing the most characteristic feature of the living area appears—the X-shaped intersection of two walls that create a pair of bent arches that separate the living room from the dining room (*17.8*).

Despite its appearance of irregularity, this plan is a variant of the octagon in a square with which the design of the house began. In the final plan, the original square encloses that part of the house containing the living room and the bedrooms, while the kitchen/dining areas at the top of the plan are an addition. This addition, however, is nothing more than an irregular piece of the original square, cut off from its rightful place, reversed, and then stuck on to the north side of the square (*fig. 23*). The interior bent arches are a visual device that happily fuses these two reunited pieces of the original geometry, while at the same time making that geometry harder to see. The intersection of the arches, incidentally, lines up with the fireplace and the east wall of the study to mark the centerline of the original square.

Moore's geometrical sleight of hand extends from the two to the three dimensional. A sheet of four sketches for the unrealized Goodman House project of 1969–70 is particularly helpful in this respect. All of the sheets of yellow trace have been taped together to keep them from slipping while the relationship of each drawing to the others is studied (*16.5*). On each separate sheet Moore drew the plan of the house at a different level (*16.7, 8, 9*). Superimposed, the four sheets tell him about the three-dimensional development of the interiors, which is complex enough to baffle all but the very few who share Moore's extraordinary mastery of three dimensions. In drawings such as these for the Goodman House, Moore pushed the transparency of yellow trace almost to its limits, to say nothing of the limits to which he pushes the ability of a flat plan to show depth. An elevation for the same house, which employs orange and black pencil, shows relationships in depths between the screen walls that would have stretched across the south side of the house, just as the orange lines of the roofs in two of his sketches

Fig. 24.   Waterfall near Fallen Leaf Lake, California

Fig. 25.   MLTW/Moore-Turnbull Faculty Club, first project University of California, Santa Barbara 1966, model

for the Klotz House reveal the relationship between the roofs and the plans of the floors below.

As Moore began his teaching career at Yale, MLTW received an important commission for a large public building: Kresge College at the University of California, Santa Cruz. The first site plans date from the fall of '66, but it was ten years and more before the building was actually completed and in use. It is important to remember, however, that the basic scheme for Santa Cruz dates from the first months in New Haven, because the concept of the street that it exemplifies had profound consequences in later designs from the same phase of Moore's career.

In plan, Kresge College as built is an irregular, reverse L that meanders down a fairly steep slope in the midst of a redwood forest (*27.2*). The upper part of the L sits astride a ridge that descends to the turn to the left in the L, while the lower part moves along against the side of a slope. The early site plans show considerable struggle with the terrain. In the final one the form of the land became the generator of the plan.

The program at Santa Cruz is complex, and the history of the design too long to go into here. What one should stress is the fact that at the same time that Moore was making his way through the intricate geometries of the Klotz House, he was also trying his hand at large-scale planning that seems deliberately to eschew geometric complexities for an apparently relaxed relationship between building and environment. The basic idea of the street that meanders uphill in an irregular path came from a study of streets in Italian hill towns and Greek island villages. These kinds of urban systems, built over centuries by human beings in touch with their landscapes, represented to architects in the mid-sixties a primeval urbanity that offered an antidote to the chilling regularity of the Corbusian *Ville Radieuse*, with its prismatic skyscrapers set on rigid grids in open and, it turned out, crime-ridden spaces. Such Cartesian logic, by 1966, hardly seemed to provide the kinds of environments that people actually wanted to live in, whereas the organically grown towns of Italy and the Greek Islands did. The exhibition organized by Bernard Rudofsky in 1965 for the Museum of Modern Art, *Architecture without Architects*, surely had an influence on Moore's thinking at this time, as it had on the works of numerous other architects. MLTW added to this, however, their own particular turns. Their steps once again mark the contour lines from the site plan, while the dormitories that flank the street have porticos broken up rhythmically (*27.4*) in exactly the same patterns we found in 1954 in the south facade of the Moore House at Pebble Beach (*1.3*). The use of rich rhythms to enliven a modestly budgeted design is not a device Moore tried only once and then forgot.

Also we find cascading down the hill at Santa Cruz a water drain that ends up in what at first seems to be a fountain that decorates the most monumental public space of the college, the piazza at the bottom of the street. Actually, the water course began at a fountain, now covered up, in the courtyard of the dining hall, located at the top of the street. The abundant rain that Santa Cruz enjoys in certain seasons courses down the street and becomes a kind of reverse fountain in the basin in the lower square (*see* Bloomer, *fig. 14*). The insertion of water into public plazas we first noted with the Seagram Building design in Moore's dissertation (*32.4,5*).

An important opportunity to use water had occurred during the mid-sixties, when MLTW joined forces with Lawrence Halprin to design Lovejoy Fountain in Portland, Oregon (plates *33.1,2*). For Lovejoy Fountain Moore and company produced a concrete variant of a falls that Moore had visited at the head of Fallen Leaf Lake, next to Lake Tahoe in the Sierras (*fig. 24*). The landscape, once again, is introduced into the urban environment. On the flat ground above the new falls, Moore placed a pavilion that consisted of square concrete piers that support a wooden roof shaped with irregular peaks that suggest a mountain landscape. One suspects that Moore's interest in Chinese painting played an important role here (he had studied Chinese art at Princeton). Below the sharp mountain peaks of the pavilion rise the mists of the waterfall, while at the bottom lies a still pool. These, obviously, are classic elements of Chinese landscape painting.

Another and smaller commission from the University of California, for the Faculty Club at Santa Barbara, came to fruition much more quickly—by 1968 it

Fig. 24

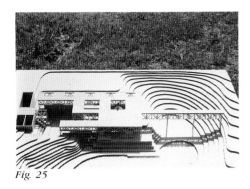
Fig. 25

was opened and deservedly heralded in the architectural press. This design, too, went through several phases. The first, published in a catalog of an exhibition of recent work by Moore and Turnbull at UCSB in the late fall of 1966, was a large concrete and glass rectangle with a shed roof supported by prominently displayed steel trusses (*fig. 25*), which surprisingly resembles Mies's project of 1952 for a giant convention hall. An undated bird's-eye-view drawing records a second stage of the design, in which the style has become Santa Barbara Spanish Colonial (plate *34.1*), of the kind Moore celebrated in his sensitive essay on Williams Mooser's Santa Barbara County Courthouse of 1926. In the bird's-eye-view project for Santa Barbara, a rectangular courtyard is penetrated by the vertical mass of, presumably, the dining hall, with its long, sloping roof that counters, as opposed to Sea Ranch, the slope of the land up from the sea.

While the geometry of this project is easy to grasp, that of the design that was actually built is not. The plan as built (*34.2*) shows a rectangular courtyard that runs north/south, parallel to the coast. At the south end the building angles away to form three sides of an irregular, fragmented polygon that seems rather arbitrarily tacked on to the rectangle of the court. This court is flanked to the west by modest structures, covered with shed roofs, that contain hotel rooms, and to the east by a flat-roofed kitchen. On the north the court opens through a portico to the swimming pools, the accompanying changing rooms, and the squash courts. At the southern end, however, the club rises up to a three-storied peak that faces the sea. From this peak, a great shed roof falls down to the east and also bends around into a second plane descending toward the south (*34.3*). This roof, which seems to be a strange intruder, actually gives the clue that explains the geometry of the whole project. One has to imagine this roof as a fragment of a great hipped roof covering an imaginary square centered on the chimney that rises beside the roof's peak to understand what Moore has done here. An alternate way to understand the Santa Barbara roof is to imagine the part of the Faculty Club under the tall roof as roughly one fourth of the Klotz House, cut from the whole and pasted onto the edge of a fairly regular rectangular courtyard. The bent arch on the south face of the Faculty Club can even be understood as a two-sided fragment of one of the interior octagons of the Klotz House, here turned into an exterior wall. The tall southern part of the club, then, is a three-dimensional fragment of a whole conceptual structure that has been connected to the relatively ordinary and unfragmented set of buildings surrounding the court. The plan also offers a clue to the conceptual whole. The diagonal wall that leads from its upper left corner into the circular entrance to the various parts of the Faculty Club and its mirror image, the diagonal wall drawn from the upper right-hand corner, show the lines of two of the ridges of the imaginary pyramidal roof centered on the chimney.

The interior of the Faculty Club is one of Moore's most felicitous (*34.6*). (One should really say "was." UCSB, like many educational institutions, does not seem to treat a great building very well.) The entrance, dark and decorated with stuffed animal heads to give a "clublike" appearance, leads to a landing from which one has an invigorating architectural choice. To the immediate left, a flight of stairs descends at a brisk clip to the dining area, while straight ahead a bridge that would have made Sant' Elia marvel flies toward a rather dark cave of a space, from which another flight zooms upward in several angular breaks. In the middle of it all hangs a brass chandelier that makes one expect the Giovanni Arnolfinis to appear at any moment. To either side of the bridge/stairs the planes of the walls are cut open to reveal spaces between the inner and outer walls that control the entrance of the vivid California light into the building. This layering of inner and outer walls creates a light trap that was surely suggested either by Kahn's project for the American Consulate in Luanda, Angola, 1959, or by Aalto's church at Imatra, 1957, or by both. The light trap creates an envelope of relatively bright light around the warm, subdued glow of the interior. Through the medium of its brilliance one can see the true strength of the light of day. Only from the level of the dining room floor, however, does the Piranesian impact of the bridge, stairs, and layered windows become clear. This dining room is flanked by bold neon banners that hang from light fixtures that suggest medieval trumpets (*34.6*).

The Church Street South low-cost housing project in New Haven gave

Moore the chance to take on a serious problem that has bedeviled almost every significant architect of this century. By the late sixties it was clear that the ideas for public housing that had originated in the 1920s, particularly in Le Corbusier's schemes for tall towers surrounded by wide greenswards, were largely failures, at least in a social sense. Jane Jacobs's book, *The Death and Life of Great American Cities*, which appeared in 1961, had dealt a mighty blow to Le Corbusier's planning schemes. Moore seems to have absorbed her arguments.

The site for the Church Street South project lay between the New Haven railroad station and the center of the city (*26.2*). New Haven in the fifties and sixties, under the vigorous leadership of Mayor Richard Lee, had made a name for itself in terms of urban renewal. Great architects had been called in to design parts of the vast rebuilding of the city, even Mies van der Rohe, who designed an elegant arrangement of steel and glass rectangles for the Church Street South site. It is in the context of New Haven's brave assault on urban blight that the Moore plan has to be seen.

There are two parts to the Church Street South project. To the north, beside the Oak Street Connector, a great surgical scar of a superhighway, rises a tall tower that provides housing for the elderly. This building is a splendid piece of architectural criticism, aimed at the Knights of Columbus tower, by Dinkeloo and Roche, across the freeway. The latter, with its four great masonry corner towers and its bridges of Cor-Ten steel, is a prime example of what Vincent Scully has labeled "paramilitary dandyism." Moore's tower is made of cheap concrete block and aluminum windows ordered out of a catalogue. Its air conditioners, painted orange, hang out the sides of its walls. The windows get wider as the tower goes up, to express the lighter load of the upper stories, but otherwise there is little of obvious architectural interest in the building, seen alone. However, its plan is an irregular octagon that suggests a square, like that of the Knights of Columbus Tower, with its corners amputated, so that Moore's tower becomes a kind of *Castrum castratum*. As far as the people who live in the tower are concerned, however, the architectural joke is beside the point. What they like are the big windows that bring in lots of light, and the stainless-steel sinks in their rooms. As one refugee from New York put it, "I feel like I'm living at the Plaza." The tower, clearly, is a sociological success. High-rise buildings restricted to the elderly do work, as Oscar Newman demonstrated in *Defensible Space*, a book that appeared in 1972, after Church Street South opened.

The southern part of Church Street South is roughly triangular in shape. Around it Moore arranged rectangular blocks of three- and four-story housing to repeat the shape of the block itself. This use of the shape of the site to dictate the plan, as we will see, becomes a common Moore device. Inside the outer wall of buildings, the triangle is repeated in a second group of housing units that leave only a small open space in the center. This space, a kind of small-scale Sienese campo is connected to the main street to the south and the tower to the north by a broad walkway that is analogous to the street that forms the spine of the Kresge College plan. Around the irregular piazza Moore arranged shops that were to serve the neighborhood—grocery, laundromat, day-care center (*26.1*). It was hoped that these shops would also attract customers from outside the project. A little triumphal arch marks the northward continuation of the street to the rest of the project and the tower for the elderly. Unfortunately, the elderly of the tower do not visit this part of the project, even though it was intended that they do their shopping in the little piazza. They are afraid to walk there, even in groups, even in daylight, because of what they see as the threat of crime. The arch and a small fountain provide Italianate urban amenities to this central, leftover space that has ambitions to become the focal point of the development. There may well be an inherent contradiction in such a method of planning. Can a leftover space be turned into the focus of that which surrounds it?

The housing itself represents a genuine effort to provide decent, visually exciting, and yet familiar surroundings for the urban poor who were to occupy it (*26.3*). In talking to prospective tenants, Moore discovered that they wanted clean, well-lit, regularly shaped rooms. Thus the interiors have none of the polygonal play or complex ceiling structures of his private houses for the well-to-do. He had hoped to be able to provide ample stoops for the tenants to sit on, to give them an urban form they were used to using extensively, but budget cuts reduced the stoops to rather mean segments of concrete circles. The stoops were part of a program to provide architectural encouragement for a street life that would give the inhabitants a sense of safety and that would prevent crime through the ability of the inhabitants to observe and thus police their own areas. They would even be able to drive their cars up to their doors and wash them, again providing the surveillance that Newman, in *Defensible Space*, proved essential to safe urban life. For reasons that still are not quite clear, Church Street South failed to give its inhabitants the safety its designers had hoped for. Someday, if we ever understand why it failed, the problem of designing low-cost housing for the poor in this country will perhaps have been brought closer to a solution.

Even if Church Street South is a social failure, it still provides a certain visual kick. The housing units aren't just bland blocks of gray concrete (*see 26.3*). The surfaces are enlivened by textured concrete block that Moore knowingly used to replicate the rusticated surfaces of the sixteenth-century buildings of Giulio Romano, one of the principal inventors of what has come in this century to be known as Mannerist architecture. A style Giulio developed for the delectation of his jaded patron, the Duke of Mantua, is, in New Haven, offered by Moore to the urban poor. The exteriors are further enlivened by a lavish use of supergraphics, particularly blue and yellow and red and yellow stripes on the fronts of houses, to get a strong architectural effect and to give the buildings low-cost personality, rather than low-cost anonimity. The entire development looked absolutely splendid when it appeared on the cover of *Progressive Architecture* in May 1972.

While Church Street South was under construction, Moore and his new New Haven partners, William Grover and Robert Harper, were approached by a developer to design a condominium resort complex for St. Simons Island, Georgia. This they christened Xanadune, in punning reference to the stately pleasure dome Kublai Khan had decreed, here to be put down by the sea among the dunes. William Hersey's perspective rendering of the main Xanadune building shows it hunkered down under its dormer-pierced hipped roof whose sheltering mass recalls late-nineteenth-century American seaside and lakeside hotels (*29.2*). That Moore intended precisely this image is made clear by a sketch, dated 9/72, of a hip-roofed nineteenth-century southern hotel (*29.3*). The Xanadune roof, however, has great holes cut out of it, in response to the open courtyards developed inside the rectangular mass of the building. In the Xanadune design, one has a prime example of Moore's fragmentation of an essentially simple geometric form. The plan and the three-dimensional image are generated from the rectangular hipped roof. This rectangle, however, is broken in a jagged "fault line" that meanders through the middle (*see 29.1*), not unlike the breaking apart of the square plan we have already seen in the Rudolph House at Captiva. Along this fault line the building splits, some of it advancing toward the sea. On the sea side, the split produces an open area that begins a tortuous path that leads to the hidden delights of patios, pools, fountains, aqueducts, and trellises inside.

Because of its strong contrast between inside and out, Xanadune is one of the best examples in Moore's work of what he calls the architectural geode, a building that has a relatively simple, monochromatic exterior that makes the surprise of a brilliantly colored interior all the greater (*29.7,8*). The interior courts at Xanadune were to be painted in lavish tropical colors, inspired by color photographs of works of the great Mexican architect José Luis Barragán, published in an architectural magazine that just happened to come to Moore's attention at the moment the Xanadune project was being discussed in the office. Unlike Barragán's colors, however, those at Xanadune are a little tawdry, as if they were taken from the set of a Gulf Coast bordello for a Tennessee Williams play. The balconies and shutters that open the individual living units onto the courtyards similarly suggest possibly illicit pleasures behind closed walls.

Even though the mass of Xanadune is broken to provide constant visual variety, the individual units were to have only four different shapes. They were also planned so that parts of each, a bedroom and bath, could be rented out separately, as if they were hotel rooms. Thus each unit has two outside doors, and can be divided into two parts. But because the parts of the building vary

Fig. 26. *Filippo Brunelleschi*
Florence Cathedral, lantern
1436 ff., exterior

Fig. 27. *Coxhead and Coxhead*
Beta Theta Pi House
University of California, Berkeley
1899, exterior

in height, the roofs hit the interior spaces at different levels, and the dormers intersect those roofs in sometimes surprising places (*29.4*). The interiors, as another perspective by Hersey makes clear, would have had none of that dull regularity that characterizes most hotel/motel architecture in this country.

Inside the courtyards, water plays a crucial role. The meandering open spaces are held together by the linear path of a screen wall, composed of arches, that also acts as an aqueduct, *alla Romana*. By the early seventies if not sooner, the pierced screen wall had become a Moore-ish leitmotif of more than occasional frequency. The pierced, flat planes of the hollow towers of his New Haven house have opened up into screens that bend and fold around spaces to direct movement and create constantly changing, fragmented views. The aqueduct/screen wall at Xanadune also marks the fault line along which the rectangle of the plan is broken and from which much of the visual excitement is generated.

Historical precedents are used here in a more straightforward way than one had generally found in Moore's work of the sixties. Giulio Romano's rustication at New Haven is paralleled at Xanadune by the Romanness of the aqueduct. Next to the aqueduct would have stood a particularly clear recollection of a key monument of western architecture. The little eight-sided gazebo with a conical roof (*29.5*) is the lantern from Brunelleschi's dome of Florence Cathedral (*fig. 26*). It is simplified, to be sure, to make it less expensive to build and to make it conform visually to the flat planes of the arches, but it is nevertheless there as a reminder of the architect's knowledge of the history of the field in which he had chosen to spend his life working. Like the staircase in the Jobson House and the telephone booth and laundromat at Kresge College (*27.5,7*), it is also a monument domesticated for middle-class twentieth-century use. Moore's bringing Brunelleschi's lantern down to the poolside at Xanadune is surely not unlike Roy Lichtenstein's re-creation of Monet's *Haystacks* and *Rouen Cathedral* in exaggeratedly large Benday dots.

A further step along the road to a more direct use of historical forms was taken by Moore Grover Harper in their unfortunately unrealized project for housing at Kingsmill on the James, near Williamsburg, Virginia (*30.2*). Here they planned to group various-sized housing units into relatively large blocks of one- and two-story units, each of which would present an individual appearance to the street. The vocabulary of the buildings was drawn from the historical architecture of Tidewater Virginia, with, of course, little Moore-ish twists to make clear that these were buildings of the 1970s rather than of the 1770s. The result would have been a strong sense of visual individuality for each unit. The idea of using disparate forms from various sources in one building may well have come from one of those early twentieth-century San Francisco architects whom Moore came to admire in his Berkeley days, Ernest Coxhead. Coxhead's Beta Theta Pi House, 1899 (*fig. 27*), just across Hearst Avenue from the Berkeley campus, appears on the exterior to be fragments of buildings from an English village, reassembled into a new whole. The somewhat quirky and decidedly picturesque effect seems to have worked its considerable charms on Moore. For the plans of the Kingsmill units, however, Moore turned to several buildings from his own past. One unit, for instance, replicates down to almost every detail the plan for his mother's house in Pebble Beach. In a particularly interesting drawing for the Kingsmill project (*30.1*), the Pebble Beach plan is joined to a smaller element, placed to one side, through the intermediary of the pairs of bent arches that separate living room and dining room in the first Rudolph House. Here Moore seems to have sliced the rectangular plan on a diagonal, almost as if it were a stalk of celery, and then put the two parts back together, using the bent arch as the principal agent of reattachment.

In the early seventies Moore grew tired of living in crime-ridden New Haven. His house was being robbed with dismaying regularity. He and his partners found an old factory in Essex, Connecticut, with a small house adjacent to it (*5*). Into the factory's upper story they moved their offices, while into the top story of the house Moore moved himself. The entrance to the house is reminiscent of the individual units at Sea Ranch. A staircase leads up to the middle of a bridge that connects a bath on one side to living quarters on the other. The single room of the living quarters, with its gabled ceiling, was left open, as were the cubes of the Sea Ranch units. To separate

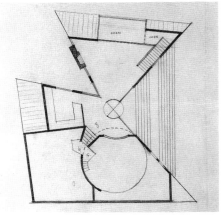

the bed from the sitting area, however, a huge plywood pyramid was built (*5.1*). The side facing the living room was cut open, much as if it were the hipped roof of Xanadune, to reveal the insides of a geode that here resembles a watermelon, because the outside of the pyramid was painted green and the inside a vibrant pink. Against the pink, as if they were seeds, were displayed Moore's personal treasures, his splendid collection of toys and electric trains. Above the pyramid's truncated top, on the ceiling, was painted the Latin inscription that encircles the pyramid on the *verso* of the dollar bill. The eye on the dollar, however, was replaced by a faceted, gold witch ball that could send its starlike shimmer scintillating across Moore's ceiling.

While many of the details here seem to have come from inspirations received by Moore and helpers during the actual construction of the pyramid, most of the basic decisions, such as the dynamic diagonal placement of the pyramid, the ball at its top, and the use of the pyramid to hide the bed on one side and to display treasures on the other are all worked out on a sheet of sketches dated 11/10/72 (*5.2*). The choice of the pyramid as a form for Moore's private house is not without significance, particularly in the light of what had already happened at Orinda and New Haven. At the first, the megaron, the king's room from a Mycenaean palace, had become the architect's living room, or bath (*see 2.4*). At New Haven, one of the towers had been called Berengaria, the name of Richard the Lion-Hearted's queen. The famous New Haven bed placed its occupant under the dome of heaven, just as Constantine had been laid to rest under the central dome of the Church of the Holy Apostles in Constantinople, or Giovanni de' Medici and his wife were placed in a sarcophagus directly under the dome of Brunelleschi's Old Sacristy in San Lorenzo in Florence. The pyramid at Essex obviously recalls the power of the pharaohs of Egypt; the toys inside are Moore's version of the miniature objects the Egyptians took with them into the afterlife. Moore's house in Los Angeles, to be designed later in the decade, is based on Bernini's Scala Regia, or royal staircase, in the Vatican Palace (*fig. 28*). Down this staircase the Pope proceeded on his *sedia gestatoria* to his palace church, St. Peter's, or from its top he welcomed important visitors to his residence. Wherever Moore decides to lay down his head for a few years, he has a way of co-opting royal prerogatives. His houses may be fun, but they are houses of hubris as well.

There are also a number of drawings, preserved thanks to the care James Volney Righter has taken of them, that show plans for a freestanding house that Moore apparently wanted to build overlooking the waterfall behind the Essex factory (*fig. 29*). Here Moore has deformed a cube with an abandon that he probably would never allow himself when faced with the reality of having to show the plan to a client. The center, if one can call it that, is occupied by a revolving door reached by climbing a triangular flight of steps to a second-story level. Once inside, a curved balcony to the left overlooks a circular swimming pool, while straight ahead lies the kitchen, with the living room to the right. A flight of steps leads down from the entrance to the pool, while another flight from the living room leads to living quarters at ground level, where another triangular room with a fireplace, and bedroom and bath are located. The grandeur of the public entrance—the forced perspective of the staircase is extraordinarily imposing—contrasts strongly with the modesty of the two little corner doors at ground level that lead directly to the pool or to the master suite.

In the New Haven years Moore's reuse of architectural ideas from the relatively distant past becomes more and more frequent, or perhaps one should say that his quotations tend to look more and more like the sources they quote. Perhaps this has something to do with his close association with Gerald Allen in those years. Allen's own designs, as we know them from *The Place of Houses*, are quite closely tied to historical precedents, more so than Moore's, even at their seemingly most derivative. The window Allen designed for the entrance to Moore's house in Essex is a quite direct quotation of a rusticated window frame by Giulio Romano, whereas Moore's rustication at Church Street South plays with the general idea of rustication, without using Giulio's forms directly. Nevertheless, the lantern of Florence Cathedral by the pool at Xanadune (*29.5*) is symptomatic of Moore's increasing fascination with classical architectural motifs in the seventies, a fasination that comes to full flower in Piazza d'Italia in New Orleans.

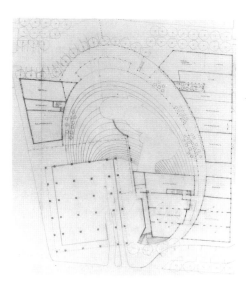

Fig. 30. Piazza d'Italia (first project)
New Orleans, Louisiana
1975–1978, plan
Ink on paper
Moore, Grover, Harper

The first schemes for the piazza were worked out in Essex, and it was from the Essex office that Moore's entry into the competition for the piazza was sent. Chad Floyd, who had been living in Pittsburgh and studying the requirements of public spaces, was called in by Moore to help with the design. The Moore, Grover, Harper entry featured an oval piazza, a motif with august Renaissance parentage, surrounded by shops (*fig. 30*). The oval was cleverly stretched across the irregular block to hide its irregularities, while the pavement pattern generated by the oval was used to suggest directions of pedestrian movement. In the open part of the space, an Italianate campanile (*35.1,3,4*) rose from a fountain with a typical contour map basin. The oval specifically was chosen to make a space that could be focused in on itself, where people could see and be seen, act and interact, in a way that might be successful, despite the fact that attempts to reproduce Italian squares in America have generally turned out to be functional failures (one thinks of Boston City Hall Plaza).

The competition was won by a New Orleans firm, Perez Associates, but the jury like the MGH scheme so much that they instructed the winners to join forces with MGH to produce a new, joint design. At this point, Moore underwent a change of venue; he moved to Los Angeles to take over the direction of the architecture school at UCLA. With him went the Piazza d'Italia job, to be worked on at Urban Innovations Group, a commercial arm of the UCLA architecture school that gives its students professional experience.

In the Los Angeles version, Piazza d'Italia underwent major changes. The fountain turned into a contour map of the Italian peninsula, from which water from the Po, Arno, and Tiber runs into a pool set into a pavement marked with concentric circles (*35.6*). Beyond the toe of the boot, and outside the pool, rises Sicily, which has the names of the participants in the project inscribed on its marble base (Moore's name is found in the neighborhood of Palermo). The vertical parts of the fountain changed from a freestanding campanile, for which a number of Moore's famous napkin drawings are preserved, into a kind of backdrop composed of curved, Moore-ish screen walls that contain witty plays on the vocabulary of classical architecture (*35.7,8,9*). The fountain became, in other words, more something to be enjoyed as a theatrical spectacle, like its main source, the splendid eighteenth-century Fontana di Trevi in Rome, than a central point in an open space. Like that of the Fontana di Trevi, the central element of Moore's fountain is an arch springing from two Corinthian columns. Like that of its source, the basin of Moore's fountain is meant to be played in (who can ever forget Anita Ekberg's dip in the Trevi in *La Dolce Vita*?). The donors of the New Orleans fountain were members of the Italian community of the city, who offered it in gratitude to the town in which they had prospered. They and their descendants could cavort over a miniature replica of the geography from which they came. Here Moore fused a sense of place and a sense of origins in a particularly magical way.

The classicizing details gone crazy show Moore's wit at its most enthralling. Nothing is quite as it should be. The more or less Corinthian columns that support the central arch have neon necking. The Ionic capitals to the right of the center are stainless steel, rather than Pentelic marble. The Doric order of the triumphal arch has voids filled with fan sprays of water where the metopes should be. Moore calls them "wetopes." On the arch itself, his collaborators applied two masks of the master, water spouting from his lips as if he were a mythological beast on a fountain in Rome. Other Doric columns have no shafts. Instead, thin streams of water dribble from the bottom of the capital to describe the cylinder of the shaft and its fluting. The space under the central arch, located at the top of the Italian Alps, was to lead to a German restaurant. Moore called the order he invented here the "deli" order. But the pun is at least a double one, recalling also Sir Edwin Lutyens's invention of what he called the Delhi Order for his Viceroy's Palace in India.

Large-scale Italianate architectural forms attract the passerby from nearby streets to the fountain. Along Poydras Street, a major thoroughfare, the campanile that was to have marked the center of the fountain in the original oval scheme now rises up in a somewhat lopsided way to challenge the boring skyscrapers around it and to suggest that something important, and even funny is going on behind it. The competition between the campanile and the towers is suggested by a witty sketch dated "1 April 76" (*35.2*). Almost as close to

Poydras Street is a sonotube temple, its concrete columns laid out in a false perspective whose vanishing point is the point in front of the fountain from which it is best viewed. Here ancient architectural forms and Renaissance perspective, both native to the Italian tradition, combine to focus on a Pop version of the Italian Baroque, with the Italian Middle Ages rising, in the form of the campanile, just a few steps away.

At the opposite end of the block from the fake perspective temple and the campanile rises a large block of masonry that bears, on the side facing the fountain, the ubiquitous town clock of every Italian village. The other side of this tower, however, becomes a resplendently rusticated Mannerist triumphal arch, trichromed in the Italian national colors (*35.11*). This arch lines up directly with a street flanked by old warehouses that is someday to become a lively commercial thoroughfare. In other words, Piazza d'Italia is not just the witty send-up of the classical language of architecture (to steal John Summerson's felicitous phrase) that it has been rightly seen to be, but it is also a careful exercise in creating relationships between the fountain and the surrounding urban space. That the fountain is now partially in ruins may in fact stem from the architects' use of fragile materials, but it is also the result of official neglect and an economic situation that has, until now, precluded the completion of the project. The circular piazza is someday to be enclosed by shops that will perhaps give it the life it now lacks. Moore is currently planning a spectacular hotel for the site (*35.12*). Even so, Piazza d'Italia has become enough of a symbol of New Orleans that is could be used for a scene in *Tightrope*, a Clint Eastwood thriller, in which the body of a murdered prostitute turns up right on top of central Italy.

The years in Los Angeles, which have come to an end only in the last year with Moore's removal to Texas, have been in many ways his most fertile. As international recognition of his importance has increased, larger and more interesting commisions have come his way. In the first years of this decade, from his drawing table (or whatever table he happened to be sitting at) have poured a string of remarkable buildings: a church, two museums, a civic center, a whole quarter of a major European city. In addition, there have been splendid, if unrealized, projects for a large hotel and a small library. Each represents a new departure for Moore, not only in terms of a new building type tackled successfully, but also in terms of a personal style that grows richer and more complex, as well as more at home with the great architecture of the past that Moore has always admired.

The additions to Lawrence Hall at Williams College are a convenient place to begin to look at the works of the last decade. Moore received the commission in the winter of 1977, but because of budgetary delays and the accompanying need to redesign the project several times, the building did not open until the fall of 1983. The earliest designs also included the addition of a swimming pool and a basketball court to the gymnasium that adjoins Lawrence Hall immediately to the west, across a narrow, but steep ravine. The whole complex also is close to the main commercial street of Williamstown, and all the early designs tried to work that fact into the scheme in one way or another. One of the happiest of the several projects submitted at this stage in the design put the new museum spaces in a large rectangular box, lit by windows placed behind beveled corners, that was slipped in between Lawrence and the gym (*51.3,4*). This project also featured a shopping arcade that led from the street to the new athletic facilities and to a marvelously curvy, irregular replay of the Spanish Steps in Rome on a steep little slope in the Berkshires. The new athletic facilities would also have been graced by another set of the "falling windows" that Moore had recently designed for his new condominium on Selby Avenue in Los Angeles (*see 6.1*). This project was put aside for financial reasons.

When planning for Lawrence Hall got underway again, the athletic facilities had been removed from the commission. The final project on which bids were submitted shows a building much in tune with its site and the architectural traditions that surrounded it (*51.5,6,7*) but no longer tied into the commercial and athletic life of the town. The original Lawrence Hall is a two-story brick octagon designed in 1846 as the college library by a talented young architect, Thomas Tefft of Providence, Rhode Island, who died much too young to make the mark on American architecture his talents promised.

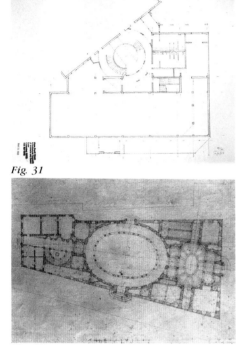

Fig. 31

Fig. 32

Fig. 34

Inside the octagon, on the upper floor, is a rotunda whose hemispherical dome is supported by eight Ionic columns. To the east and west of the octagon, wings were added in 1889, while the T-shaped building to the south appeared in 1925. (The space between the T and the west wing was filled in 1937.) To the south of the T, the land drops off steeply. Moore decided to place the main space of the new addition, a large gallery, on a line drawn along the top of this slope. Here again the shape of the site dictated the shape of the building. The new building meets the old at less than a 45-degree angle at the southwest corner of the T, thereby creating a geometrically somewhat irregular situation (see **51.1**). On the northeast end of the new gallery Moore added a second gallery, at right angles to the first. The angle of intersection of these two masses is lined up precisely with the center of the interior of Tefft's rotunda.

On the axis thus created with Tefft's octagon, Moore designed an octagonal east end for the large gallery. The axis between the two octagons was the primary feature to tie the disparate elements of the design together. There were several schemes for this axis, the most arresting of which was one that placed inside the irregular trapezoid left between the old south wall of the T and the new galleries a pair of semicircular staircases, one rising up to the level of the galleries, the other descending to a floor with classrooms and offices. Although the drawings for the entire scheme seem not to have been preserved, those with the circular staircase are recorded in photographs (fig. 31). Here one can see the new octagon at the end of the new gallery, preceded by a smaller octagon that forms a buffer zone between gallery and staircase. The stairwell would have been connected to the old building by a bridge, which would have debouched into an oval gallery carved out of the space of the old T. To the north of the oval, still continuing on the north/south axis, would have been a square gallery, followed by the originial Tefft rotunda. No more sophisticated promenade of spaces has ever come from Moore's pen than these. The source for this promenade seems clear: one of Borromini's projects for the Palazzo Carpegna in Rome, which was published in 1979 by Anthony Blunt in his Borromini. In this particular project (fig. 32) Borromini joined large and small spaces on a long axis that held the entire irregular mass of the building together. Particularly noteworthy for our purposes are the irregular octagon of the entrance hall that is joined to an oval courtyard, beyond which a semicircular staircase rises alongside the corridor that marks the axis. Moore seems to have devoured this book shortly after it was published, and to have used several of its illustrations as sources for his own work. We will see more of Borromini's drawings come into play when we discuss the designs for the Beverly Hills Civic Center.

During the course of refining the design to meet the client's needs, the Borrominilike plan disappeared. Indeed, even the walls that would have defined the octagon at the east end of the new large gallery disappeared. The octagonal shape was preserved, however, in the polygonal exterior, and an octagonal dome was planned to float over the end of the gallery. In the budget cuts that followed the submission of the bids, that octagonal vault, and indeed the entire shed roof over the new galleries, was lopped off, together with some twenty feet of the west end of the three-story mass. The resulting change in proportion and roof line produced a final building considerably changed from the one envisioned in the model (figs. 33, 34).

From the south side of the building Moore cantilevered the art faculty offices out in the saddlebag conformation (**51.13**) he has been using since the Bonham House (see **12.1**). The roof line of the "bag" is interrupted by a large gable that rises over the large window that lights an interior lounge. Below the window, two pairs of columns flank a staircase that leads up to a lower entrance. The columns, however, do not rise high enough to meet their capitals, which hang from the cantilevered floor of the bag above. Dubbed the "Ironic Order" by Whitney Stoddard, these columns are a particularly hilarious joke on the ancient orders, but, as Moore's jokes do, they also make an architectural point. The shafts do not meet the capitals because the cantilevered floor needs no support from the columns. On the other hand, the staircase did need markers to emphasize its role as a principal entrance to the building. The pairs of columns, with their capitals hanging above, act like upside-down exclamation points, in Spanish, that gleefully announce that entrance.

Fig. 35

The commission for the Hood Museum at Dartmouth College presented Moore and his partner in Essex with a similar problem—joining new gallery space to already existing buildings. But the buildings at Dartmouth that surrounded the site for the Hood were vastly different in style from the countrified Federal that presented itself in Williamstown. The Dartmouth site is dominated by the huge bulk of Wallace Harrison's Hopkins Center, a red brick and concrete version, somewhat scaled down, of his Metropolitan Opera House at Lincoln Center, New York, the buildings of which Moore had subjected to rather biting ridicule in a magazine piece of the 1960s. To either side of the "Hop" rise imposing structures—the quadrangular bulk of the Hanover Inn to the west, the turreted Romanesque mass of Wilson to the east.

One of the first problems Moore confronted was where to site the new addition. In a series of design sessions held in public on the Dartmouth campus in the summer of 1980, Moore at first played with the idea of putting the Hood between the Hop and the Inn. He saw this version of the Hood as a one-eyed mansarded monster, moving aggressively northward from the facade of the Hop toward the green (*56.1*). The one great window seems to be an echo of the large round-arched windows by Harrison that overlook a terrace between the Hop and the Inn, but which Moore's addition would have replaced (*fig. 35*). From this phase of the design comes a particularly beautiful Moore drawing that shows the roof of the Hop peeking above splendidly inventive screen walls that hide the lower part of a facade that Moore clearly does not much like.

In the public design sessions, Moore used small models of various parts of the proposed new structures (*56.6,7,8,9*). These could be taken apart and recombined with other models, or other parts, at the suggestion of the local participants. The shapes were always controlled by Moore and his assistants, but where they were placed, and how they related to each other, could be shifted, to give the participants in the design process a sense that they had had some effect on the way the building finally came out. Included in these models were not only suggested parts for the facade, but also buildings to be placed in a courtyard behind and to the east of the Hop, such as the circular "Bower of Bliss," a snack bar, and the "Temple of Chair Storage," a semigrandiose fragment of a structure, but with very mundane functions.

The site finally selected, however, was not between the Hop and the Inn, but rather between the Hop and Wilson Hall. For this area, too, there are several schemes, which developed as a suite of galleries running south from Wilson, with a screen wall and an octagonal pavilion intervening between Wilson and the Hopkins Center, a project which is preserved in another splendid drawing by Moore (*56.10*). The final plan bridged the space between Hopkins and Wilson with a rather severe concrete gate that simultaneously provides a connecting corridor between the two older buildings and allows passage from the area of the green into the courtyard that actually leads into the Hood Museum (*56.18*). Once past the gate, one can choose between a path that leads straight down to a basement entrance or one that rises up a gently curved ramp to enter the Hood in the side of the tower with the gilded, Bramantesque topknot that rises directly ahead (*56.20*). To the left, as one moves up the ramp, are the concrete surrounds of the windows that must, from their stepped form in the style of Aalto, light a staircase inside.

The door to the Hood leads into one of Moore's most successful revolving-door vestibules (*56.22*), of the type he has been using at least since the Santa Barbara Faculty Club (*see 34.5*). At Dartmouth the vestibule is a polygon set inside the square of the tower. Four faces of the polygon allow circulation in four different directions; this hall is planned to be a principal node of communication on the campus. Students are expected to pass through it on their way to their mailboxes, or to the snack bar in the Hopkins Center. On the way, they may even be tempted to look at a work of art in the museum.

The massing and plan of the Hood (*56.16,17*) are reminiscent, as we shall see, of the plan and massing of St. Matthew's in Pacific Palisades, a building that had already been designed when the project for the Hood got underway. The main gallery of the Hood, the roof of which rises high above the rest of the building, is analogous to the nave of St. Matthew's. The smaller galleries, under lower roofs, intersect the main gallery at an oblique angle, something in the manner of skewed dwarf transepts. Over the main gallery soars the polygonal

Fig. 36. Andrea Palladio
Plan for villa
(From A. Palladio, I Quattro Libri
dell'Architettura, Venice, 1570, plate LVII)

Fig. 37. Richard Morris Hunt
Griswold House
Newport, Rhode Island
1863, plan

Fig. 38. MLTW/Moore-Turnbull
Tempchin House
Bethesda, Maryland
1968, plan

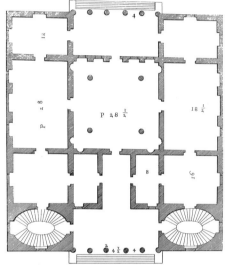

Fig. 36

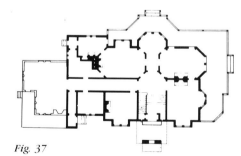

Fig. 37

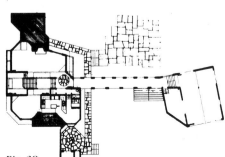

Fig. 38

arch of a mighty truss-cum-light-bridge (**56.24**). This is the last, for the moment, in a long series of great roof trusses that run from the Moore House in Orinda (*see* **2.1,3**) through the trusses of the roofs at St. Matthew's (**56.13,14**).

The Hood has a somberness of color and a heaviness of mass that is not typical of Moore's earlier work. Partly, one suspects, this is in response to the massiveness of the surrounding buildings, including even Harrison's Hopkins Center. In part, however, one senses a change in style at work here, a change toward greater bulk, toward a greater sense of solidity than one was accustomed to find in the taut, thin surfaces of the earlier phases of his career. Particularly notable in this respect are the tops of the concrete piers that surround the edge of the stairwell in the main gallery (**56.24**). At the opening of the museum, one wag suggested that they represented the necks of the Dartmouth line.

Out back, one can see this heaviness carried out in the great round arch that supports the staircase of a fire escape (**56.19**). (Leave it to Mr. Moore to give so mundane a function so great a form.) Here a bent arch, descended from the one at the Santa Barbara Faculty Club, is no longer a thin plane folded in space. Instead, it has become a noble, heavy form, almost Richardsonian in its massiveness, that is able to turn the great size and arched roof of the Hopkins Center into a background structure.

A number of other important stylistic shifts occurred in the late seventies and early eighties in Moore's work. There is a movement from some of the almost obsessive irregularity that one finds in the works of the late sixties, such as the Klotz House, or even more extremely in the magnificently eroded project for the Goodman House, dated "12/9/69" (**16.6**), toward more symmetrical Palladian plans. The second Rudolph House (Rudolph II), in Williamstown, Massachusetts, designed in 1979, is one of the best cases in point. The site for the house is a rather steep slope running down toward the west. The earliest scheme for this house, sketched out by Robert Harper, shows an asymmetrical plan that respected the slope—a "modernist" concatenation of rectangular boxes disposed to accommodate the functions of the house on the topography of the site (**19.1**). Moore's first sketch, now lost, combined elements of sixteenth-century Italian designs, particularly the three-story nymphaeum of the Villa Giulia in Rome, with a plan reminiscent of Palladio. The nymphaeum was deliberately set into the hill so that the slope sliced diagonally through its regular Renaissance elevation. Aspects of Moore's design are preserved in the two sheets of sketches, dated "5/25/79," made by Harper (**19.2,3**). The U-shaped main floor is arranged around a square courtyard with a circular pavement pattern. This gives on to a rectangular entrance placed very close to a pair of curved steps, reminiscent of those at the Villa Giulia, that give access to a swimming pool placed north of the house. The house broadens to the south to accommodate bedrooms on the west and a garage on the east. This design was too wide to set into the slope without digging away a good part of the site. In the next version the width was greatly reduced, producing the present compact scheme, centered on a square sitting room topped by an octagonal dome (**19.4**). This scheme, with an octagon placed in the middle of a square, is uncannily close to an early design for the Rudolph House (**17.2**). The difference between the move from symmetry to asymmetry in the planning of that house, and the opposite movement here, is symptomatic of some of the changes that Moore's thinking underwent in the seventies. The un-Moore-ish regularity of the whole scheme, however, is to be attributed to Harper's considerable role in its design. He was on the scene, while Moore was largely on the West Coast.

An interest in Palladian symmetry manifests itself in the pages of *The Place of Houses*, which Moore, together with Donlyn Lyndon and Gerald Allen, published in 1974. Included in the work are plans of villas by Palladio, and one of these, Plate LVII from Palladio's *Quattro Libri* (*fig. 36*), is clearly the principal source for the plan of Rudolph II. In the same book, the authors reproduce a plan of the Griswold House by the nineteenth-century American architect Richard Morris Hunt, which has an almost perfectly symmetrical core (*fig. 37*). This symmetry is largely retained in a design by Allen, the Smyth House, but it is massaged away in the Tempchin House, a Moore plan that depends on the same source (*fig. 38*). One imagines that if Moore had had a greater hand in the plan of Rudolph II, it would have been more irregular, like

Fig. 39.   Robert Harper
Rudolph II House
Williamstown, Massachusetts
1979–1981, elevation of corner pavilion
Pencil on yellow trace

Fig. 40.   Urban Innovations Group
Licht House
Mill Valley, California
1977–1979, exterior

Fig. 41.   Licht House
1977–1979, interior, staircase from dining
room

Fig. 42.   Licht House
1977–1979, interior, dining room and living
room from staircase

Fig. 39

Fig. 40

Fig. 41

Fig. 42

the Tempchin House, than four-square, like the Palladian villa from which it descends. The geometric regularity of Sammis Hall at the Cold Spring Harbor Laboratories (*see* **52**) also bespeaks a larger role for Harper than for Moore in its design, even though Moore was certainly involved in the planning of Sammis, just as he was in Rudolph II.

If one compares the second Rudolph House with the Johnson House at Sea Ranch (*see Bloomer, fig. 8*), one can see the same basic elements handled in vastly different ways. In both there is a long axis that unites house with land and site, but the axis at Rudolph II is straight. There is the pyramidal roof that slopes to a projecting entrance porch, but at Rudolph II the roof is punctured by four chimneys—only one functions—derived from Stratford, the ancestral home of the Lees; its corners are broken up by the separate slopes of the roofs of the pavilions and the entrance porch is a semicircular portico with white columns. At Rudolph II the outside is not covered in one taut, monochromatic skin. Instead, the walls of the square that lies at the heart of the plan are covered with brick, while the parts that either extend beyond the core, or are cut out of it, are covered in pink stucco (*19.11,12*). At the Johnson Sea Ranch House, the ancillary spaces around the octagon expand as function dictates, to produce an irregular exterior that gives little clue to the presence of the regular octagon at its core. At Rudolph II, the functions are forced into the preconceived, symmetrical shapes of the square-corner pavilions. But, like the Johnson House, the second Rudolph House saves its central octagonal core for a surprise. Only the rather open, asymmetrical space shared by the kitchen and the dining room at Rudolph II has that sense of fused spaces with ambiguous edges that one finds in the Johnson House. At Rudolph II the square plan of the dining room pavilion is expressed toward the interior by the intersection of two beams overhead, while the space below is allowed to flow freely from one area to another.

The dominant interior feature of Rudolph II is the central dome (*19.13*). Eight-sided, it seems to float over the square room below, although it is actually supported by concealed steel rods. Where Brunelleschi had placed ribs between the eight sides of his dome for Florence Cathedral, Moore and Harper have left empty spaces. In this splendid contradiction of static expectations, one finds light where one expects structure. (One finds the Moore-ish touch in sketches for the dome of the second Rudolph House by one of the members of the staff of Moore, Grover, Harper, James Childress (*19.6*). If these domes had been drawn by Moore himself, however, he probably would have "massaged" their shapes more vigorously.) Similarly, on the outside, at the corners of the pavilions, one finds pilasters which, in their Renaissance prototypes, would have been metonymic representations of the structural function of the corner of the wall they mark. Here, however, the pilasters are not solids, but planes of glass (*fig. 39*). The structure at the corner is dissolved, as done by Gropius at the Fagus Werk in 1911, or as done by Moore in his own house at Orinda in 1962. If the term postmodern (can't we find a less oxymoronic phrase?) has any meaning at all, it should certainly apply to this detail, which wittily manages to combine both a modern and a classical resolution of the corner in one contradictory form.

Designed at the same time as Rudolph II, but totally different in effect, is the Licht House in Mill Valley, California (*figs. 40, 41, 42*). They are different not just because Moore was working with different associates on the two projects, but primarily because he was working with clients whose personalities and tastes were very different. The Licht House has a relaxed H plan (Stratford invoked once again, but very differently) that cascades down a gentle slope from bedroom and study above, past entrance landing, to living room, dining room, kitchen, and studio below. The symmetrical source here is converted into a set of asymmetrical steps that hug the slope of the site. The exterior is Bay Area board and batten (*fig. 40*), and the interior is, at the Lichts' request, simple and all white (*figs. 41, 42*). They had previously lived in an all-white Cliff May interior in Los Angeles, and they wanted to repeat this feature. The Lichts and the Rudolphs are both retired couples with taste, intelligence, and an interest in art—they are, in many ways, ideal Moore clients. Their tastes, however, run in very different directions from one another, and from their architect's as well, a fact to which Moore was sensitive. He did not force them to live in buildings that conformed to his tastes, but rather he provided them with sympathetic stage sets on which they could perform the

Fig. 43. Charles W. Moore
Sketches for Ocala, Florida, housing project
1971
Pencil on yellow paper

dramas of their lives, as they saw fit.

If Palladian traditions, indigenous to New England, were invoked for the second Rudolph House, and California traditions for the Lichts, then traditions specific to Berlin were invoked in the designs for the Tegel Harbor competition of 1980, which Moore, Ruble, Yudell, up against a field of international architects, won. In doing so, they probably became the first American architects ever to have the chance to design an entire quarter of a major European city.

The requirements for the Tegel Harbor competition were complex. The designer was to provide housing and cultural and recreation centers. Ruble and Yudell laid out one of the first sketches for the site plan, which featured an angular complex of apartments, with rather knobby joints (*54.1*). At the east end of the long, narrow plot of ground they arranged the buildings of the cultural complex in stepped blocks separated by a curving path. The recreation center is in the shape of a boat moored in the river, and the bank of the river has been cut back in graceful curves. The existence of this boat is prefigured in an earlier sketch, where a stern-wheeler steams up to a less elegantly curved shore. At the northwest corner of the apartment blocks stands a housing tower, simultaneously curved and angular in plan. John Ruble, in an elevation drawing of this tower (*54.3*), noted its debt to local twentieth-century traditions in the inscription "SHAROUN!" (Hans Scharoun is the architect of the Berlin Philharmonic, 1956–63, the jagged profile of which Ruble's drawing recalls.)

A later stage in the design shows certain crucial changes introduced by Moore, particularly in the plan of the housing elements (*54.2*). Gone are the angles and knobby elbows. Instead, the line of the buildings flows like the line of the riverbank. Here the stream that Moore introduced into the Seagram Building plaza in his dissertation has become a full-fledged building. One may also see here, of course, a reference to the eighteenth-century Lansdowne Crescent, Bath (Moore is quite fond of eighteenth- and nineteenth-century British residential crescents). The sinuous curvature of the housing at Berlin has reappeared, on a smaller scale, in the plan of the Miglio House at Sea Ranch, designed in early 1984 (*21*).

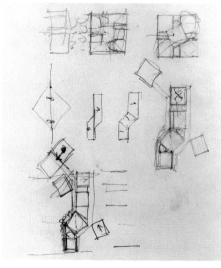

The origins of this kind of serpentine planning go back to Moore's work of the early seventies. A sketch for the Ocala project of 1971 demonstrates, amazingly enough, that the Miglio and Berlin plans ultimately derived from the simple idea of a square rotated inside a larger square (*fig. 43*). In this sketch Moore begins, in the middle sketch at the top, with what he would call a doughnut plan, a square within a square. He then rotates the smaller square and separates the corners into irregular, almost square spaces close in size to the one in the center. This move leaves narrow, four-sided spaces between the corner spaces. The final step involves dismembering the parts and rearranging them in a linear grouping with a jog in the line caused by the rotated square. Only one further step—"massaging" the corners of the rotated square into curves—produces both the Berlin and the Miglio plans. Such is the way Mr. Moore's mind works.

The boatlike recreation center at Berlin (*54.4,5,6*), which unfortunately will probably not be built, presents us with another of the images that have obsessed Moore in the past decade. The source is what Moore calls "the boat of the Empress of China," a great marble fake barge, with pavilions atop, built by the Dowager Empress in a lake in the gardens of the summer palace in Peking. Moore knows equally well Isola Bella in Lake Como, that "boat" that contains the splendid baroque gardens of the Borromeo family. In the late seventies Moore, Grover, Harper built a concrete boat on the banks of the Miami River in Dayton, Ohio, as part of their Riverdesign project (*50*). From this boat, rock bands entertain the Dayton citizenry on warm evenings. The fountain in the Beverly Hills Civic Center, as we shall see, was also to be graced by one, or even two such boats (*55.10*). The conceit is a splendid one, creating a kind of Pirandellian play between illusion and reality, a play that would have been further complicated at Berlin by the fact that the boat would have contained swimming pools, laid out in curved patterns that suggested that the pools were part of the river system, somehow contained within the riverboat.

The glass exterior for this boat also allowed Moore to play with another

Fig. 44. Karl Friedrich Schinkel
Bauakademie Berlin
1831–1836, exterior, elevation
(From K. F. Schinkel, Sammlung
Architektonischer Entwürfe, *Berlin, 1873, 117)*

aspect of Berlin architectural traditions, the penchant for glass walls that a number of early twentieth-century Berlin architects showed, from the relatively restrained work of Gropius and Mies in the teens and twenties to the extravagant dreams of Paul Scheerbart's *Glasarchitektur* of 1914. At the same time, he suggests those ocean liners that Le Corbusier so greatly admired in the pages of *Vers une architecture*, while the sharply angled bridges that join the boat to the shore hint at the sci-fi fantasies of the Archigram group, particularly Ron Herron's Walking City. In Moore's rec-boat, we have at least a quadruple entendre.

For the buildings in the cultural center Moore turned to one of his principal heroes, the great Berlin classicist of the early nineteenth century, Karl Friedrich Schinkel. It is hardly surprising that the forms of such civilizing structures as the Music School at Tegel Harbor (*54.*7) should be drawn largely from the civilized Schinkel. The sources are not so much Schinkel's most rhetorical designs, such as the Altes Museum, but rather his more mundane educational institutions, such as the Bauakademie, which seem to offer Moore appropriate prototypes for the Tegel Harbor situation (*fig. 44*).

The library, however, ventures outside Berlin, at least in part, for its sources. When Moore thinks about libraries, he turns to Aalto. Like most of the libraries of Aalto, Moore's at Berlin will be lit by light introduced in the center of the roof by a light hood created by raising one side of the roof higher than the other (*54.*8,9). This was an idea Moore first played with in 1954, in the Chung Wha Girl's School in Seoul (*43*), and to which he was to return in the eighties in the room for the secretarial staff in his building at the University of California, Irvine (*59.1*). For the Berlin library, however, the roof is to be curved, like that of Aalto's library at Rovaniemi, 1963–68. In plan (*54.8*), the regular rectangle of the Tegel Harbor library is subdivided by a circular entrance hall (one of Moore's revolving door entrances) from which two curved walls emanate. The one to the right, a flattened curve that moves diagonally through the reading room, will hold the bookcases. The imagery of the river flows once again (*54.11*). The books become a stream of knowledge flowing through the community, or, perhaps, even the tail of a spermatozoon that fertilizes the minds of the Tegelhafener.

In the project for the San Juan Capistrano, California, Library competition of 1982, Moore, again working with Ruble and Yudell, drew even more extensively on Aalto as a source for his design (*58.1,3*). In plan the San Juan Capistrano project is extraordinarily close to Aalto's at Seinäjoki, 1963–65. In both bookshelves fan out in a radial pattern from a central control desk, while offices and other types of rooms have rectangular plans. Moore's fan shape, however, is completely encased in rectilinear walls, so that the exterior could maintain the Spanish Colonial flavor the competition rules called for. The junctures between fan and rectangle were used by Moore to create picturesque irregular courtyards for outdoor reading. The typical Moore all-covering roof would have been supported by an interior truss system. The truss itself would have been absolutely regular, but the supports would have been irregularly spaced, to fit them inconspicuously into the bookshelves, whose positions were determined by the radial pattern emanating from the desk of the all-seeing librarian (*58.1*). Two different systems clash here, in a way that simultaneously solves the architectural problem and makes the conflict clear. The tension thus produced characterizes much of Moore's work, particularly the designs of the past few years.

There would also have been something churchlike about the open truss under the roof, a sense that would have been enhanced by the painted decorations that Moore intended to apply to the trusses, which are reminiscent of those one finds on the wooden beams that support the ceiling of the church inside the ruins of the famous San Juan Capistrano mission, which is only a block away from the library. Indeed, the play of straight and semicircular walls on the terrace just outside the library, when seen in relation to the truss inside, recalls the juncture of apse, transept, and nave in the main church of the town, which is located diagonally across the street from the library. Here the library appears as a kind of temple of knowledge, an idea that can hardly be foreign to Moore. Among the buildings of the past that Moore likes best is Thomas Jefferson's campus for the University of Virginia at Charlottesville. There, of course, the ensemble is dominated by the library,

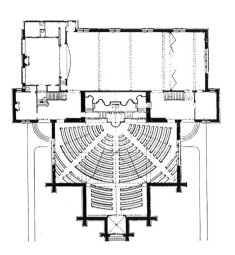

*Fig. 45. Cram, Wentworth and Goodhue
Unitarian Church (project)
Somerville, Massachusetts
Plan
(From American Architect and Building News,
October 6, 1894)*

Jefferson's version of the Pantheon in Rome, transformed also into a temple of knowledge. At San Juan Capistrano Moore seems to have taken Jefferson's concept to heart, but to have changed the architectural vocabulary into something developed out of the local religious vernacular.

The integration of contradictory forms into what Robert Venturi might call a "difficult whole" was achieved by Moore with singular mastery at St. Matthew's Episcopal Church in Pacific Palisades, California. The commission was awarded to Moore in 1979, and the church opened its doors in 1983. The role of the congregation in planning this church is discussed in detail elsewhere in these pages by Richard Song. Here I would like to address the problem the congregation set the architect: a church with semicircular seating placed inside a cruciform shape. At first thought, the problem seems incapable of solution. It had been faced in late nineteenth-century American church designs, such as a proposal for a Unitarian Church in Somerville, Massachusetts, by Cram, Wentworth and Goodhue, that appeared in the *American Architect and Building News* of October 6, 1894 (*fig. 45*), but Moore may not have been aware of these earlier schemes.

Moore has often said that the architectural activity should be placed overhead, to get it out of the way of the functions that go on below. That is precisely what he did at St. Matthew's. The cruciform roof is held up by a system of steel trusses that float over the circular seating below. The trusses are supported from below by two pairs of steel I-beams that rise from the floor to form a pair of arches placed toward either end of the nave (*53.14*). The triangular peaks of these arches hold up a truss that runs the length of the nave and supports the shed roof over the nave. From the bottom of this truss is hung, at right angles to it, a second truss that supports the lower roofs of the dwarf transepts. The transept truss is stabilized, according to some accounts, by the network of raylike ribs that connect the nave and transept trusses at the crossing (*53.15*), and the transept roof is also stabilized by the walls that rise in a diagonal line from piers placed toward the ends of the transepts (*53.13*).

In this way, the actual structures that rise up from the floor can be placed so far apart that plenty of room is left in between for the semicircular pews, whose radii fan out from the altar (*53.6*). The architectural problem, then, is literally left hanging in suspension, as if it were an unstable chemical solution. We see the contradictory systems, one on top of the other, each sufficient unto itself, and yet each perfectly comfortable with the contradictory other. Moore has named this manner of designing with seemingly irreconcilable opposites "immaculate collision." The apparent ease with which this is accomplished belies the considerable sweat that must have been expended in finding the solution. Part of the success lies in the mediating role provided by the octagonal walls within which the suspension of the cross takes place. They provide a shape that is both centralizing and angular. Part of the success is also due to the generosity of the size of the interior, so that the play between the seats and the cross does not impose itself too claustrophobically on the viewer. Part of it also has to do with the abundant light that is allowed into the interior, creating a spiritual experience that is far more moving than one has any right to expect from a building designed at the tail end of the twentieth century in a cushy corner of Lotus Land. And part of it has to do with the very clever manipulation of the relationship between color and light. The walls of the church are painted a rather pale pink, which is broken up by the darker pink lines that frame the oak battens that rise, with a Gothic eagerness for verticality, from floor to ceiling. The congregation wanted not only a great deal of light and wood in their church, but also stained glass. Because the latter did not fit the budget, Moore manipulated the color of the walls to give the effect of stained glass. Anyone who has visited one of the great Gothic cathedrals of France that still has its stained glass in place will recall how the light that enters the church through the stained glass takes on a kind of palpable color that washes over the surfaces of the vaults and tints them pale pink, if the color of the glass through which the light has passed is predominantly red. The pink walls at St. Matthew's imitate the effect of stained glass on the light inside the church, even though no stained glass is present.

The foursquare bell tower that now marks the entrance to St. Matthew's is rather more hard-edged than what Moore apparently wanted on the site. A

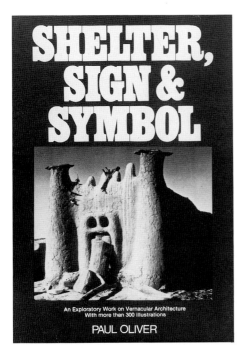

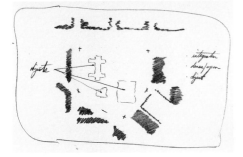

sketch for his preferred version of the campanile shows a rather slinky form attached to a wall that wound around the edges of the church and its parking lot (**53.2**). Typical of Moore is the source for the facelike features of the campanile, apparently the photo of a Dogon building in Africa that graced the cover of a book on vernacular architecture around the world that appeared first in 1977 and came out in a paperback version in 1980 (*fig. 46*), presumably the year of the drawing in question. The vernacular African entrance, with its mysteriously deep eyes and mouth, was simply co-opted for the bell tower of an altogether WASP church.

Moore, working with Urban Innovations Group, won the competition in 1982 for the new Beverly Hills Civic Center. In some ways, this is perhaps the most challenging commission he has ever received, and it called forth one of his most inventive plans. Because a particularly fine set of drawings for this project, from Moore's hand, have been preserved, thanks to the foresight of Stephen Harby, we can observe his mind and working methods here in particularly close detail.

The UIG office began the process of laying out the problem, as a small sketch by Richard Best demonstrates (*fig. 47*). The new Civic Center was to be placed on two irregularly shaped blocks that contained important structures which had to be incorporated into the design. The old City Hall, with its H-shaped plan and tall tower, would remain the dominant vertical object. The fire station near it had a handsome Art Deco exterior that would have been a shame to lose. The exterior of the library, on the other block, of a gaucheness that could be covered over in good conscience, imposed a squarish mass which could not be eliminated without greatly increasing the budget for the project. Best's sketch shows the shapes of the two blocks and the three built objects within them that had to be dealt with.

A drawing by Stephen Harby (**55.11**) shows one of Moore's assistants struggling with the difficult problem presented by the site. Harby sets up two pedestrian axes, one in line with the center of the back of the City Hall, and the other moving diagonally from northeast to southwest to tie the blocks together. These axes then cross a third, the vehicular axis of Rexford Drive, the street that separates the two blocks. Harby used an open fragment of an octagon, focused on a monument directly in line with City Hall, to fuse the pedestrian axes, while Best's drawing used a trapezoid to mediate between City Hall and a circular plaza that joins rather awkwardly with the L created by the library and a new community center.

Our first record of Moore's intervention is on a sheet of 8½-by-11-inch lined paper, on which he sketched the problem at dinner one night with Harby and Peter Becker, with whom he collaborated on the writing of a guidebook to Los Angeles. The drawing is lost, but fortunately it has been preserved in a Xerox sheet. Moore drew the two blocks and the existing buildings, then defined the leftover space between them in a series of curved lines that enclose an amorphously shaped space. From this sketch was developed a large drawing that shows his ideas from the dinner table in more detail (**55.3**). At the southeast corner two towers form an entrance that is marked on the plan by an arrow. This entrance leads to an irregularly shaped court between City Hall and the fire station. The fire station is connected to the opposite block by a (domed?) bridge that then meanders around the north side of the library to the irregular space opposite the back of City Hall. A long rectangular structure terminates the design to the west, while a zigzag building that houses the police station sits to the north and is connected to the City Hall by a second bridge. The edge of the leftover spaces is marked by curvilinear forms that suggest the wandering path of the border of an English romantic garden; no geometry yet controls the leftover space between the buildings. (One recalls that Moore often focuses on voids, or leftover spaces, as in the piazza at Church Street South (*see 26.1*) or the entrance hall of the Williams Art Building (*see 51.9*). Moore's conceptual understanding that the site presented him with a problem of fusing two different axes is shown in the quickly sketched overlapping grids in the upper left corner of the drawing, a solution, one recalls, already presaged in his design made for Peressutti in 1956 for a cultural center at Chichén Itzá (*see 44*).

The next step in the design is the crucial one. A diagonal axis drawn across the two blocks is developed as a sequence of oval and round spaces

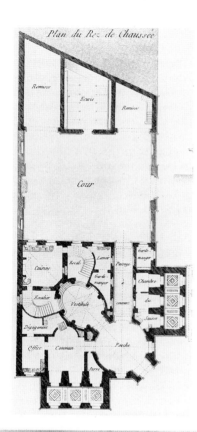

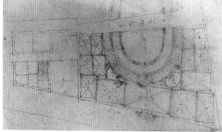

that fit in between the structures, both those already standing and those to be built (55.4). The ovals and circles are not all centered on the axial line, but clearly a geometric concept has come into being that only wants refinement to produce a coherent design. This solution of lining up circles and ovals on the diagonal axis may well have been suggested to Moore by the plan of Claude-Nicolas Ledoux's Hôtel de Montmorency in Paris (Ledoux being an architect much admired by Moore). There the great late-eighteenth-century French architect developed a sequence of circle, oval, and square in a diagonal line from the corner entrance to the back corner of the building (fig. 48). If the Ledoux plan is indeed Moore's source, it was chosen with particular aptness; the model fitted the problem at hand. This, of course, is almost always the case with Moore's use of historical precedents.

The rest of the drawings in this group largely show the working out of the "Ledoux" solution in ever more sophisticated ways. Of particular importance is a sketch that concentrates on the central part of the axis (55.5). The southern bridge, linking the library to the opposite block, is now gone, leaving only one bridge connecting the police station and City Hall. The focus of the whole axial progression is now a large oval which crosses the street to unite both blocks. This idea has a very specific historical source, another of Borromini's projects for the Palazzo Carpegna, Rome. When Count Carpegna managed to acquire property across the street from the complete block he had already purchased, he asked Borromini to come up with a plan to unite the two parcels. Borromini's ingenious solution was to take the oval court, which he had planned for the center of the palace on one block (see fig. 32), turn its long axis ninety degrees, open it up to the outside world, and stretch it across the street to the newly acquired property (fig. 49). Fortunately for us, what Borromini was never allowed to build, Charles Moore is being allowed to construct. Borromini's brillant idea will become Moore's entirely appropriate solution to a very different, yet very similar problem. Through Moore's oval that spans the street pass both pedestrian axes, as well as the vehicular axis of Crescent Drive.

This sketch also announces another idea of some importance for the final plan: mediating between the shape of the oval and the surrounding rectangular structures via a screen of palm trees, planted in a kind of Tinker-Toy pattern (drawn clearly in the upper left of the sketch). The palm trees are joined in two subsequent drawings by a narrow watercourse that marks the diagonal axis the ovals and circles follow. Of these drawings, the one in colored pencil seems to follow the one in pencil. In another pencil sketch (55.6) the ovals and circles all have their centers more or less on the axis. One oval, however, breaks away from the axis to wander rather aimlessly off to the north edge of the right-hand block. In another sketch (55.7) the axis is finally completely straight, with the exception of the wanderer to the north, the open spaces are all now ovals, and an oval island appears in the fountain north of the library. This oval fountain, with a smaller oval inside it, reappears in a particularly handsome large sketch (55.8) that shows a circle beyond the fountain, in which a starburst pattern has been drawn, perhaps as a vault over a circular ramp for cars to drive up into the rectangular garage that marks the eastern edge of the site. In this same sketch, the oval wandering off to the north is suppressed and replaced by another one of those wandering paths that often indicate that Moore has not quite made up his mind what to do with a space.

The fountain, as one might imagine, received considerable attention from Moore. Two drawings show him working out elaborate Baroque details in plan. One with two ovals (55.9) shows a series of curved terraces rising from the street level. (The curves respond, in part, to the curved roadway immediately to the south, which was put in to allow cars to get into the garage to the east.) At the point of intersection of the two ovals, he constructs an oval platform which leads into a series of steps that literally flow down toward the water in the fountain. The steps take on the flow pattern of moving water which the still water of the pool cannot have. Just below and to the right of the fountain an even wavier set of steps offers access from the fountain area to the garage. In the second drawing (55.10), apparently traced over the first, only the edge of the steps descending to the water is recorded. Here most attention is paid to the groups of columns that will flank the terrace leading to the stairs, columns that will support domed pavilions sporting the now ubiquitous Moore

Fig. 51.   Beverly Hills Civic Center
1982–, elevation of tower
Pencil on yellow trace

Fig. 52.   Francesco Borromini
Sant'Agnese in Piazza Navona, Rome
1653–1657, facade, elevation, detail of tower
(Courtesy The Albertina, Vienna, no. 59a)

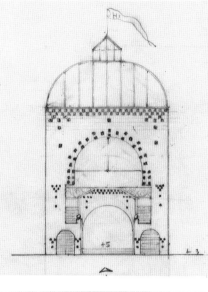

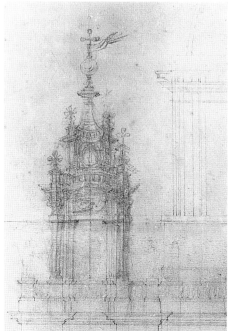

pennants that always fly from left to right. Moored in the pool are two little masonry boats—the Empress of China's, now doubled.

What this pool and its surrounding pavilions might have looked like is shown in one of the most charming sketches to have come from Moore's hand (*fig. 50*). Three pennant-bedecked towers show his inventiveness with these kinds of festive forms. The drawing is quick and assured, the tower tops blocked out by crisscrossing horizontal and vertical lines that meet in firmly pressed points. Detail is only suggested; the overall massing is what is important. There is a lightness and litheness of form that shows Moore at his best in this sort of design. To appreciate the particularly personal qualities of his drawing, one has only to compare this sketch with one made by someone in the UIG office in imitation of his manner, also for a pavilion at Beverly Hills (*fig. 51*). To understand where Moore learned to draw little towers like these, one has to turn once again to Borromini. An elevation of the facade of Sant'Agnese in Piazza Navona, Rome, which was published in Anthony Blunt's *Borromini*, includes a left-hand tower that combines most of the elements we find in Moore's drawing (*fig. 52*). Here he seems to have taken in Borromini's drawing style—an admirable one to imitate, one might add—with what Moore has called "the gulps of a piranha fish."

The fountain, as finally designed for the competition project, was much more suggestive of the Art Deco qualities of the exterior of the City Hall and also perhaps of certain extravagant movie-palace designs of the same era (*55.12*). This sheet of sketches also allows us to see the soft, suggestive nature of Moore's drawing on the left against the very similar but harder-edged lines drawn on the same sheet by someone else in the office. Also, where Moore suggests depth by gentle smudging and gently varying line weight, the other draftsman varies the line thicknesses harshly and makes shadows with bold, closely packed crosshatches. The smoky quality of Moore's drawing here may also have to do with a similar quality one finds in Borromini's charcoal drawings. Certainly Moore is now light-years away from the style of the drawings for the Pebble Beach House of 1955 (*see 1*) or the Jobson House of 1961 (*see 11*).

The way Moore uses the work of his assistants in the design phase of a project is made particularly clear by a pair of drawings that study the elevations of the walls of the new structures to be built in a style that deliberately takes off from that of the old City Hall. An office drawing with elevation and section of a three-story segment of wall shows an arcade below, surmounted by rectangular windows flanked by thick piers (*fig. 53*). The windows are joined by a strip of masonry that rises from the top of a rather exaggerated keystone at the top of the arch. Over this drawing Moore traced the modifications he wanted to make (*fig. 54*). The parts not redrawn will be left as shown, but the parts redrawn, between the piers, are changed considerably, and for the better. The grid of squares suggested by the panes of glass in the top window becomes a theme on which Moore invents variations by adding decorative bands of smaller tile squares above and below the windows, a decorative drip of the same squares on the face of the vertical that joins the windows, and, particularly subtle in its effect, two tiny squares at the springing of the arch below. The keystone almost entirely disappears. All that is left are three narrow verticals that tie the arch to the windows above much more successfully and at the same time mirror the stepped designs at the tops of the piers. Moore's intervention, through relatively minor changes, fuses the parts into an ambiguous, considerably less bulky and considerably more satisfactory, whole.

Lest the discussion of Moore's work for Beverly Hills turn exclusively on artistic issues, we should consider Moore's plan for the police station. The importance of this plan (*55.15*) lies in the fact that Moore drew it just before the final drawings were made to be submitted to the competition jury. In this plan, Moore carefully worked out all of the positions of the doors into the countless rooms the program called for. His intention was to make the plan look good, to make it clear that careful architectural thought had even gone into what must have seemed to all the entrants the least interesting part of the project. Moore's action here is another example of his careful presentation of his own work in the best possible light, and of his care for seemingly unimportant detail when he knows such care matters.

The library plan was also worked out by Moore himself (*55.16*). Again he went back to the Aalto prototype he had already used for the San Juan

*Fig. 53. Beverly Hills Civic Center
1982–, elevation
Pencil on yellow trace*

*Fig. 54. Beverly Hills Civic Center
Elevation, traced over figure 53
Pencil on yellow trace
Drawing by Charles W. Moore*

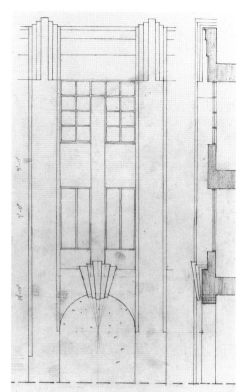

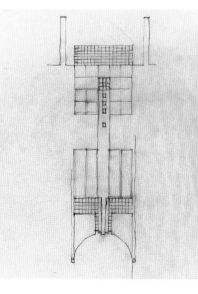

Capistrano competition. Particularly elegant here is the way the shelves and tables are mixed near the door and the curved line along which the main group of stacks is cut. Aalto himself could not have handled this curve with greater finesse.

If Moore has seemed more classical or more baroque or more vernacular or more of any number of stylistic modes, in recent years, one may also say that his work has grown, especially in his fantasy drawings and in his projects for various forms of public amusement, ever more fluid. The little pavilions sketched, after Borromini, for Beverly Hills are but a foretaste of the fused delights of the pavilions, drawn with limpid, looping lines and the most seductively colored pencils, that Moore devised for an amusement park to be built on the Hudson River opposite New York (*40.2,3*). Although the project seems moribund, the drawings for it certainly are not. The mixture of styles, sources, and shapes in those pavilions, in which each new structure seems to comment on the one that came before and to suggest the one to come next, stands as the visual embodiment of the mind that created the pavilions. Each is distinct but part of the continuous flow of architectural ideas produced by a restless imagination. The Wonder Wall of the New Orleans World's Fair (*37.1,2,3*) is the product of the same imagination, but perhaps slightly less fluid in its conception, since it is the product of a moment some three years earlier. The cut-paper model on a blue mirror of the Wonder Wall, however, easily foreshadows some of the delights of the New Jersey Amusement Park, as do even the ins and outs of the screen wall with which Moore once proposed to cover the front of the Hopkins Center at Dartmouth (*56.3*). Here we see the paper-flat screen walls of the early seventies—creatures given shape by the foam core out of which they were made—turned into sequences of rotund rotundas, domed and festively flagged into a broken silhouette line that is the vertical counterpart of the dance movements of the pavilions in plan. It is the rollicking movement of Gaudí's roof on the Casa Milá that we sense here, as well, perhaps, as something of the fantasy of the chimney pots.

Moore is an unusual figure in today's architectural scene for any number of reasons. Hardly without ego, he is nevertheless able to make that ego subservient to the desires of the client, or at least to take pride in the fact that his buildings fit the personalities of his clients rather than replicate his personality on whatever piece of land the client owns. Moore is apparently unable to work on his own. One of his partners once said, "The muse simply does not strike Charles unless someone is sitting across the table from him." He needs a straight man to play against, but he also enjoys having someone else to look after boring details. Ultimately, his art is a gregarious one, made for people to enjoy, even in the process of its being designed.

Moore's need to surround himself with a host of collaborators and followers brings to mind one artist from the past with whom Moore seems to have much in common, Peter Paul Rubens. It is not that any particular stylistic parallels exist between the work of the painter and that of Moore, but rather that there seem to be certain parallels in the personality and intellect that inform their work, in the charged vitality of their lives and work, that ultimately give a similar sense of satisfaction from that work. Rubens liked to create paintings of large size in large numbers. He seems to have felt a compulsion to be productive. This meant making use of a lot of assistants and collaborators. The same is true of Moore. He has a compulsion for getting buildings built. In the case of both, this practice can lead to variations in artistic quality. Moore, however, differs from Rubens in that Rubens seems rarely, if ever, to have incorporated the ideas of his collaborators into his work, whereas Moore tends to welcome ideas from collaborators with wide ranges of talents and interests. Moore works today, as Rubens did in the past, in what most of us would find chaotic circumstances, yet he is able to keep several activities going at once.

Like Rubens, Moore has a phenomenal memory and an encyclopedic knowledge of the art or architecture of the past (as well as being splendidly learned in general). He knowingly makes use of a wide range of sources, almost invariably because the use of a particular source adds a new and more complex dimension of meaning to the work in which it is reused. As he has matured, Moore has expanded his repertoire of available sources, but he also has a tendency to return to ideas once used successfully, even long in the past, if those ideas can be reworked to fit a new situation.

Yet Moore has suffered from the point of his work being misunderstood, partly because of an instinct for joy that can be mistaken for an instinct for frivolity. Rubens is sometimes thought of as a weak-minded master of acres of overabundant pink flesh. Anyone who knows his life, however, knows that he was a scholar and an intellectual. Anyone who knows his art knows that it is filled with complex ideas and an extraordinary sensitivity to human feeling. Moore is sometimes seen as the master of the architectural joke, a genial designer of clever structures that may be a bit too coy for their own good. But anyone who knows his life knows that he too is a man of learning and intellect. Anyone who looks seriously into his work will find it filled with complex architectural ideas and an extraordinary sensitivity to the feelings humans want their architecture to evoke.

Buildings and Projects: 1949–1986

The buildings and projects illustrated in this volume have been subdivided into four categories chosen by Charles Moore himself. The first, *Houses for the Architect*, contains his own houses. The number of houses is large because Moore has been remarkably peripatetic. In these buildings are worked out many ideas he later used in structures created for others. These houses form the core of his work. The second category, *Houses As the Center of the World,* contains single-family houses designed for others, followed by housing projects. The third, *Frivolous and Serious Play*, is made up mostly, but not exclusively, of large outdoor public projects in which people are asked to participate in the architectural experience, rather than simply observe. The last, *Fitting*, the largest and most inclusive, contains a variety of building types. What holds them together in one category is the fact that each is concerned with fitting into its environment, in the broadest sense. For some, environment may mean landscape, for others, older buildings. For all, there is the question of fitting the building to local architectural traditions, as well as to the function it must serve. Within each category, the buildings are arranged chronologically. A final group of plates presents a selection of drawings of architectural fantasies that Moore has been doing since at least 1971. These last are highly personal expressions of architectural ideas that seem to have informed his built work more and more directly in recent years.

Houses for the Architect

1. Moore House 1954–1955
2. Moore House 1962
3. Moore House 1963–1965
4. Moore House 1966 *Renovation*
5. Moore House 1970–1975 *Renovation*
6. Moore, Rogger, Hofflander Condominium 1975–1978
7. Moore Cabin 1983
8. Moore House 1985– *Renovation*

Houses As the Center of the World

9. Jones House 1949 *Project*
10. Arnold House 1954 *Project*
11. Jobson House 1961
12. Bonham House 1961–1962
13. Jenkins House 1963 *Project*
14. Otus House 1963 *Project*
15. Klotz House 1967–1970
16. Goodman House 1969 *Project*
17. Rudolph House I 1970–1971
18. Burns House 1972–1974
19. Rudolph House II 1979–1981
20. Kwee House 1981–1984
21. Miglio House 1984–1986
22. Hoffman House 1985–
23. Inn at Cannery Row 1958 *Project*
24. West Plaza Condominium 1962 *Project*
25. Monte Vista Apartments 1963
26. Church Street South 1966–1969
27. Kresge College 1964–1974
28. Whitman Village 1971–1975
29. Xanadune 1972 *Project*
30. Kingsmill on the James 1974 *Project*
31. Parador 1982 *Project*

Frivolous and Serious Play

32. Ph.D. Project 1957
33. Lovejoy Fountain 1965–1966
34. Faculty Club, University of California 1966–1968
35. Piazza d'Italia 1975–1978
36. Indiana Landing 1980–1982 *Project*
37. Wonderwall 1982–1984 *Dismantled*
38. Centennial Pavilion 1982–1984 *Dismantled*
39. Copley Square 1984 *Project*
40. Amusement Park 1985
41. 1992 Chicago World's Fair 1985 *Project*

Fitting

42. Yun Chon Chapel 1954 *Project*
43. Chung Wha Girls' Middle and High School 1954 *Destroyed*
44. Cultural Center 1956 *Project*
45. Jewish Community Center 1957 *Project*
46. Retail Milk Products Drive-in 1960 *Project*
47. Porte Cochere for Dr. and Mrs. Seymour Pastron 1961
48. Sea Ranch Condominium 1963–1965
49. Jones Laboratory 1974–1977
50. Riverdesign 1976
51. Williams College Museum of Art 1977–1983, 1984–1986
52. Sammis Hall 1978–1981
53. St. Matthew's Episcopal Church 1979–1983
54. Tegel Harbor Housing 1980–
55. Beverly Hills Civic Center 1982–
56. Hood Museum, Dartmouth College 1981–1985
57. Hermann Park 1982–
58. San Juan Capistrano Library · 1982 *Project*
59. Alumni Center, University of California 1983–1985

Fantasy Drawings

Houses for the Architect

1. Moore House   1954–1955
Pebble Beach, California
Single-family dwelling

SOUTH

1

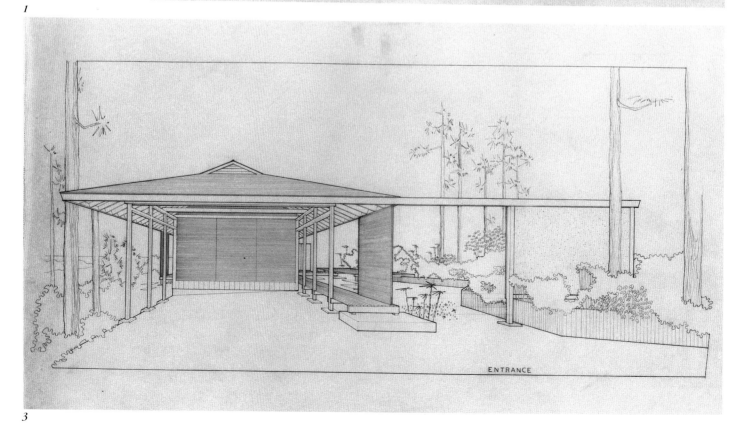

ENTRANCE

3

1. *Perspective, south side*
   Pencil on white paper, 18" × 23.5"
   Drawing by Charles W. Moore

2. *Perspective, entrance*
   Pencil on white paper, 18" × 23.5"
   Drawing by Charles W. Moore

3. *Perspective, garden*
   Pencil on white paper, 18" × 23.5"
   Drawing by Charles W. Moore

4. *Plan, section A-A, and construction details*
   18" × 23.5"
   Drawing by Charles W. Moore

2

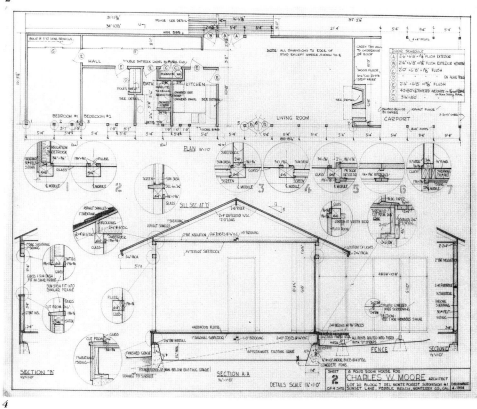

4

5. Plan and section
  Ink and watercolor on paper, 30" × 22.5"

2. Moore House 1962
Orinda, California
Single-family dwelling

1. Plan and section
Ink and watercolor on paper, 30" × 22.5"

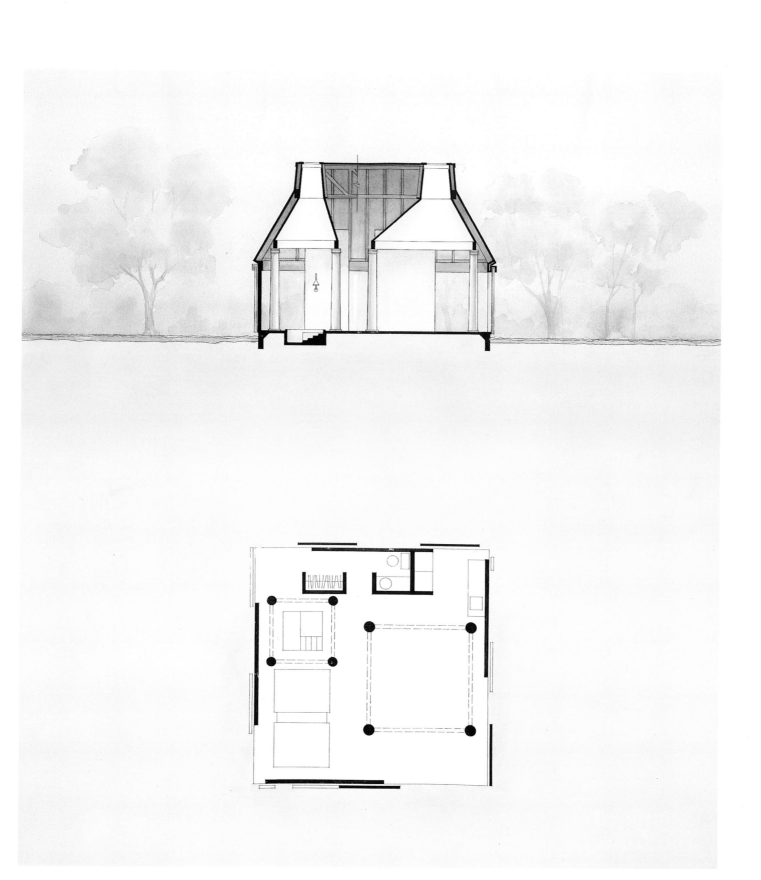

2. Exterior view
   (Photograph © Morley Baer)

3. Longitudinal and cross sections
   Blueprint and typewriter
   Drawing by Charles W. Moore

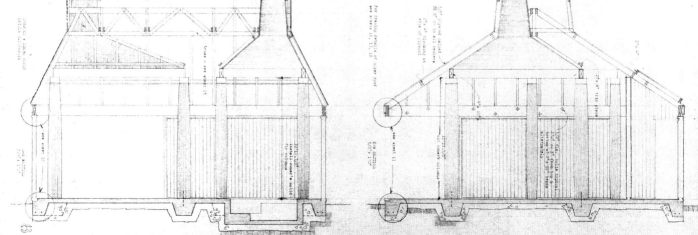

4. Interior, bath
  (Photograph © Morley Baer)

5. Isometric

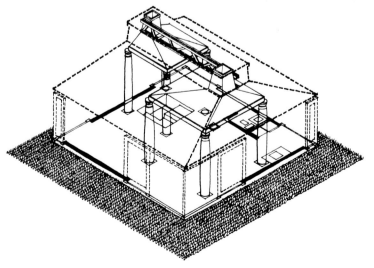

3. Moore House   1963–1965
Sea Ranch, California
Condominium
Moore, Lyndon, Turnbull, Whitaker

1. Elevations

2. Plan

3. Interior
(Photograph © Morley Baer)

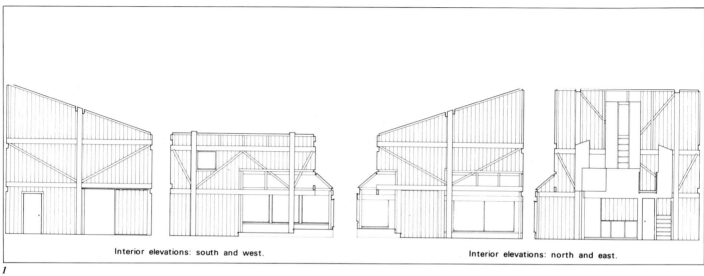

Interior elevations: south and west.   Interior elevations: north and east.

1

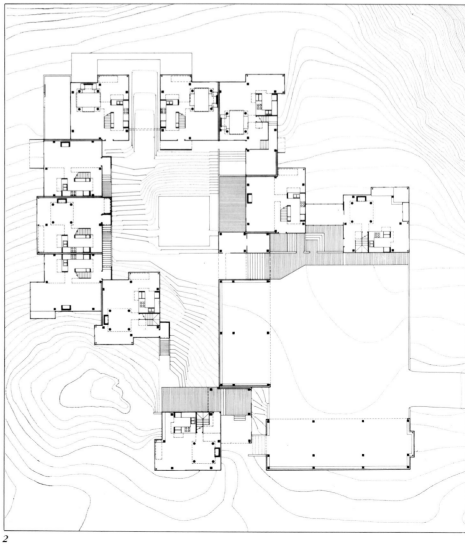

2

3

4. Moore House   1966   *Renovation*
New Haven, Connecticut
Single-family dwelling

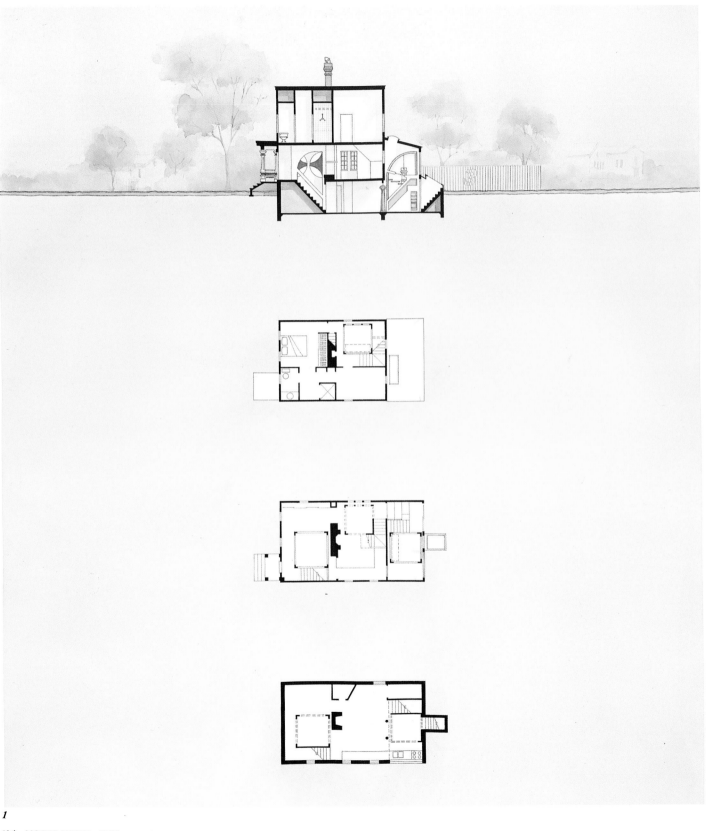

1

1. *Plan and section*
   Ink and watercolor on paper, 30" × 22.5"

2. *Interior*
   (Photograph by John Hill)

3. *Interior, bedroom*
   (Photograph © Norman McGrath)

4. *Interior of Howard, with the architect*
   (Photograph by John Hill)

2

3

4

5. Moore House 1970–1975 *Renovation*
Essex, Connecticut
Single-family dwelling

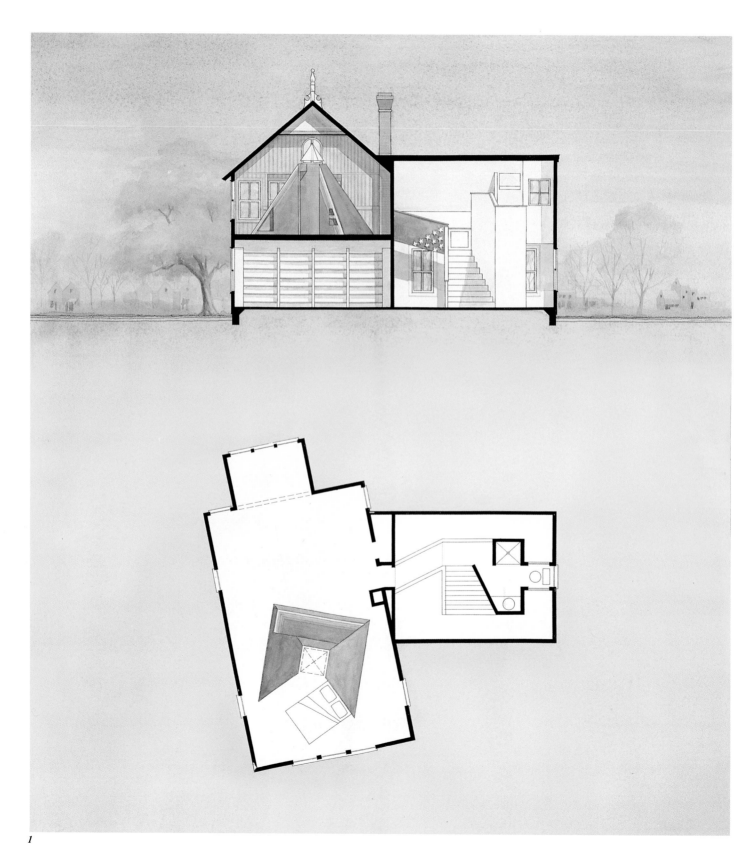

1

1. Plan and section
   Ink and watercolor on paper, 30" by 22.5"

2. Plans and sections with details of pyramid, 1972
   Pencil on lined paper, 11" × 8.5"
   Drawing by Charles W. Moore

3. Plan
   Pencil on yellow trace, 11" × 8.5"
   Drawing by Charles W. Moore

4. Exterior

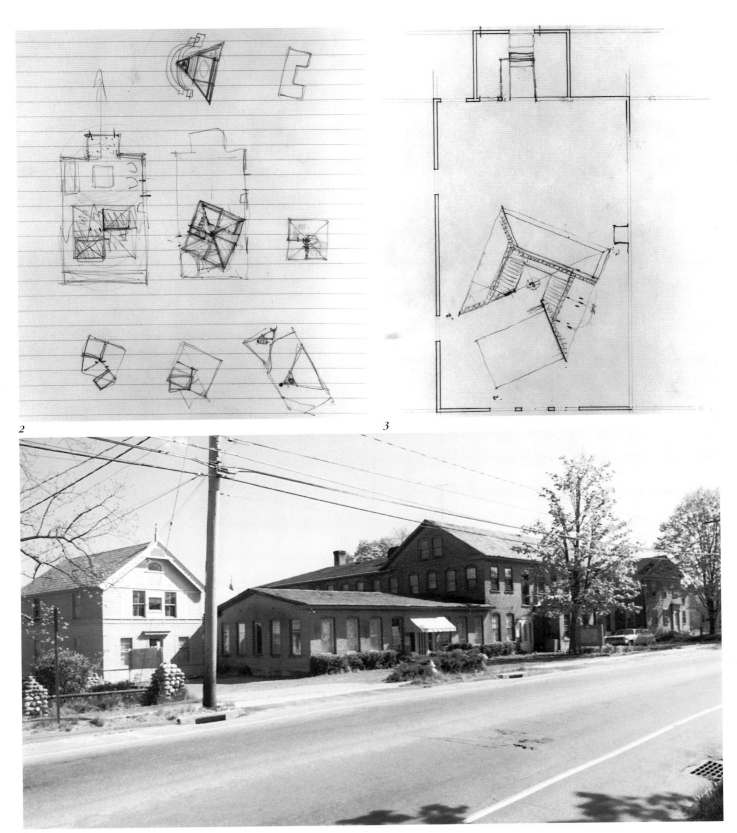

2

3

4

6. Moore, Rogger, Hofflander
Condominium 1975–1978
Los Angeles, California
Condominium
Charles W. Moore with Richard Chylinski
and Urban Innovations Group

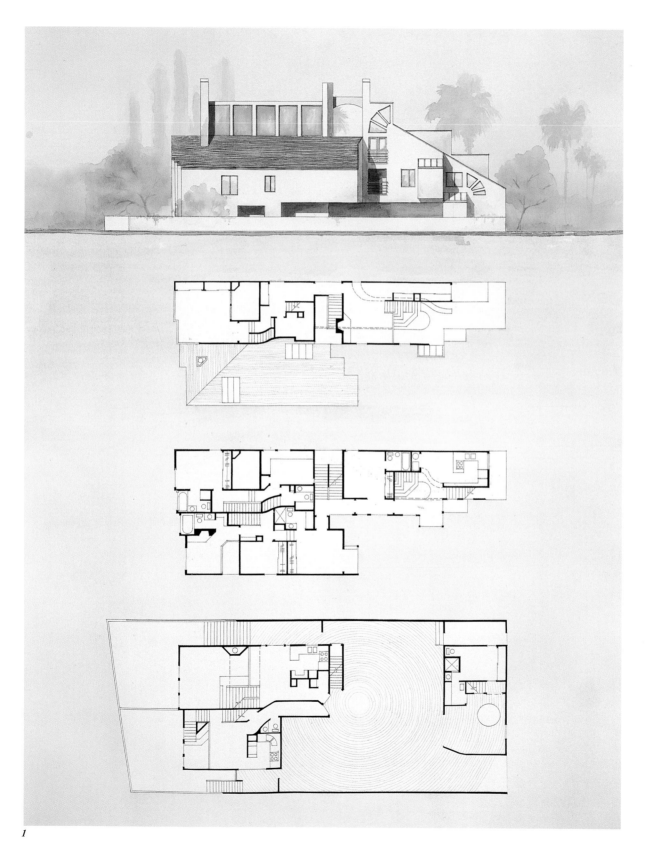

1

1. *Plan and section*
   Ink and watercolor on paper, 30" × 22.5"

2. *Exterior*
   (Photograph by John Nicolais)

3. *Exterior detail*
   (Photograph by John Nicolais)

4. *Exterior detail*
   (Photograph by John Nicolais)

2

3

4

5. *Interior, second-floor area and stairs*
   (Photograph by Tim Street-Porter)

6. *Interior, stairwell from second floor*
   (Photograph by Tim Street-Porter)

7. *Interior, third floor*
   (Photograph by Tim Street-Porter)

7. Moore Cabin   1983
Pine Mountain, California
Single-family dwelling

1. Plan and section
Ink and watercolor on paper, 30" × 22.5"

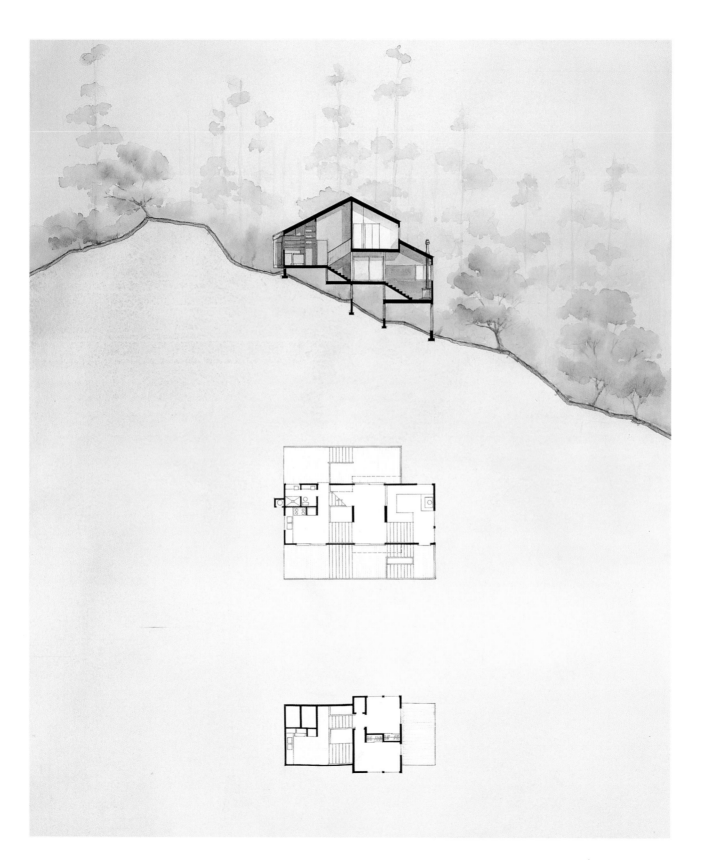

8. Moore House   1985–

Austin, Texas
Single-family dwelling
Charles W. Moore with Arthur Andersson
and Richard Dodge

1. Plan and section
Ink and watercolor on paper, 30″ × 22.5″

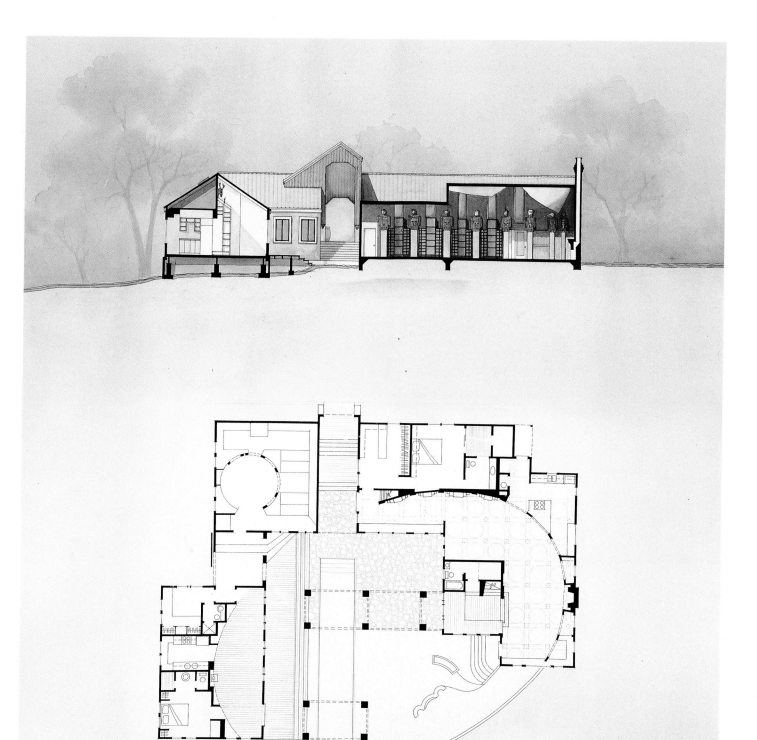

9. Jones House 1949 *Project*

Eugene, Oregon
Single-family dwelling
Charles W. Moore

1. Plan
Blueprint, 22.5" × 30"
Drawing by Charles W. Moore

2. Elevations, north, south, east, west
Blueprint, 22.5" × 30"
Drawing by Charles W. Moore

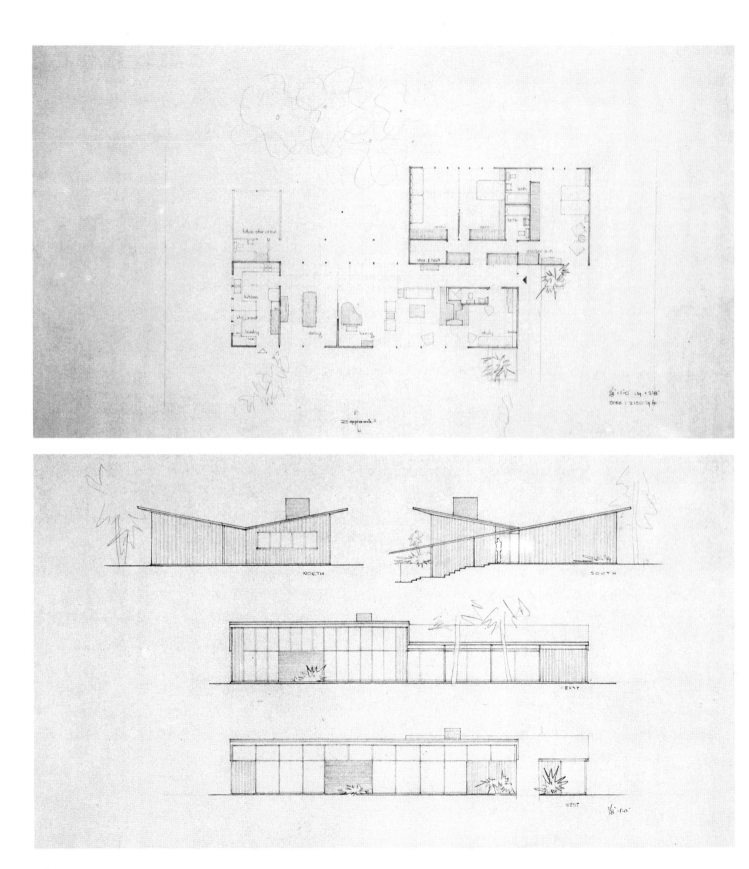

10. Arnold House 1954 *Project*

Carmel, California
Single-family dwelling
Charles W. Moore

1. Plan
Pencil on white trace, 13" × 18"
Drawing by Charles W. Moore

2. Perspective
Blueprint, 13" × 26"
Drawing by Charles W. Moore

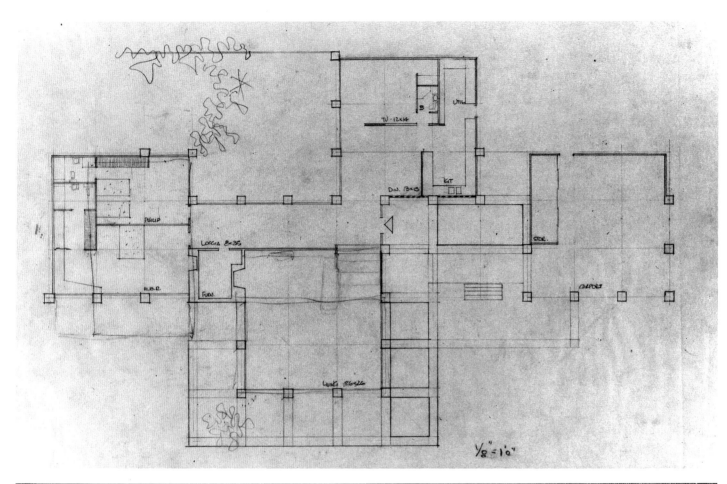

11. Jobson House   1961

Palo Colorado Canyon, California
Single-family dwelling
Charles W. Moore with Peter Hopkinson

1. Site plan
   Pencil on white paper, 15" × 15"
   Drawing by Charles W. Moore

2. Floor plan
   Pencil on white paper, 15" × 15"
   Drawing by Charles W. Moore

3. North elevation
   Pencil on white trace, 15" × 15"
   Drawing by Charles W. Moore

4. South elevation
   Pencil on white trace, 15" × 15"
   Drawing by Charles W. Moore

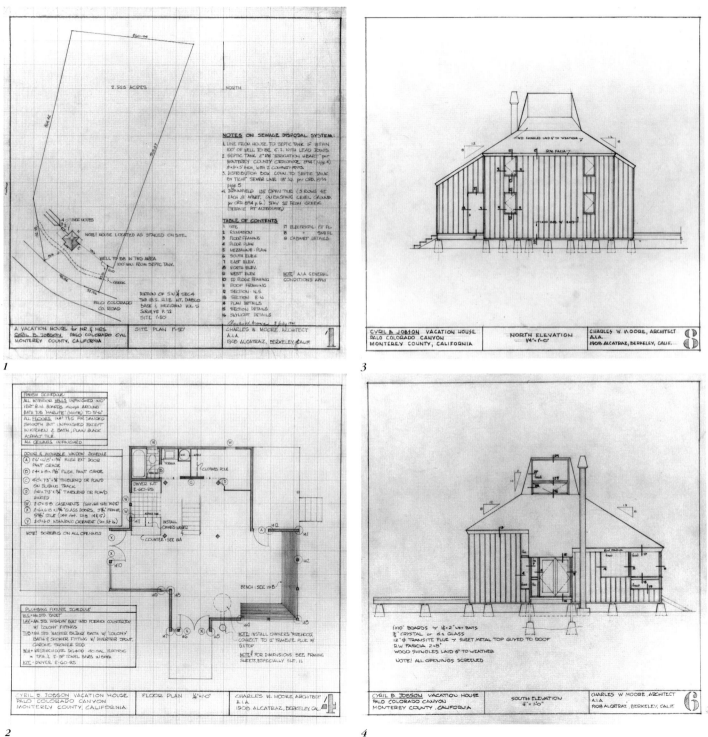

1

2

3

4

5. *East elevation*
   Pencil on white trace, 15" × 15"
   Drawing by Charles W. Moore

6. *West elevation*
   Pencil on white paper, 15" × 15"
   Drawing by Charles W. Moore

7. *North-south section*
   Pencil on white paper, 15" × 15"
   Drawing by Charles W. Moore

8. *East-west section*
   Pencil on white paper, 15" × 15"
   Drawing by Charles W. Moore

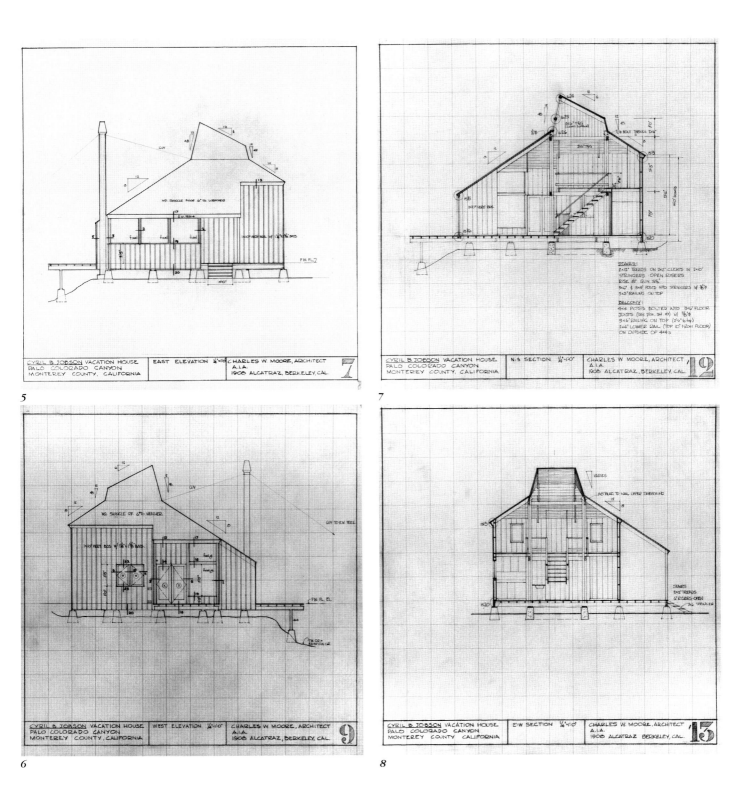

5

6

7

8

9. South exterior, with interior view of
   stairwell from entrance
   (Photograph © Morley Baer)

10. Isometric

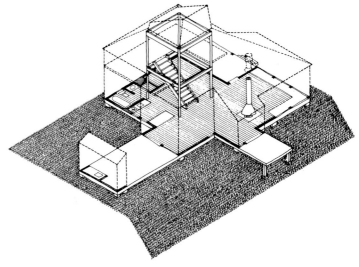

11. Interior, living room and entrance
   (Photograph © Morley Baer)

12. Bonham House   1961–1962
Santa Cruz, California
Single-family dwelling
Charles W. Moore with Warren Fuller

1

1. Plan and section
  Ink and watercolor on paper, 30″ × 22.5″

2. Exterior
  (Photograph © Morley Baer)

3. Isometric

2

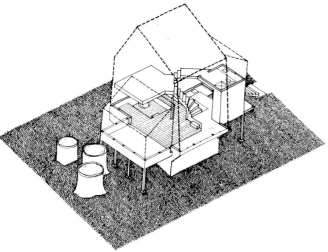

4. Exterior
(Photograph © Morley Baer)

13. Jenkins House 1963 *Project*
St. Helena, California
Single-family dwelling
Moore, Lyndon, Turnbull, Whitaker

1. Plan and section
Ink and watercolor on paper, 30" × 22.5"

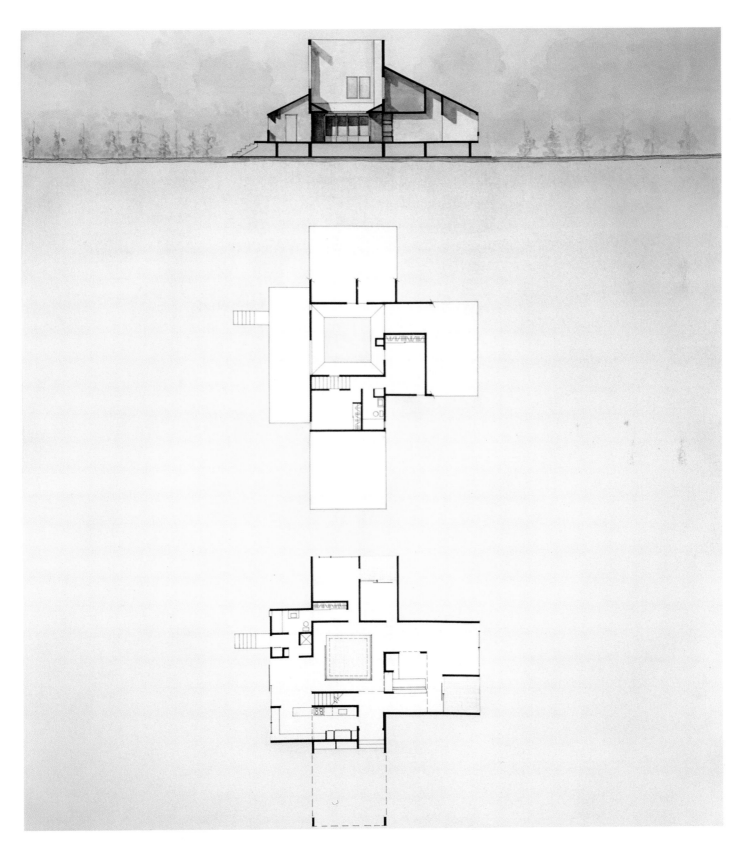

14. Otus House 1963 *Project*
Berkeley, California
Single-family dwelling
Moore, Lyndon, Turnbull,
Whitaker/Charles W. Moore
with Warren Fuller

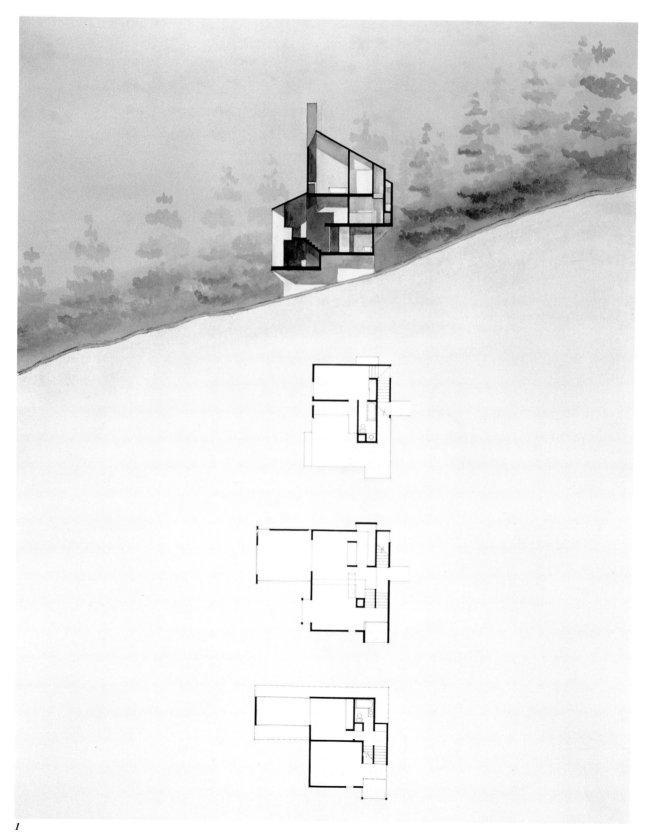

1

1. *Plan and section*
   Ink and watercolor on paper, 30" × 22.5"

2. *Model*
   (Photograph courtesy Turnbull Associates)

3. *Perspective, June 1963*
   Ink on white paper, 21" × 25"

2

3

15. Klotz House 1967–1970

Westerly, Rhode Island
Single-family dwelling
MLTW/Moore-Turnbull
with William Grover and Marvin Buchanan

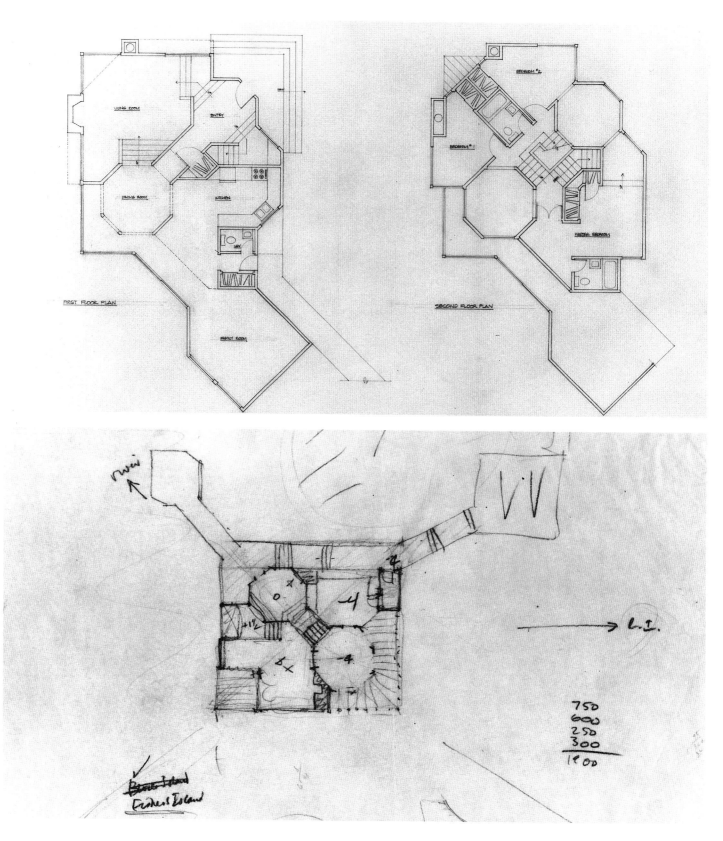

1. *Plans, first and second floor,*
   March 10, 1967
   Pencil on white paper, 24" × 36"
   Drawing by Edward Johnson

2. *Plan with notations of landscape elements*
   Pencil and colored pencil on yellow trace,
   12" × 18"
   Drawing by Charles W. Moore

3. *Plans, first floor and superimposed roof;*
   elevation, roof; plan, roof
   Black and orange pencil on yellow trace,
   18" × 44"
   Drawing by Charles W. Moore and others

4. *Plan with superimposed roof*
   Black and orange pencil on yellow trace,
   17.5" × 25"
   Drawing by Charles W. Moore and others

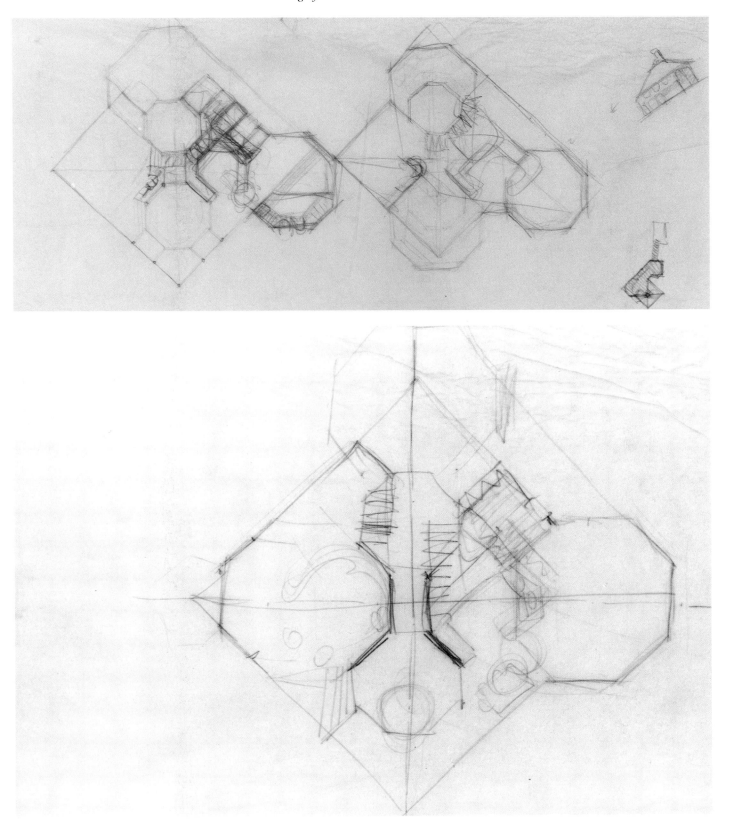

5. *Plan, ground floor, as built*
   Ink on white paper, 24" × 33"

6. *Plan, second floor, as built*
   Ink on white paper, 24" × 33"

7. *Plan, attic floor, as built*
   Ink on white paper, 25" × 34"

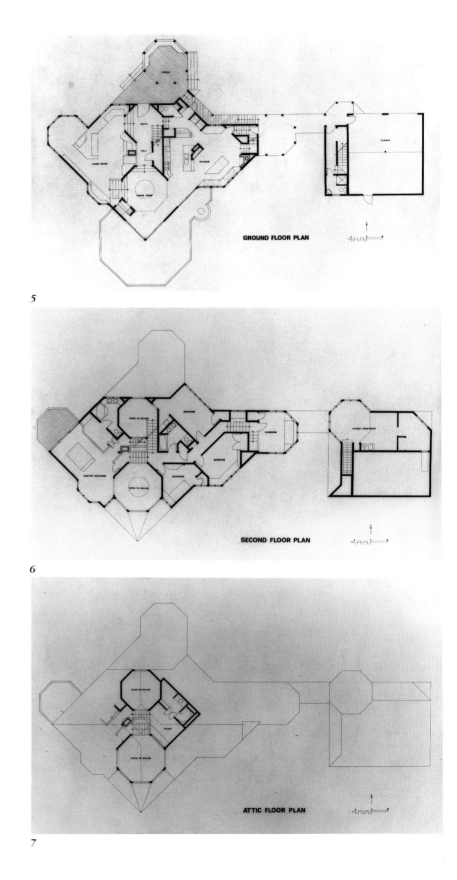

GROUND FLOOR PLAN

5

SECOND FLOOR PLAN

6

ATTIC FLOOR PLAN

7

8. *North-south cross section with interior*
   elevation, as built
   Black and red ink on yellow trace,
   22″ × 14″

9. *Play tower, fence and sandbox; plan,*
   elevation, two perspectives and
   construction detail
   Pencil on yellow trace, 10″ × 8″
   Drawing by Charles W. Moore
   (Collection of Mr. and Mrs. Paul Klotz)

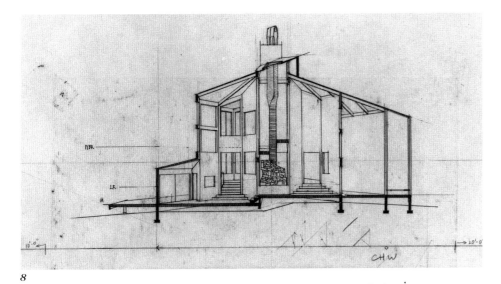

8

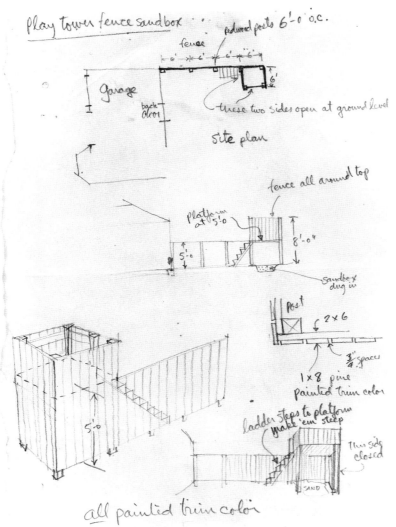

9

11. Exterior
(Photograph by Bill Maris)

16. Goodman House 1969 *Project*
Montauk, New York
Single-family dwelling
MLTW/Moore-Turnbull

1. Plan (first overlay), roof
   Pencil on yellow trace, 11.5" × 9.5"
   Drawing by Charles W. Moore

2. Plan (second overlay), upper level
   Pencil on yellow trace, 12.5" × 11.5"
   Drawing by Charles W. Moore

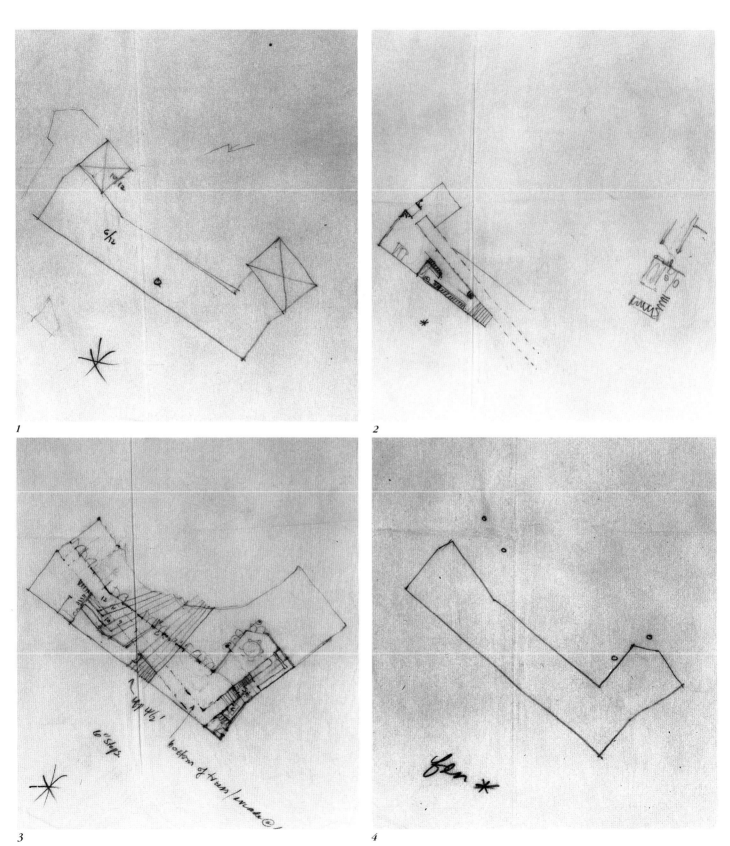

1

2

3

4

3. Plan (third overlay), main floor
   Pencil on yellow trace, 13" × 13.5"
   Drawing by Charles W. Moore

4. Plan (fourth overlay), foundation
   Pencil on yellow trace, 13" × 11.5"
   Drawing by Charles W. Moore

5. Plan with four overlays
   Pencil on yellow trace, 13.5" × 15"
   Drawing by Charles W. Moore

6. Plan, December 9, 1969
   Pencil on white trace, 12" × 14"
   Drawing by Charles W. Moore

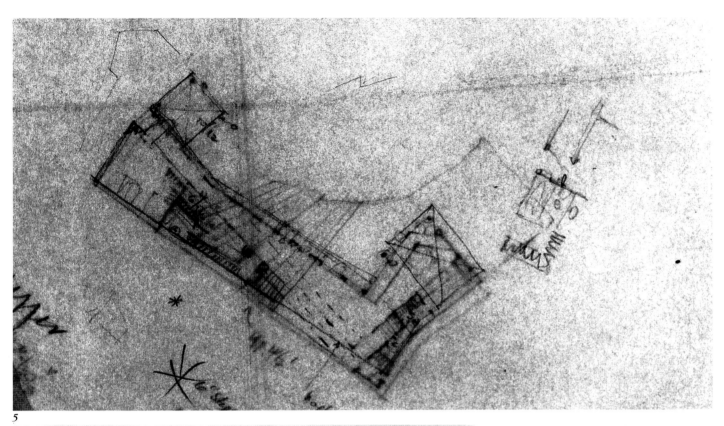

5

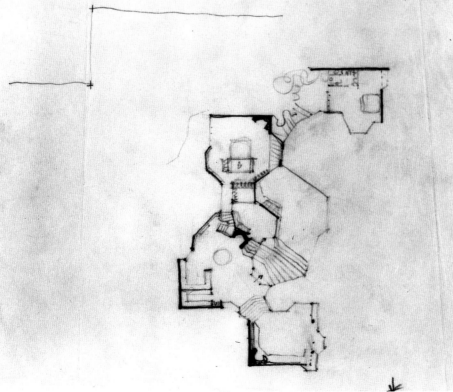

6

7. *Plan, first floor*
   Pencil on white trace, 6.5" × 10"
   Drawing by Charles W. Moore

8. *Plan, second floor*
   Pencil on trace, 6.5" × 9.5"
   Drawing by Charles W. Moore

9. *Elevation*
   Black and red pencil
   Drawing by Charles W. Moore

7

8

9

17. Rudolph House I   1970–1971
Captiva, Florida
Single-family dwelling
Charles W. Moore Associates
with James Volney Righter

1. Sketches of house, roof, and garage plans
Pencil on white trace, 12" × 23"
Drawing by Charles W. Moore

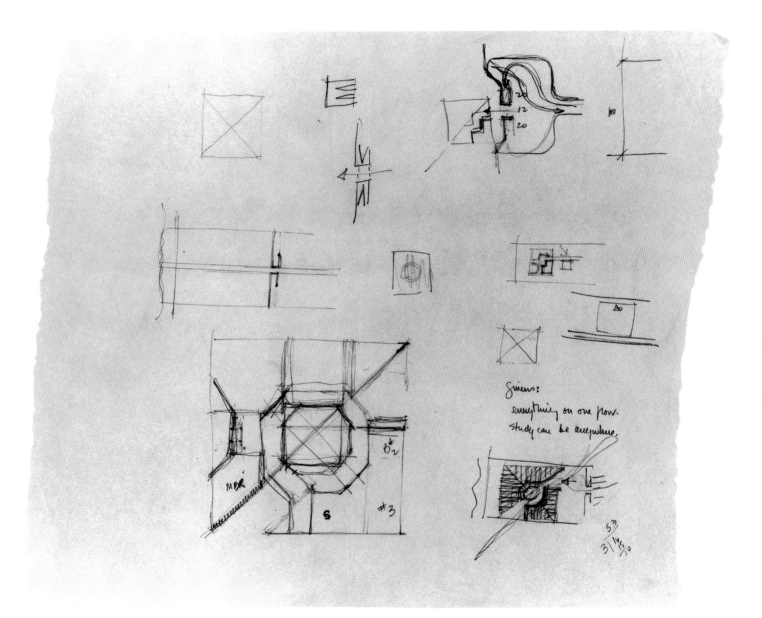

2. Plan, July 3, 1970
   Pencil on white trace, 12" × 17.5"
   Drawing by James Volney Righter

3. Sketches of floor plans, July 9, 1970
   Pen on paper, 8.5" × 11"
   Drawing by Charles W. Moore

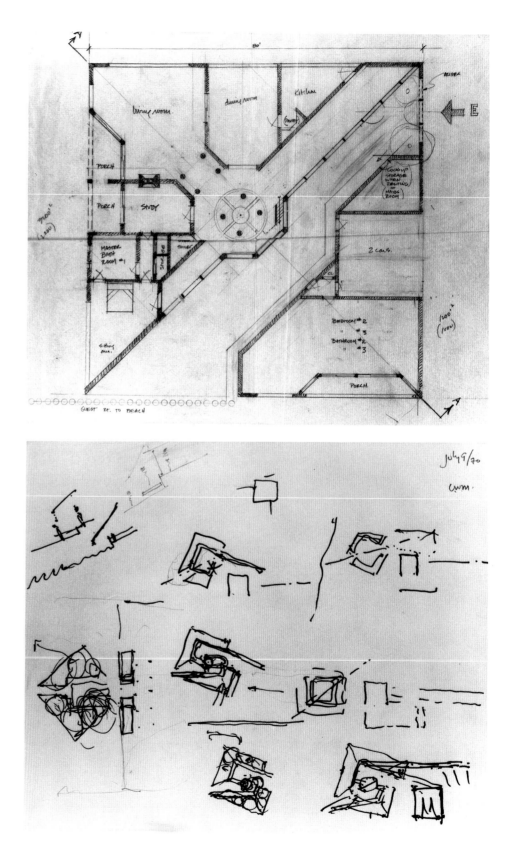

4. Plan
   Pencil on trace, 12" × 12.5"
   Drawing by Charles W. Moore

5. Plan, bird's-eye view
   Pencil on white trace, 14" × 12"
   Drawing by Charles W. Moore

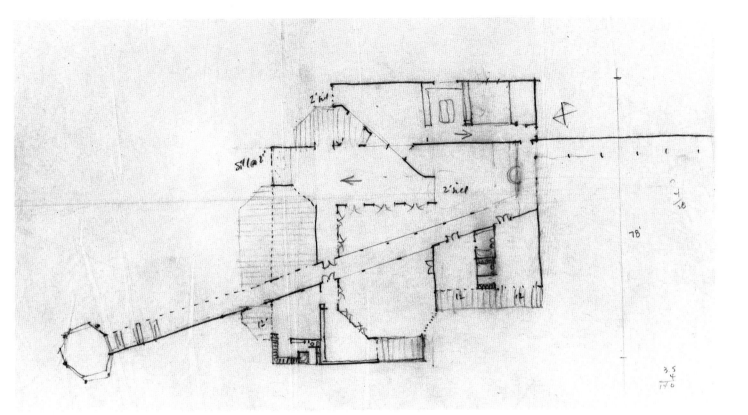

6. *Exterior view from beach*
   (Photograph by H. Richard Archer)

7. *Interior*
   (Photograph by William H. Pierson)

8. *Interior*
   (Photograph by William H. Pierson)

9. *Interior*
   (Photograph by William H. Pierson)

18. Burns House 1972–1974
Santa Monica, California
Single-family dwelling
Charles W. Moore with Richard Chylinski

1

1. Plan and section
  Ink and watercolor on paper, 30" × 22.5"

2. Exterior by day
  (Photograph © Morley Baer)

2

3. Exterior by night
  (Photograph © Morley Baer)

4. *Interior with stair*
   (Photograph © Morley Baer)

5. *Interior, living room with organ*
   (Photograph © Morley Baer)

19. Rudolph House II   1979–1981

Williamstown, Massachusetts
Single-family dwelling
Moore, Grover, Harper with Robert Harper

1. Plans and section
Ink on graph paper, 11″ × 8.5″
Drawing by Robert Harper

2. Plan, three levels, May 25, 1979
Pencil on white trace, 11″ × 5″
Drawing by Robert Harper

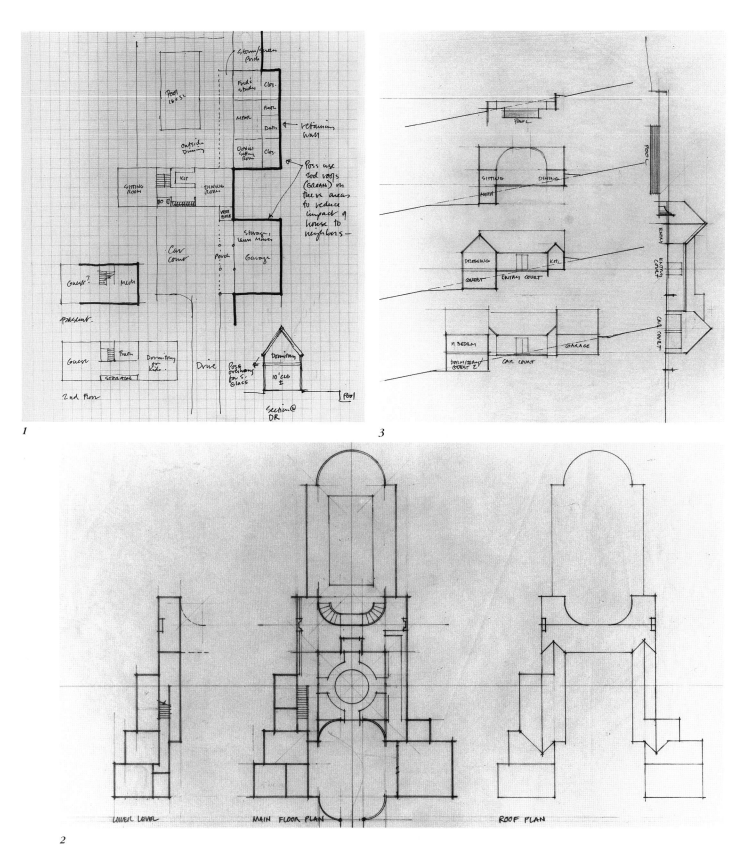

1

3

2

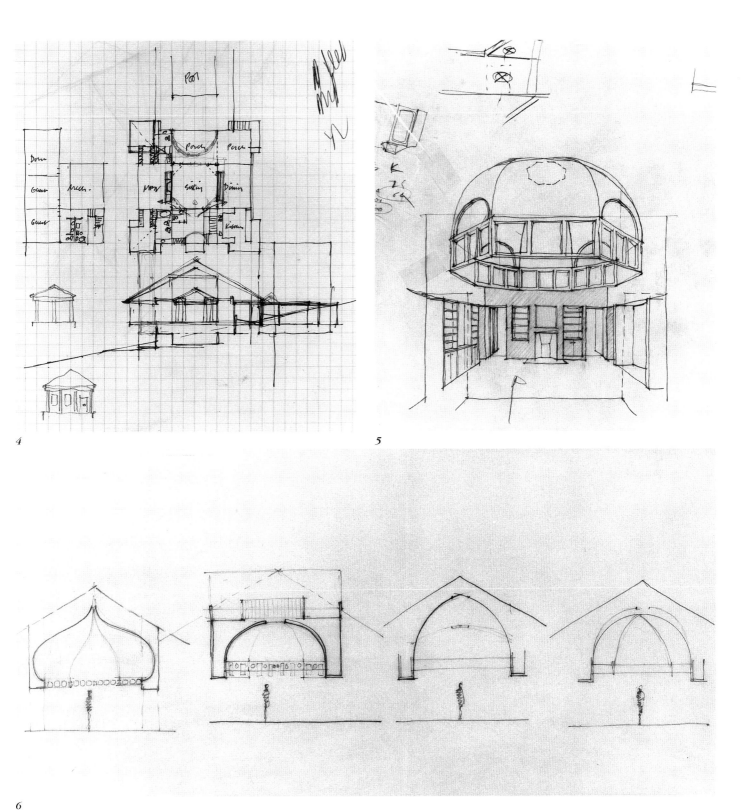

3. *Five sections, May 25, 1979*
   Pencil on yellow trace, 14" × 11"
   Drawing by Robert Harper

4. *Two plans and elevation*
   Ink and pencil on graph paper, 11" × 8.5"
   Drawing by Robert Harper

5. *Perspective of living room with dome*
   Pencil on yellow trace, 14" × 17"
   Drawing by Robert Harper

6. *Four sketches for dome*
   Pencil on yellow trace, 14" × 33.5"
   Drawing by James Childress

4

5

6

7. *Model*
   (Photograph by Amanda Merullo)

8. *Model*
   (Photograph by Amanda Merullo)

9. *Plan*
   Ink on vellum, 18" × 33.5"

10. *Section*
    Ink on vellum, 18" × 33.5"

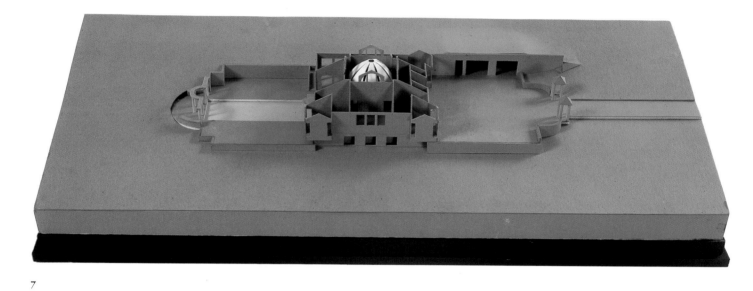

7

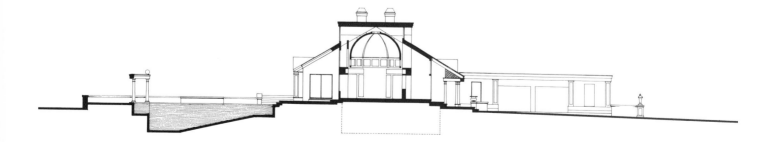

9

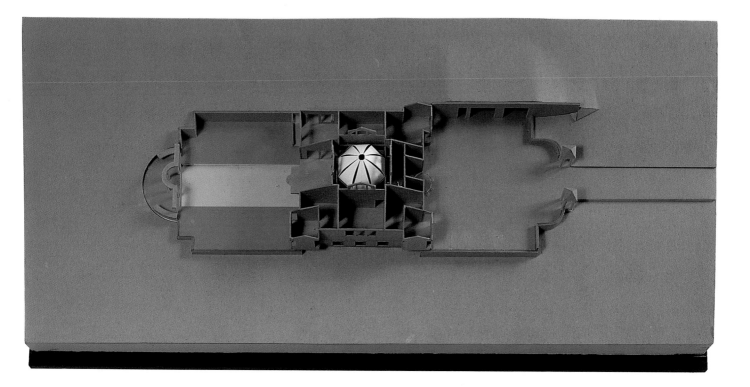

8

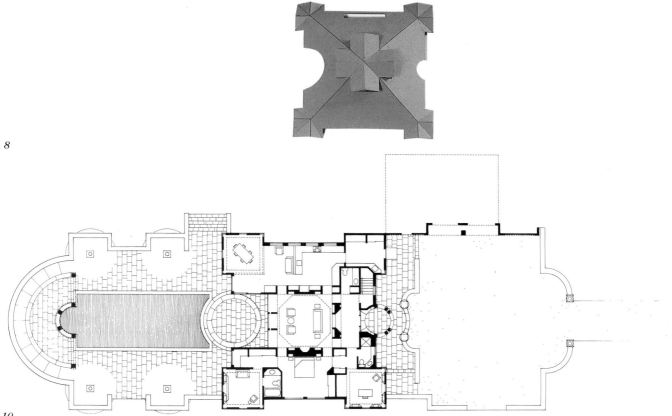

10

11. *Exterior, entrance from south*
   (Photograph © Joseph G. Standart III)

12. *Exterior, with pool, from north*
   (Photograph © Joseph G. Standart III)

13. *Interior, living room with dome*
   (Photograph © Joseph G. Standart III)

20. Kwee House   1981–1984
Singapore
Single-family dwelling
Moore, Ruble, Yudell

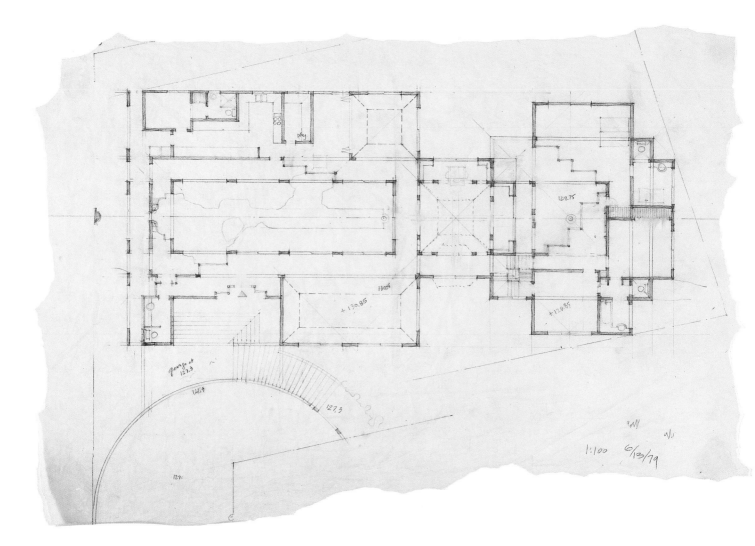

1

1. Plan
   Pencil on yellow trace, 14" × 20"

2. Axonometric
   Ink and watercolor on paper, 21" × 21"

Following pages

3. Interior
   (Photograph courtesy Moore, Ruble, Yudell)

4. Interior
   (Photograph courtesy Moore, Ruble, Yudell)

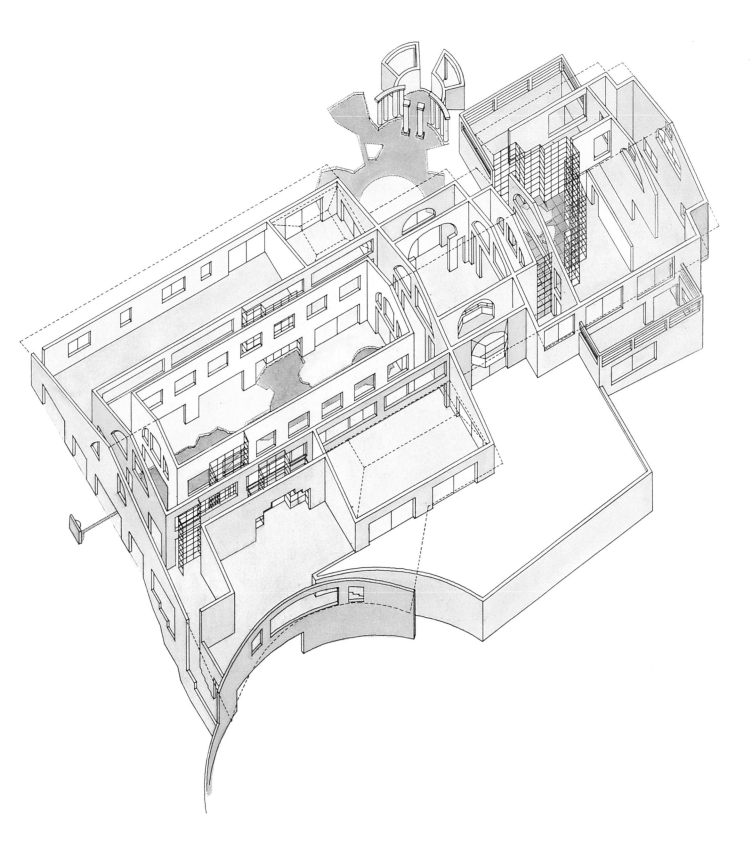

2

3

4

21. Miglio House   1984–1986
Sea Ranch, California
Single-family dwelling
Charles W. Moore
and Urban Innovations Group

1. Plan and section
Ink and watercolor on paper, 30" × 22"

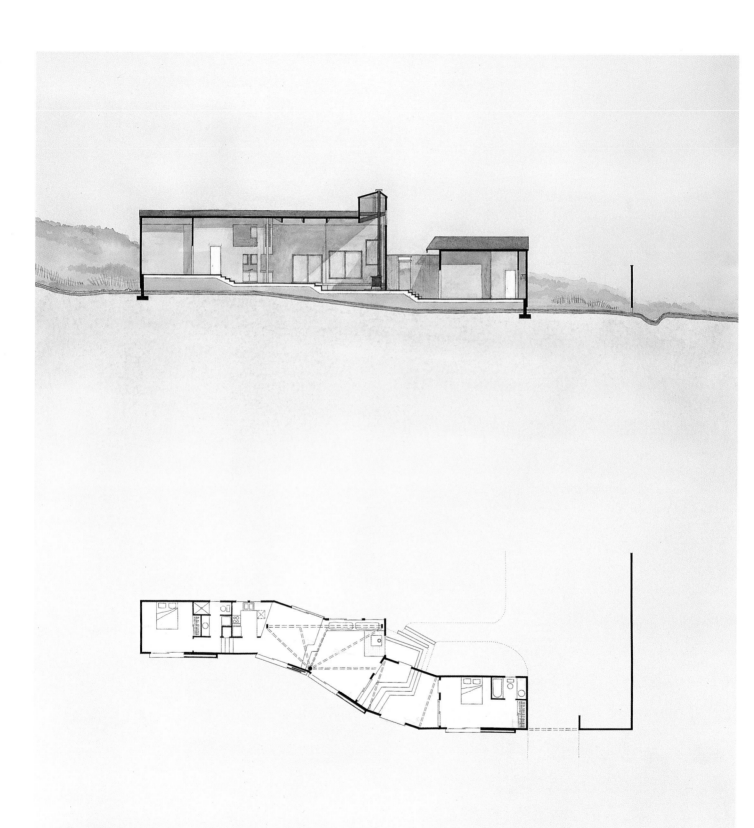

22. Hoffman House   1985–
Dallas, Texas
Single-family dwelling
Charles W. Moore
with Arthur Andersson and Paul Lamb

1. Plan and section
Ink and watercolor on paper, 30" × 22.5"
Drawing by Charles W. Moore

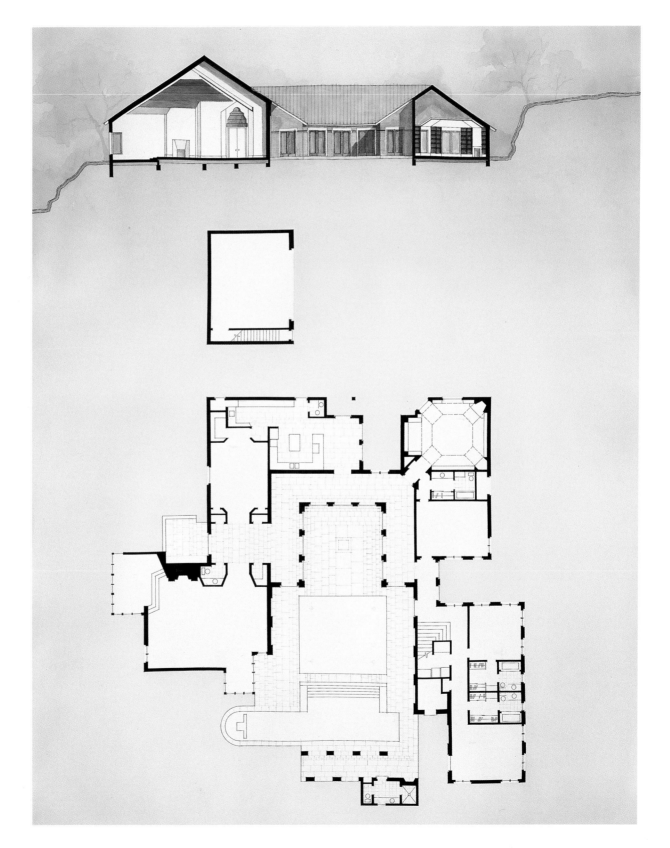

23. Inn at Cannery Row   1958   *Project*
Monterey, California
Hotel
Wallace Holm, Architect
with Charles W. Moore

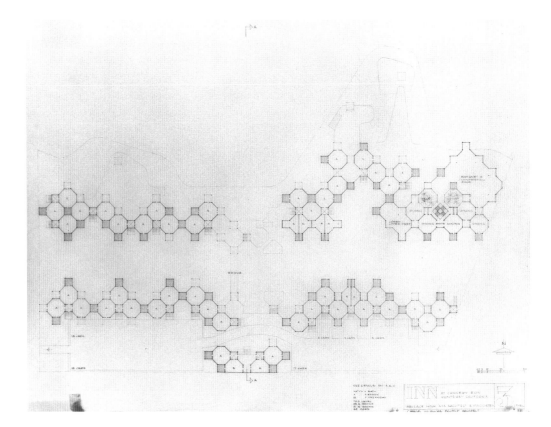

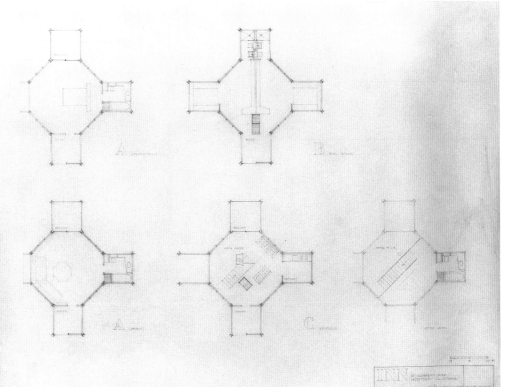

1. *Plan, third level*
   Pencil on white trace, 29" × 36"
   Drawing by Charles W. Moore

2. *Room plans*
   Pencil on white trace, 29" × 36"
   Drawing by Charles W. Moore

3. *Section A-A*
   Pencil on white trace, 30" × 36"
   Drawing by Charles W. Moore

4. *Perspective*
   Ink on white paper, 30" × 36"
   Drawing by Charles W. Moore
   (Photograph courtesy Turnbull Associates)

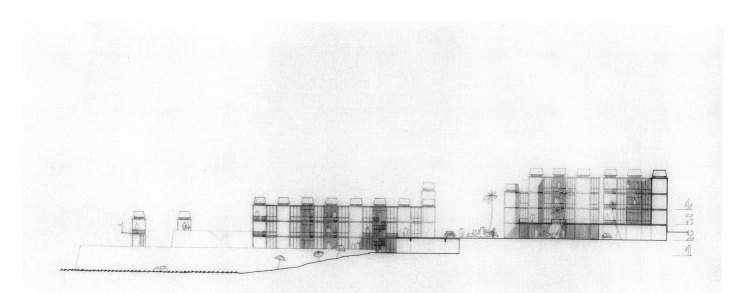

24. West Plaza Condominium 1962 *Project*
Coronado, California
Charles W. Moore
with Donlyn Lyndon and William Turnbull

1. *Model, Scheme 1*

3. *Elevation, Scheme 3*

2. *Model, Scheme 2*
   (Photograph by Amanda Merullo)

4. *Model, Scheme 3*
   (Photograph by Amanda Merullo)

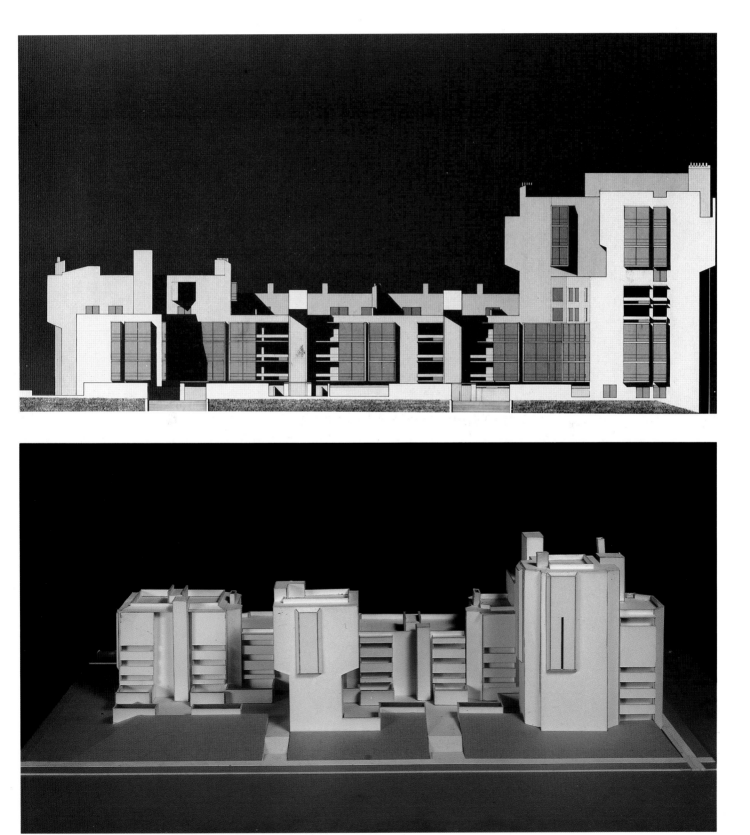

25. Monte Vista Apartments   1963
Monterey, California
Moore, Lyndon, Turnbull, Whitaker

1. Four elevations, May 6, 1963
Blueprint with color pencil, 24" × 41"

2. Exterior
(Photograph © Morley Baer)

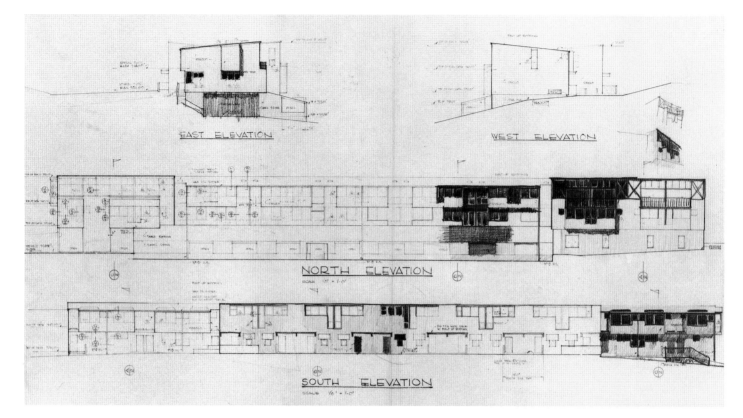

26. Church Street South   1966–1969
New Haven, Connecticut
Public housing
MLTW/Moore-Turnbull
with Marvin Buchanan and Donald Whitaker

1. Plan of laundromat plaza
Pencil on yellow trace, 12" × 32"
Drawing by Charles W. Moore

2. Aerial view
(Photograph by Aerial Photos International, Inc.)

3. Exterior
(Photograph © Norman McGrath)

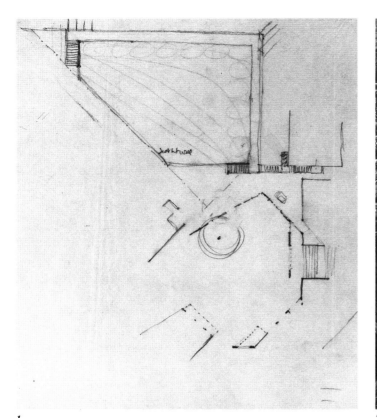

1

2

3

27. Kresge College   1966–1974
University of California at Santa Cruz
Residential college
MLTW/Moore-Turnbull
with Marvin Buchanan, Robert Calderwood,
and Robert Simpson

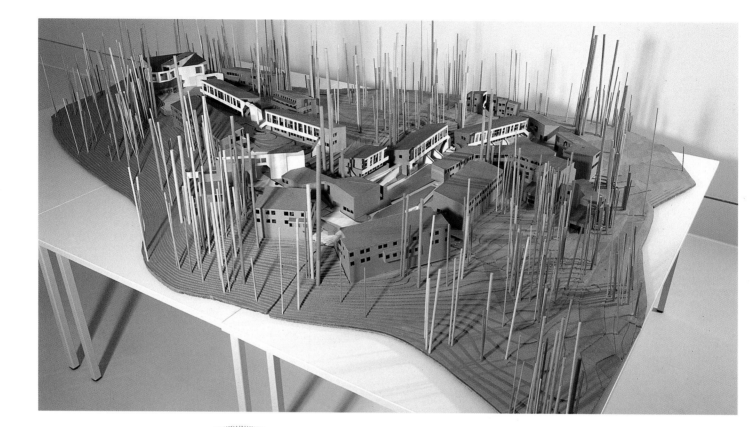

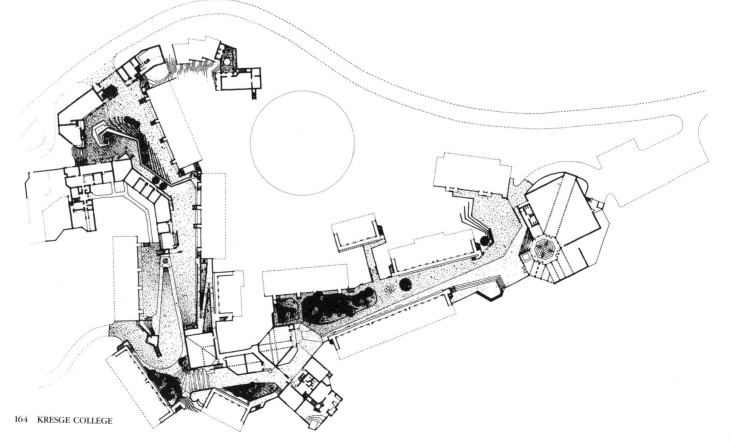

1. Model
   (Photograph courtesy Deutsches
   Architekturmuseum, Frankfurt)

3. Administrative buildings

4. Ramp for the disabled

2. Site plan
   Ink and watercolor on paper, 30″ × 40″

5. *Telephone booth*

6. *Dormitory*

7. *Laundromat*

28. Whitman Village   1971–1975
Huntington, New York
Public housing
Charles W. Moore Associates
with Robert Harper

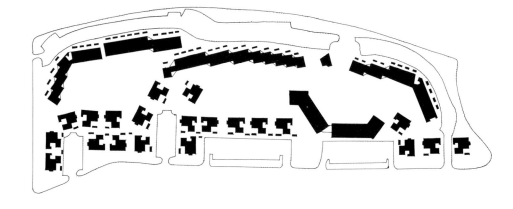

1. *Exterior, roofscape*
   (Photograph © Norman McGrath)

2. *Plan*

3. *Exterior*
   (Photograph © Norman McGrath)

4. *Exterior*
   (Photograph © Norman McGrath)

29. Xanadune 1972 *Project*
St. Simons Island, Georgia
Condominium
Charles W. Moore Associates
with Richard Oliver, Mary Ann Rumney,
and Robert Yudell

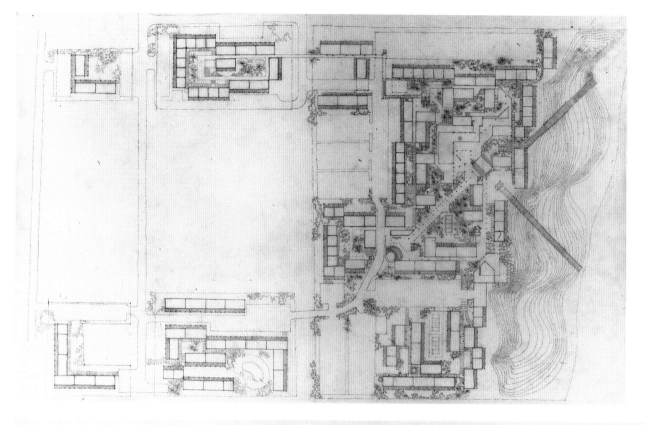

1. *Site plan, October 2, 1972*
   Pencil on white paper, 48" × 30"
   Drawing by Charles W. Moore

2. *Perspective exterior, October 12, 1972*
   Ink on white paper, 24" × 33"
   Drawing by William Hersey

3. *Sections and elevation of old southern*
   hotel, September 1972
   Pencil on yellow trace, 11" × 12"
   Drawing by Charles W. Moore

4. *Sections and roof plans, September 1972*
   Pencil on yellow trace, 9.5" × 16.5"
   Drawing by Charles W. Moore

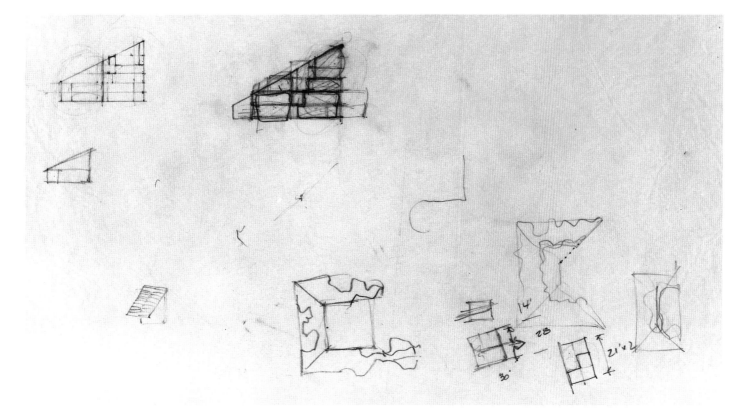

5. *Perspective, interior court, November 16,*
   1972
   Ink on white paper, 21" × 30.5"
   Drawing by William Hersey

6. *Perspective, interior of apartment, October*
   12, 1972
   Ink on white paper, 22" × 25"
   Drawing by William Hersey

7. Model
  (Photograph by Amanda Merullo)

8. Model
  (Photograph by Amanda Merullo)

30. Kingsmill on the James   1974   *Project*

Williamsburg, Virginia
Housing project
Charles W. Moore Associates
with Robert Harper, William Grover,
and Glenn Arbonies

1. Plan and section
Pencil on yellow trace, 14" × 31.5"
Drawing by Charles W. Moore

2. Model
(Photograph by Amanda Merullo)

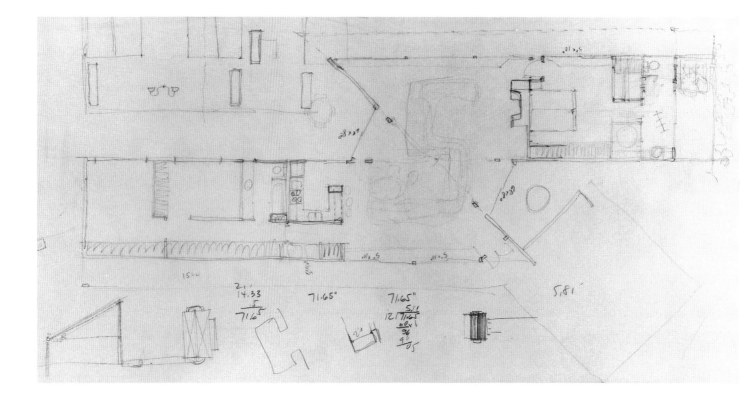

31. Parador 1982 *Project*
San Juan Capistrano, California
Hotel
Moore, Ruble, Yudell

1. Isometric
  Ink and watercolor on paper, 21" × 28.5"
  (Photograph courtesy Deutsches
  Architekturmuseum, Frankfurt)

2. Elevation
  Ink and watercolor on paper, 21" × 28.5"
  (Photograph courtesy Deutsches
  Architekturmuseum, Frankfurt)

3. Perspective
  Ink and watercolor on paper, 21" × 28.5"
  (Photograph courtesy Deutsches
  Architekturmuseum, Frankfurt)

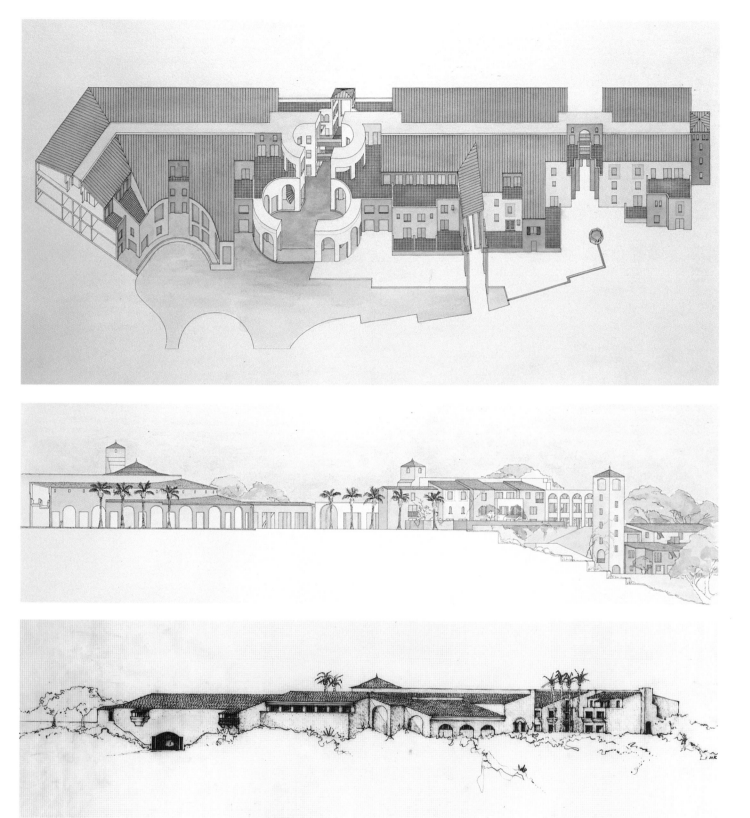

32. Ph.D. Project   1957
Princeton University
Charles W. Moore

1. *Glen Canyon Dam, Arizona*
View number 6, four perspectives
Drawing by Charles W. Moore
(Courtesy Princeton University School
of Architecture)

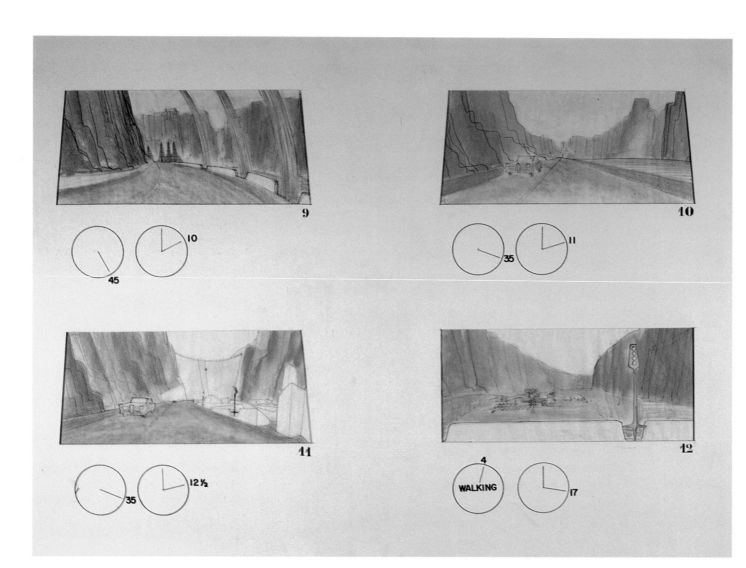

2. *Lever House, New York City*
   Courtyard
   Drawing by Charles W. Moore
   (Courtesy Princeton University School
   of Architecture)

3. *Lever House, New York City*
   Plan
   Drawing by Charles W. Moore
   (Courtesy Princeton University School
   of Architecture)

4. *Seagram Building Plaza, New York City*
   Perspective
   Drawing by Charles W. Moore
   (Courtesy Princeton University School
   of Architecture)

5. *Seagram Building Plaza, New York City*
   Plan
   Drawing by Charles W. Moore
   (Courtesy Princeton University School
   of Architecture)

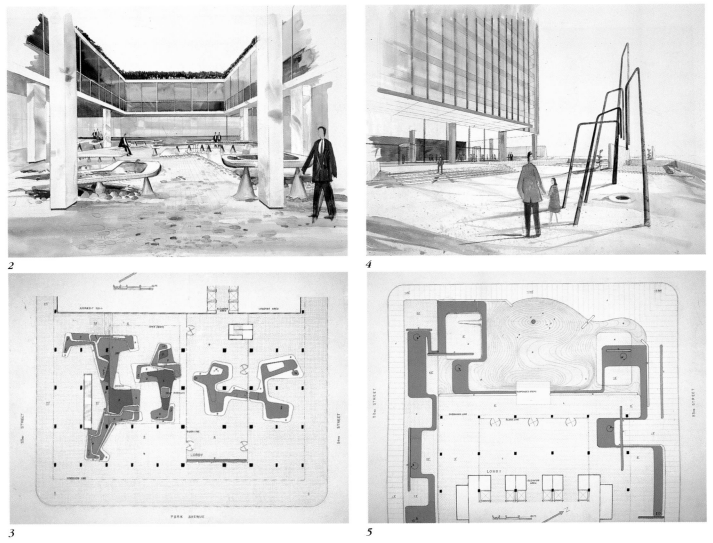

2

4

3

5

33. Lovejoy Fountain   1965–1966

Portland, Oregon
Fountain/waterfall in public park
Lawrence Halprin and Associates
with Moore, Lyndon, Turnbull, Whitaker
and Urban Innovations Group

1. Plan
Ink on paper, 22.5" × 30"

2. Fountain
(Photograph © Morley Baer)

34. Faculty Club, University of California
1966–1968
Santa Barbara, California
MLTW/Moore-Turnbull
with Donlyn Lyndon, Marvin Buchanan,
and Bruce Beebe

1. Bird's-eye view
Ink on white paper, 18" × 27"

2. Plan
Ink and watercolor on paper, 30" × 40"

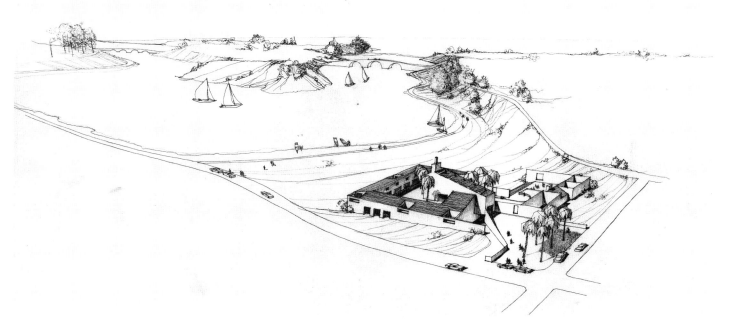

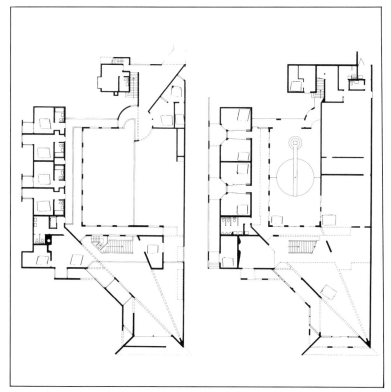

3. *Exterior, view from southwest*

4. *Exterior, view of entrance from courtyard*

5. *Exterior, view of entrance from terrace*

6. *Interior*
   (Photograph © Morley Baer)

3

4

5

35. Piazza d'Italia   1975–1978
New Orleans, Louisiana
Piazza/square
Charles W. Moore Associates
and Urban Innovations Group
with August Perez Associates

1. *Elevation studies for campanile and arcade*
   Ink on napkin, 5" × 10"
   Drawing by Charles W. Moore

2. *Elevation study of campanile, second*
   project, April 1, 1976
   Ink and watercolor on paper, 22.5" × 30"
   Drawing by Charles W. Moore

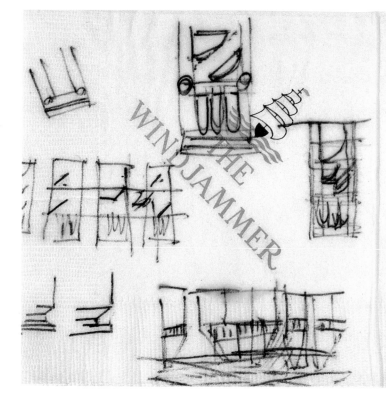

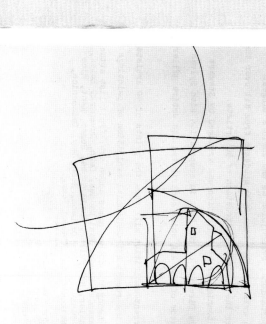

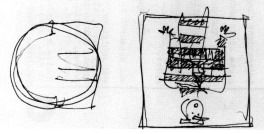

3. *Campanile, four elevations*
   Pencil on yellow trace, 14" × 16"
   Drawing by Charles W. Moore

4. *Elevations of campanile*
   Pen on napkin, 4" × 4"
   Drawing by Charles W. Moore

5. *Campanile and arcades*
   Ink on paper bag, 10" × 7"
   Drawing by Charles W. Moore

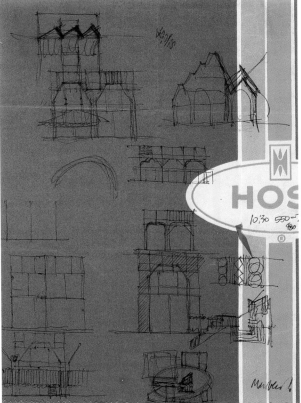

6. *Plan of second project*
   Ink on paper, 30" × 40"
   Drawing by William Hersey

7. *View by daylight*
   (Photograph © Norman McGrath)

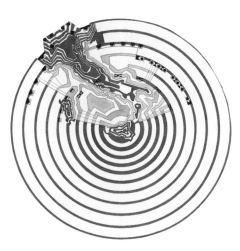

8. *View at night*
   (Photograph © Norman McGrath)

9. *Perspective of second project*
   Ink on paper, 27" × 19"
   Drawing by William Hersey

10. *Detail, central arch*
    (Photograph © Norman McGrath)

11. Triumphal Arch viewed from Lafayette Street

12. *Elevation of Hotel Piazza d'Italia*
    and office building
    Project, 1985
    Ink and watercolor on paper, 22.5" x 30"
    Drawing by Arthur Andersson

13. *Model*
    (Courtesy Deutsches Architekturmuseum,
    Frankfurt)

36. Indiana Landing   1980–1982   *Project*
Indianapolis, Indiana
Amusement Park
Charles W. Moore
and James Winkler, Stephen Harby,
and George Harris;
and Edgardo Contini of Urban Innovations Group
with Howard Beedles, Tammen and Bergendoff

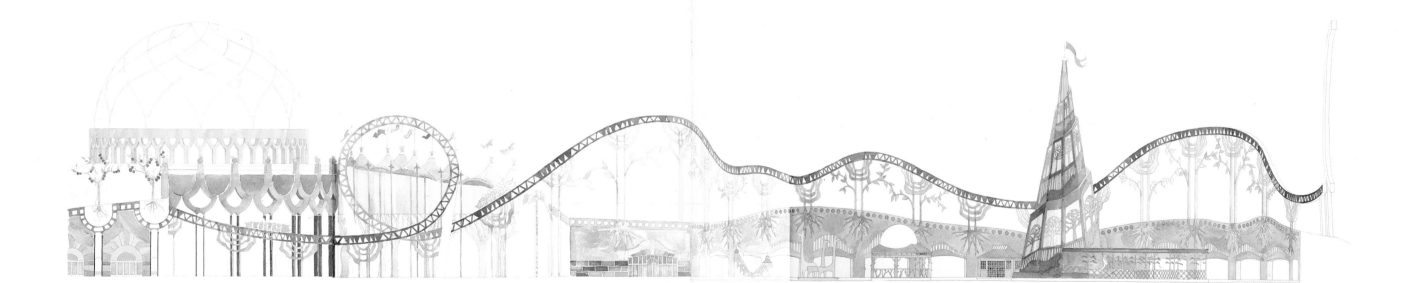

37. Wonderwall 1982–1984 *Dismantled*
New Orleans, Louisiana
World's Fair
Charles W. Moore and William Turnbull
with August Perez Associates, Kent Bloomer,
Leonard Salvato, and Arthur Andersson
and Urban Innovations Group

1. Elevation
Ink and watercolor on paper, 18″ × 116″

2. Elevation
Ink and watercolor on paper, 18″ × 116″

3. Elevation
Ink and watercolor on paper, 18″ × 116″

4. Model

5. Model

Following pages

6. Detail
   (Photograph by Donald M. Bradburn)

7. Detail
   (Photograph by Donald M. Bradburn)

38. Centennial Pavilion   1982–1984   *Dismantled*
New Orleans, Louisiana
World's Fair
Charles W. Moore and William Turnbull
with August Perez Associates
with Arthur Andersson and Leonard Salvato

1. Elevation
Ink and watercolor on paper
Drawing by Arthur Andersson

39. Copley Square 1984 *Project*
Boston, Massachusetts
Lyndon/Buchanan with the collaboration of
Charles Moore, William Turnbull,
William Hersey, Christopher Noll, and
Alice Wingwall

1. Plan
Ink and watercolor on paper, 24″ × 36″
Drawing by William Hersey and others

2. Perspective
Ink and watercolor on paper, 24″ × 36″
Drawing by William Hersey and others

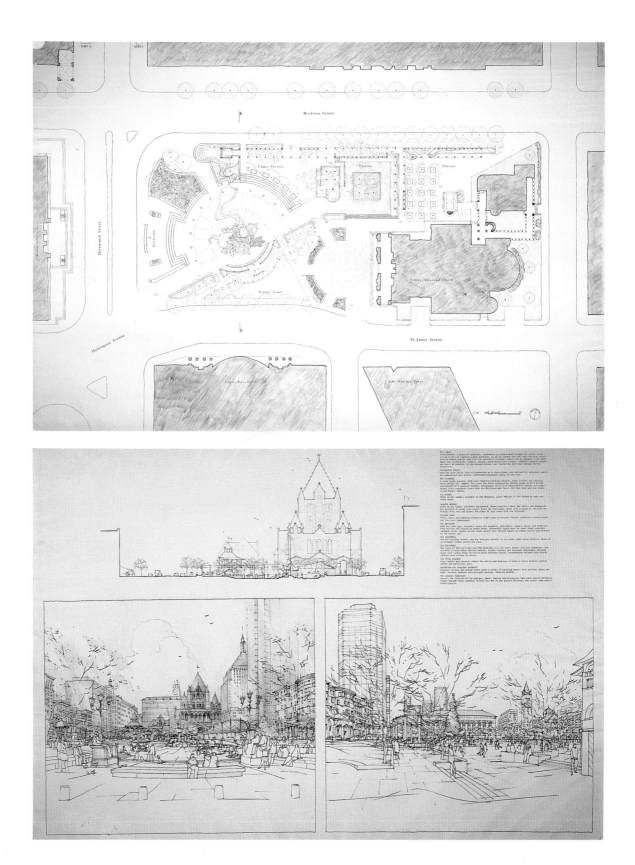

40. Amusement Park   1985

New Jersey
Charles W. Moore, Arthur Andersson,
and Charles Lamb, with Centerbrook,
J.P.C. Floyd, and James Childress

1. Site plan
Colored pencil on yellow trace, 24" × 78"
(Courtesy Centerbrook Associates)

2. Plan with train
Colored pencil on yellow trace, 14" × 24"
Drawing by Charles W. Moore

3. Elevations
Pencil on yellow trace, 5" × 16"
Drawing by Charles W. Moore

41. 1992 Chicago World's Fair   1985   *Project*

Chicago, Illinois
SOM, Stanley Tigerman, Thomas Beeby,
Robert A.M. Stern, Jacquelin Robertson,
and Charles W. Moore, with Renzo Zecchetto

1. Plan
Ink and watercolor on paper, 30″ × 40″

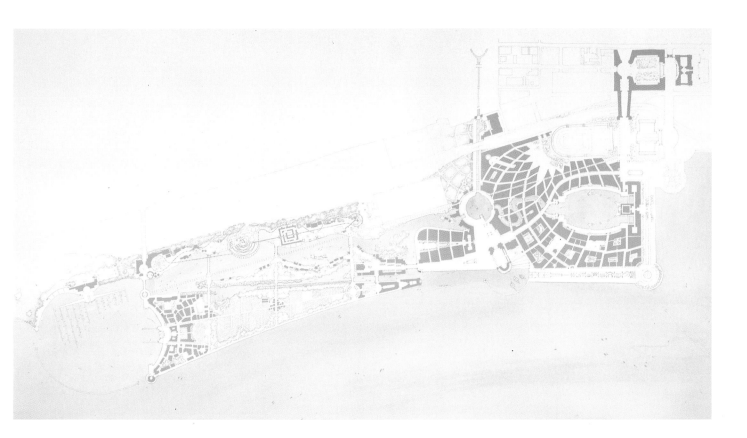

Fitting

42. Yun Chon Chapel 1954 *Project*
Yun Chon, Korea
Lieutenant Charles W. Moore

1. Plan and elevations
Blueprint, 21" × 30"

2. Sections
Blueprint, 21" × 30"

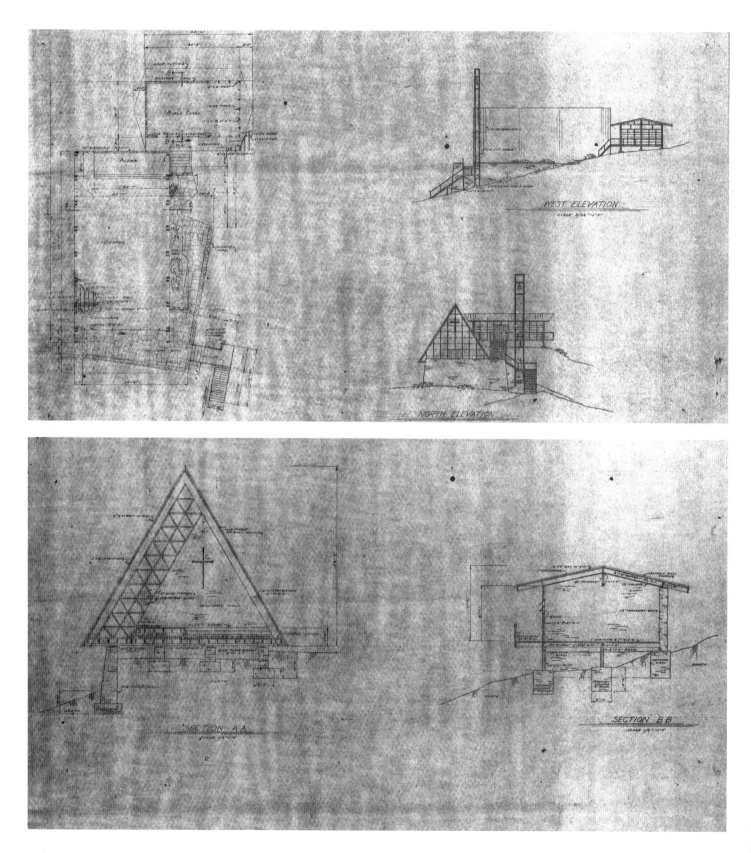

43. Chung Wha Girls' Middle and High School 1954 *Destroyed*
Seoul, Korea
Lieutenant Charles W. Moore

1. Plan, elevations, and sections
Blueprint, 20" × 27"
Drawing by Charles W. Moore

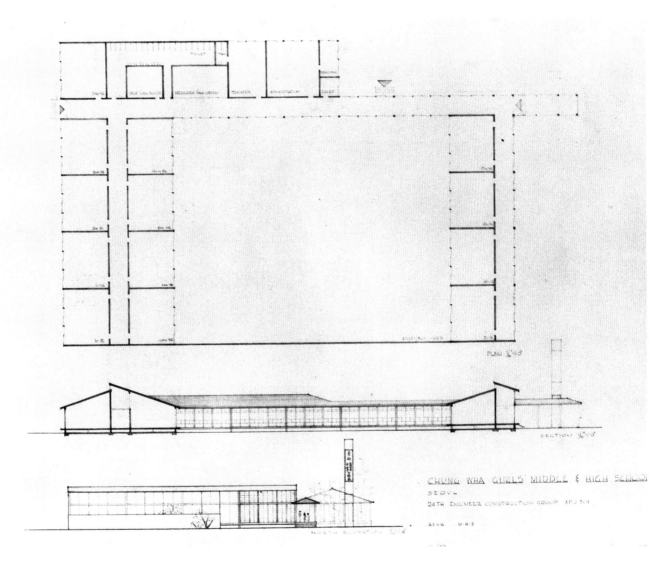

44. Cultural Center 1956 *Project*
Chichén Itzá, Mexico
Charles W. Moore

1. Bird's-eye view
Ink on paper, 19.5" × 26"
Drawing by Charles W. Moore

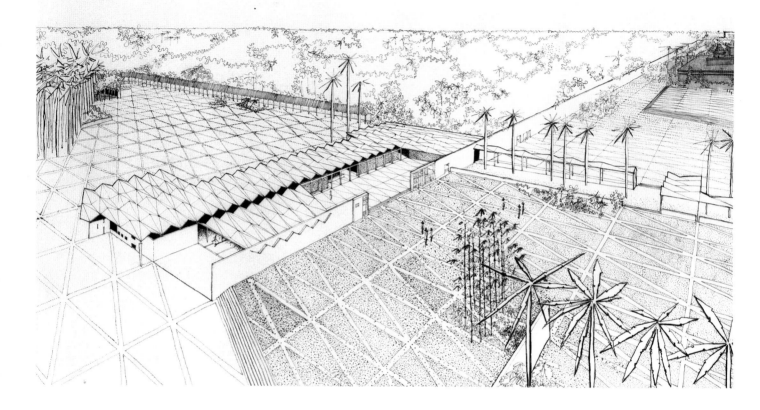

45. Jewish Community Center 1957 *Project*
Seaside, California
Charles W. Moore

1. Perspective
Ink on white trace, 18″ × 24″
Drawing by Charles W. Moore

2. Plan
Ink on white trace, 18″ × 24″
Drawing by Charles W. Moore

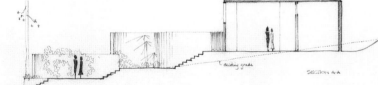

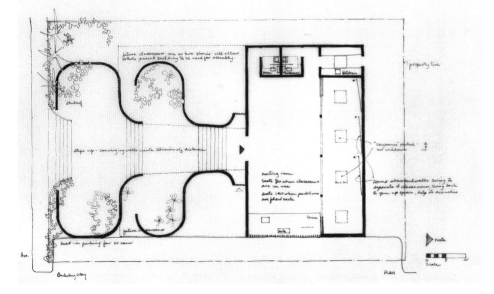

46. Retail Milk Products Drive-in
1960 *Project*
Pacific Grove, California
Commercial development
Charles W. Moore

1. Plan and perspective
Ink on white paper, 24" × 31"
Drawing by Charles W. Moore

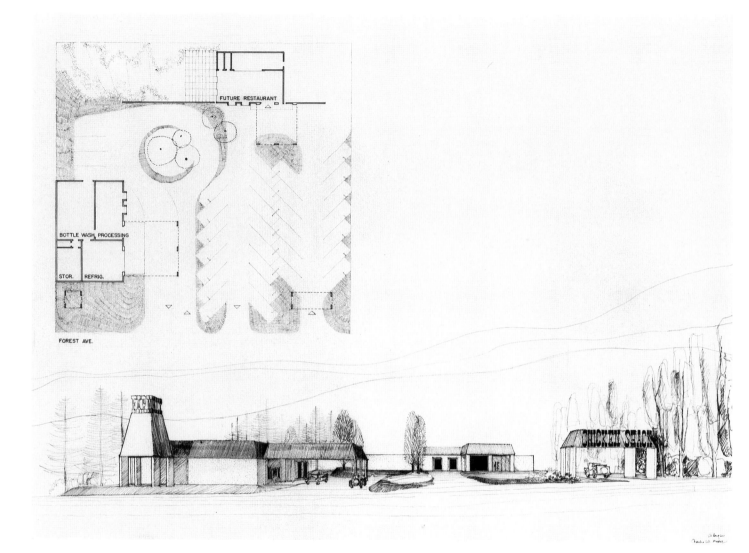

**47. Porte Cochere
for Dr. and Mrs. Seymour Pastron   1961**
Los Angeles, California
Charles W. Moore

1. Perspective, entrance
Pencil on white paper, 14″ × 18″
Drawing by Charles W. Moore

PORTE COCHÈRE for DR & MRS SEYMOUR PASTRON
LOS ANGELES, CALIFORNIA

48. Sea Ranch Condominium   1963–1965
Sea Ranch, California
Moore, Lyndon, Turnbull, Whitaker

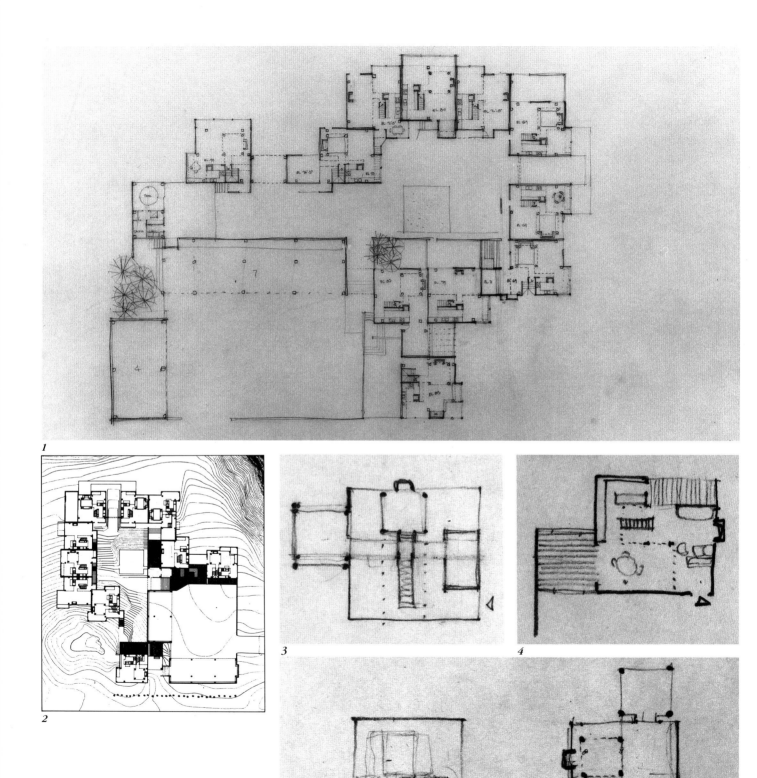

1

2

3

4

5

1. *Plan of condominium, June 20, 1964*
   Pencil on white trace, 42" × 26"
   Drawing by Charles W. Moore
   and William Turnbull

2. *Plan, as built*

3. *Plan of unit 4*
   Pencil on yellow trace, 6" × 6"
   Drawing by Charles W. Moore

4. *Plan of single unit*
   Pencil on yellow trace, 12" × 11"
   Drawing by Charles W. Moore

5. *Plans of single unit*
   Pencil on yellow trace, 17" × 14"
   Drawing by Charles W. Moore

6. *Axonometric plan of bathroom and kitchen*
   unit
   Pencil on yellow trace, 14.5" × 23"
   Drawing by William Turnbull

7. *Interior perspective of single unit*
   Pencil on yellow trace, 13" × 23"

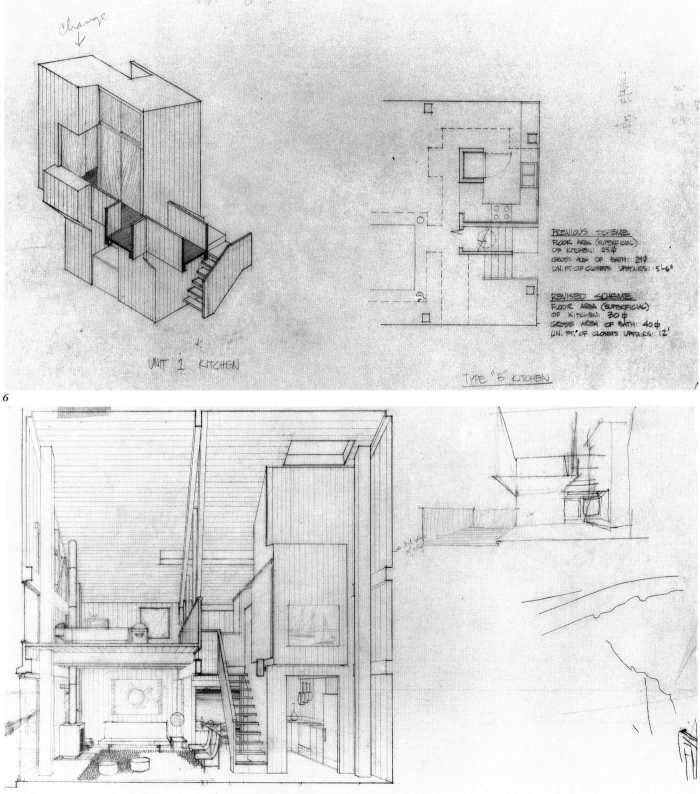

8. *North elevation*
   Pencil on white trace, 12" × 27"
   Drawing by Charles W. Moore
   and William Turnbull

9. *South elevation*
   Pencil on white trace, 12" × 27"
   Drawing by Charles W. Moore
   and William Turnbull

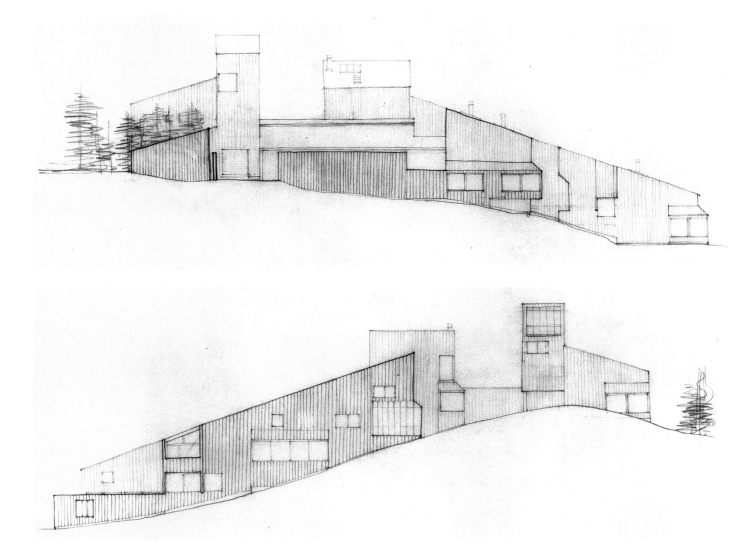

10. *East elevation*
    Pencil on trace, 12" × 25"
    Drawing by Charles W. Moore
    and William Turnbull

11. *West elevation*
    Pencil on trace, 12" × 27"
    Drawing by Charles W. Moore
    and William Turnbull

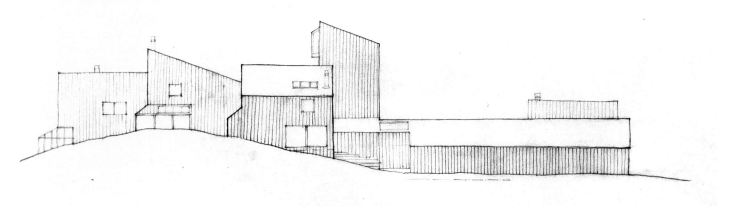

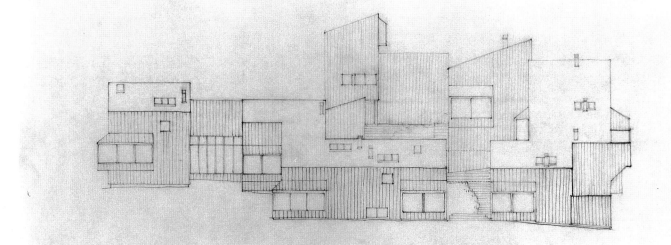

12. *Exterior from south*

13. *Exterior from northwest*
   (Photograph © Morley Baer)

14. *Exterior from north*

15. *Exterior of courtyard*

49. Jones Laboratory   1974–1977
Cold Spring Harbor, New York
Laboratory for cancer research
Moore, Grover, Harper

1. *South and east elevations*
   Ink on vellum, 18″ × 33.5″

2. *North and west elevations*
   Ink on vellum, 18″ × 33.5″

3. *Plan*
   Ink on vellum, 15″ × 27″

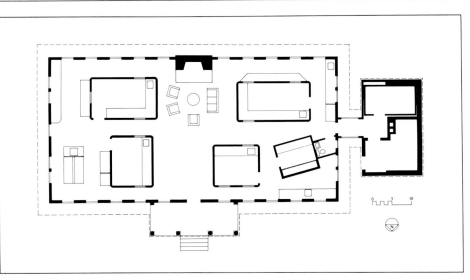

50. Riverdesign 1976
Dayton, Ohio
Project for public park, designed on television
Moore, Grover, Harper with Lorenz and Williams

1. Aerial view of riverfront with bandstand
and floating fountain
(Photograph courtesy Centerbrook)

51. Williams College Museum of Art and Art Department (Lawrence Hall) Additions 1977–1983, 1984–1986

Williamstown, Massachusetts
Art museum extension and addition
to art department
Moore, Grover, Harper/Centerbrook
with Robert Harper

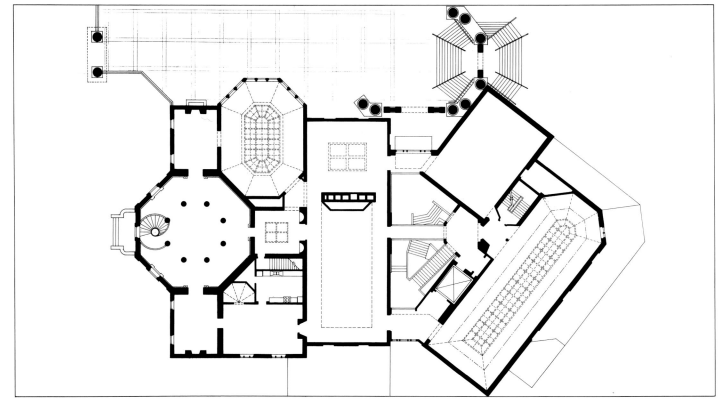

1. Section, as built
   Ink and watercolor on paper, 22.5" × 30"
   Drawing by Centerbrook

3. Early project, view from north
   Ink and watercolor on paper, 11" × 17.5"
   Drawing by William Hersey

2. Plan, as built
   Ink on paper, 22.5" × 30"
   Drawing by Centerbrook

4. Early project, bird's-eye view from west
   Ink and watercolor on paper, 15" × 22"
   Drawing by William Hersey

5. *Early project, model*
   View from north

6. *Early project, model*
   View from east

7. *Early project, model*
   View from southeast

5

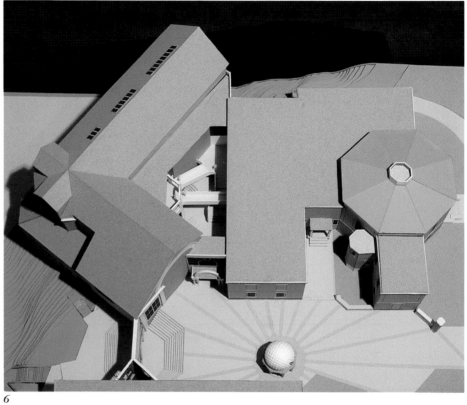

6

7

8. *Project for polychromy in atrium, 1985*
   Watercolor, 11" × 8.5"
   Drawing by Charles W. Moore

9. *Axonometric*
   Ink and watercolor on paper, 22.5" × 30"

10. *Bird's-eye view of courtyard,*
    with proposed sculpture by Patrick
    and Anne Poirier, 1985
    Ink on trace, 12" × TK
    Drawing by Charles W. Moore

8

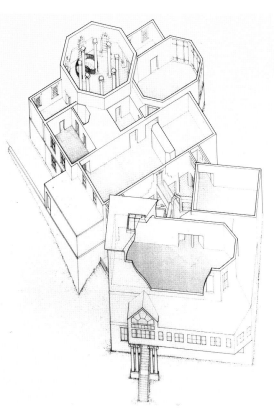

9

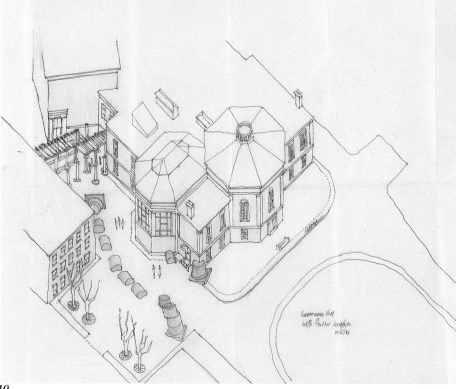

10

11. *Model, with proposed sculpture*
by Patrick and Anne Poirier
(Photograph by Amanda Merullo)

12. *Model*
   (Photograph by Amanda Merullo)

13. Exterior from southeast
(Photograph © Norman McGrath)

14. *Interior, entry level looking north*
    (Photograph © Norman McGrath)

16. *View of stairwell*
    (Photograph © Norman McGrath)

15. *Interior, entry level looking south*
    (Photograph © Norman McGrath)

17. *Upstairs hallway*
    (Photograph by Ralph Lieberman)

52. Sammis Hall   1978–1981
Cold Spring Harbor, New York
Residential hall/conference center
Moore, Grover, Harper

1

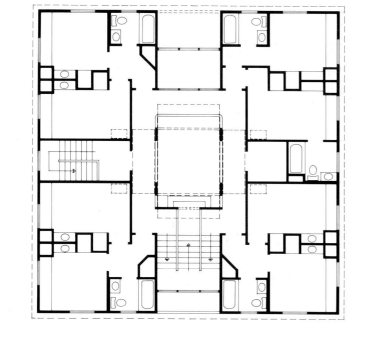

2

3

1. *Elevation*
   Ink on vellum, 13" × 32"
   Drawing by Centerbrook

2. *Plan, second floor*
   Ink on vellum, 17" × 17"

3. *Perspective*
   Ink on vellum, 16" × 14"
   Drawing by Centerbrook

4. *Model*
   25" × 20" × 20"
   (Photograph by Amanda Merullo)

5. *Model with roof removed, showing interior*
   25" × 20" × 20"
   (Photograph by Amanda Merullo)

4

5

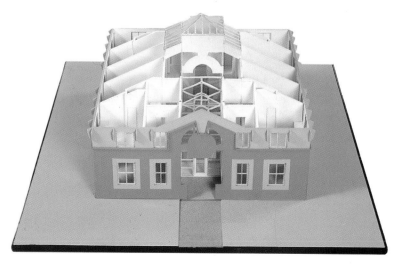

53. St. Matthew's Episcopal Church
1979–1983
Pacific Palisades, California
Moore, Ruble, Yudell

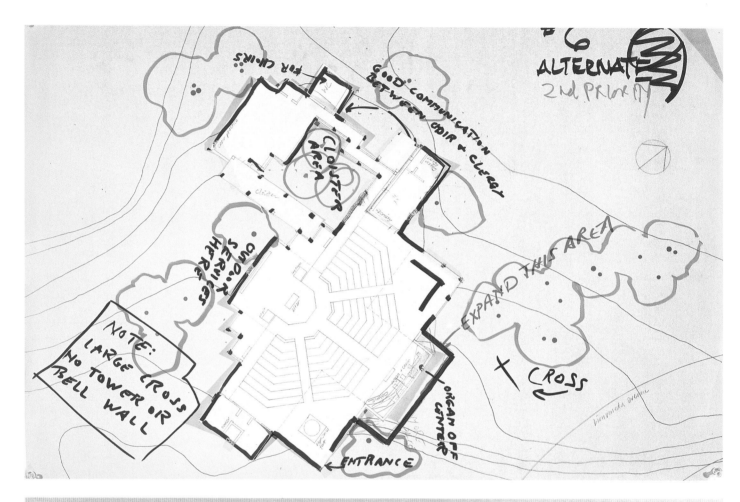

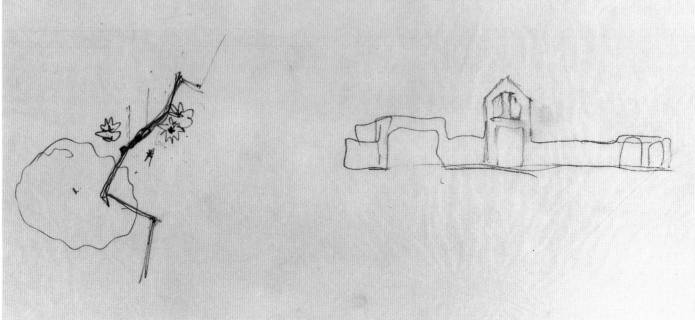

1. *Workshop drawing*
   Magic marker and collage on blueprint,
   24" × 36"
   Drawing by parishioners

2. *Plan and elevation of screen wall with*
   bell tower
   Pencil on yellow trace, 12" × 24"
   Drawing by Charles W. Moore

3. *Model*
   66" × 27.5" × 26"
   (Photograph by Amanda Merullo)

4. *Model*
   66" × 27.5" × 26"
   (Photograph by Amanda Merullo)

5. Elevation
   Ink and watercolor on paper, 27" × 40"

6. Site plan
  Ink and watercolor on paper, 27″ × 40″

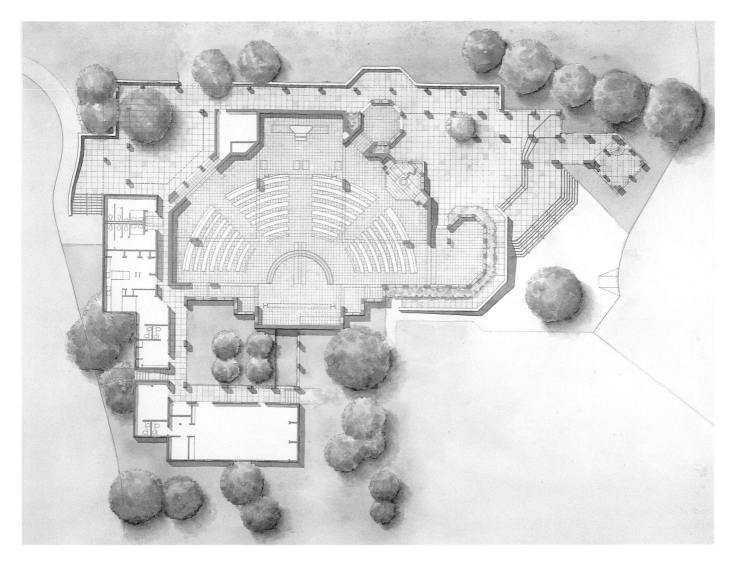

7. *Drawing for reredos*
   Pencil on yellow trace, 12" × 13"
   Drawing by Charles W. Moore

8. *Perspective, interior*
   Watercolor on paper, 18" × 12"
   Drawing by Charles W. Moore
   (Courtesy Max Protech)

9. *Axonometric of interior with roof trusses*
   Ink and pencil on acetate, 24" × 36"

10. *Section*
    Ink and watercolor on paper, 27" × 40"

7

8

9

10

11. Model of altar
29" × 29" × 10"
(Photograph by Amanda Merullo)

12. Exterior from south

13. Interior from northwest

14. Interior from narthex

15. Interior, detail of roof trusses

54. Tegel Harbor Housing 1980–
Berlin, West Germany
Public housing
Moore, Ruble, Yudell

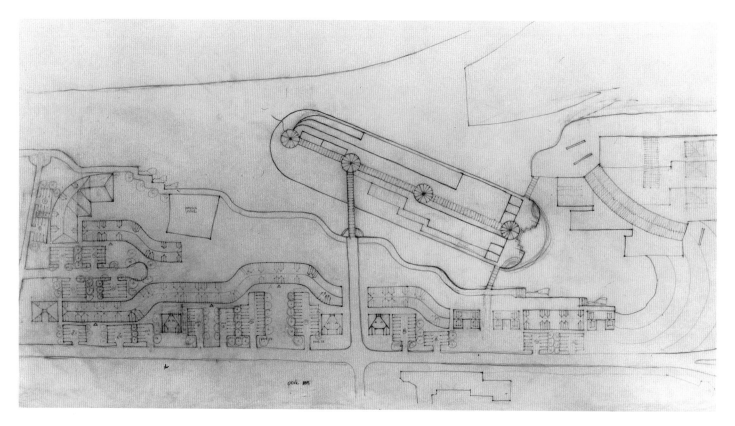

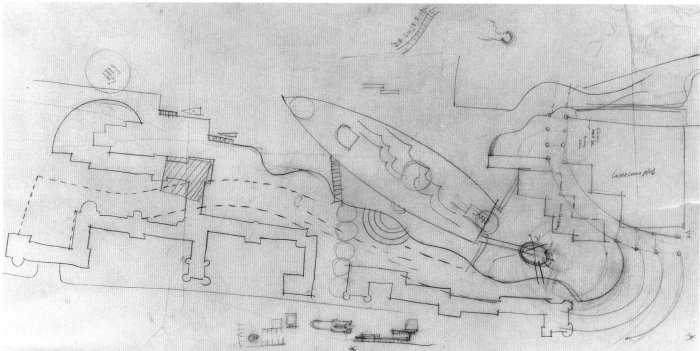

1. *Housing, preliminary plan*
   Pencil on yellow trace, 24″ × 49″
   Drawing by Charles W. Moore and others

2. *Housing, preliminary plan*
   Pencil on yellow trace, 24″ × 59″
   Drawing by John Ruble and Robert Yudell

3. *Tower housing, elevation*
   Pencil on yellow trace, 12″ × 18″
   Drawing by John Ruble

4. *Plan*
   Pencil on yellow trace, 11″ × 22″

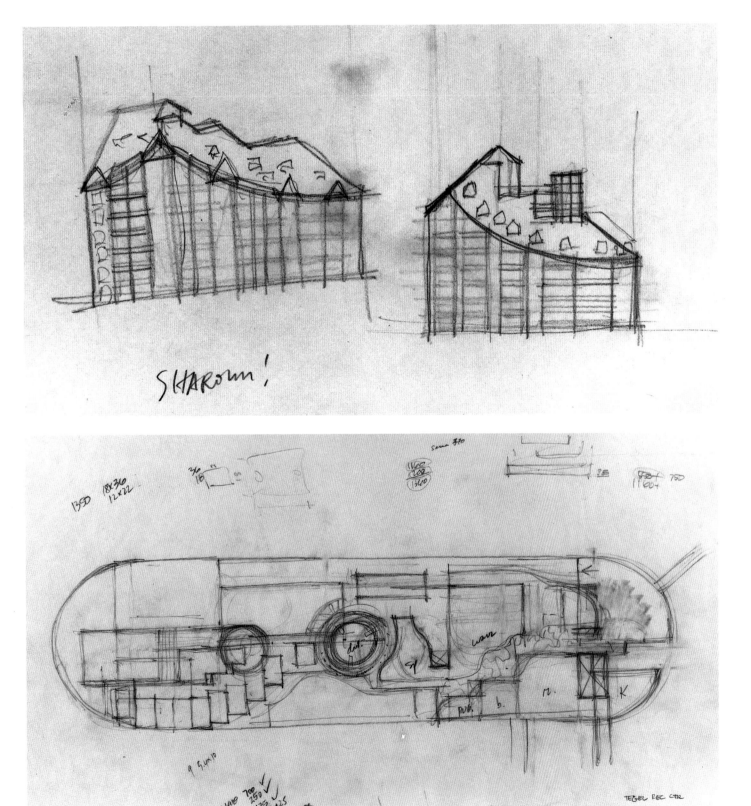

5. *Recreation center, plan*
   Colored pencil on yellow trace, 12" × 20"
   Drawing by Charles W. Moore

6. *Recreation center, elevation*
   Ink and pencil on yellow trace, 12" × 19"
   Drawing by Charles W. Moore

7. *Music school, elevation*
   Pencil on yellow trace, 12" × 16"
   Drawing by Charles W. Moore

5

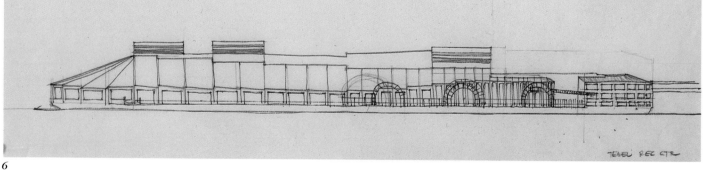

6

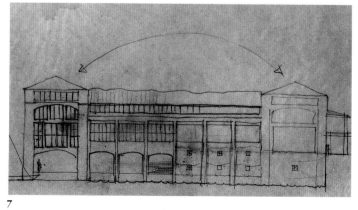

7

8. Library, site plan
   Ink and watercolor on paper, 26″ × 40″

9. Library, elevation
   Ink and watercolor on paper, 28″ × 40″

10. Library, section
    Pencil on yellow trace, 12″ × 14″
    Drawing by Charles W. Moore

11. Library and adult school, plan
    Pencil on white trace, 12″ × 12″
    Drawing by Charles W. Moore

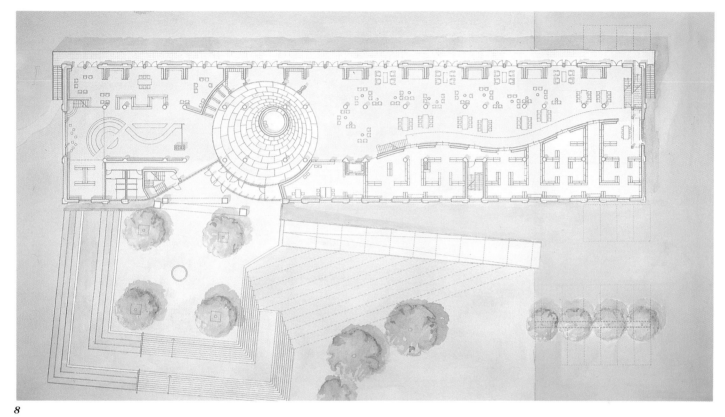

8

9

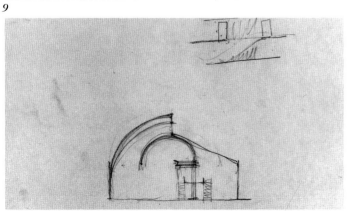

10

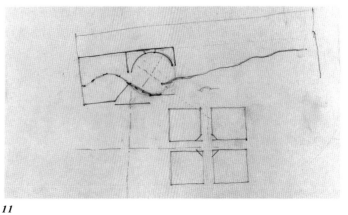

11

12. Library, section and perspective
Ink and watercolor on paper, 28" × 40"

13. Site plan
Ink and watercolor on paper, 28" × 40"

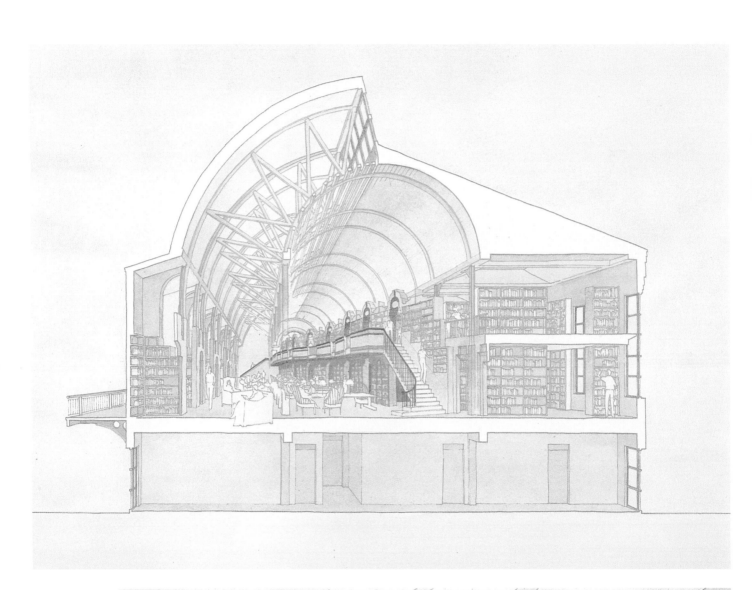

14. *Housing, model*
    (Photograph by Amanda Merullo)

15. Housing, elevation
   Ink and watercolor on paper, 25" × 89"

16. Strasse 7, elevation
   Ink and watercolor on paper, 18" × 107"

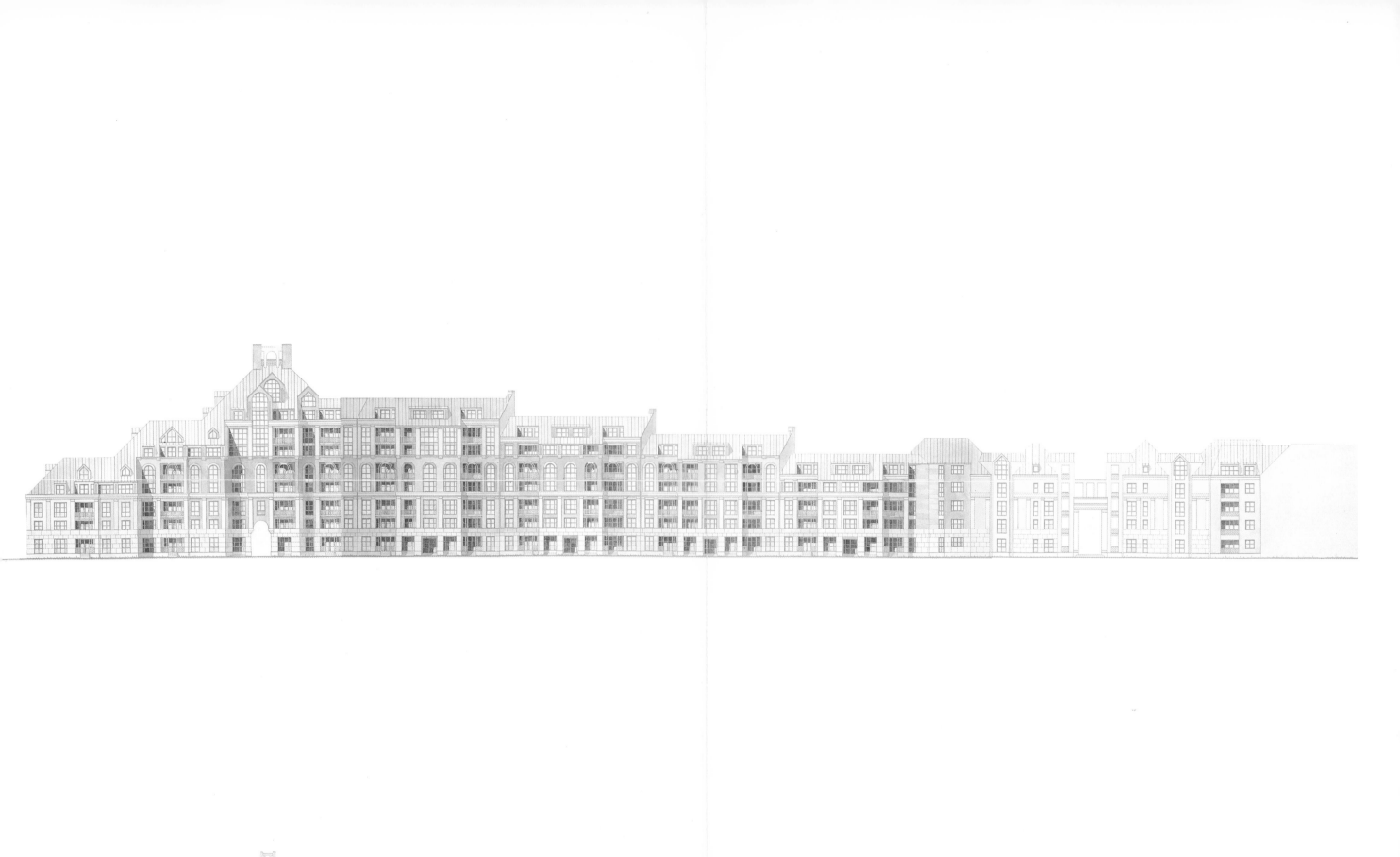

55. Beverly Hills Civic Center   1982–

Beverly Hills, California
Charles W. Moore
and Urban Innovations Group
in association with Albert C. Martin and Associates

1. Elevation
Ink and watercolor on paper, 32″ × 114″

2. Theater side section
Ink and watercolor on paper, 32″ × 114″

3. *Plan after lost sketch*
   Pencil on yellow trace, 24″ × 36″
   Drawing by Charles W. Moore

4. *Plan with five ovals on wandering axis*
   Pencil on yellow trace, 18″ × 24″
   Drawing by Charles W. Moore

5. *Partial plan with three ovals*
   and palm trees
   Pencil on yellow trace, 18″ × 27″
   Drawing by Charles W. Moore

6. *Plan with five ovals and watercourse*
   Pencil on yellow trace, 18″ × 37″
   Drawing by Charles W. Moore

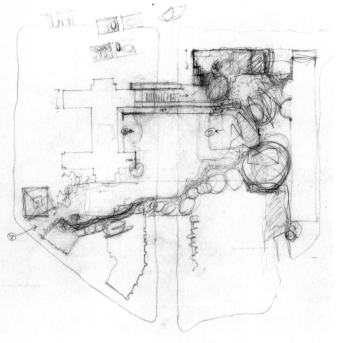

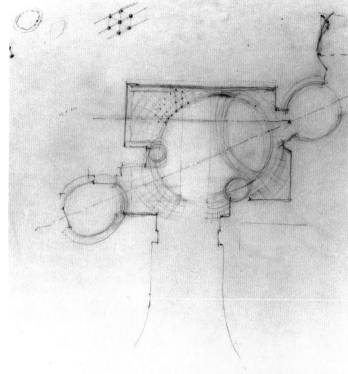

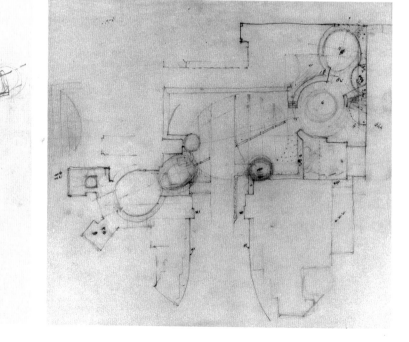

7. Plan with five ovals
   Pencil on yellow trace, 18" × 26"
   Drawing by Charles W. Moore

8. Plan with two ovals and circle
   with starburst pattern
   Pencil on yellow trace, 18" × 39"
   Drawing by Charles W. Moore

9. Plan of large ovals and fountain area
   Pencil on yellow trace, 18" × 25"
   Drawing by Charles W. Moore

10. Plan of oval fountain with two boats
    Pencil on yellow trace, 19" × 18"
    Drawing by Charles W. Moore

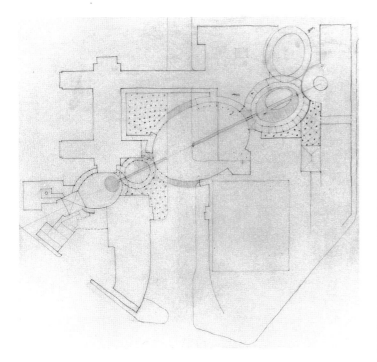

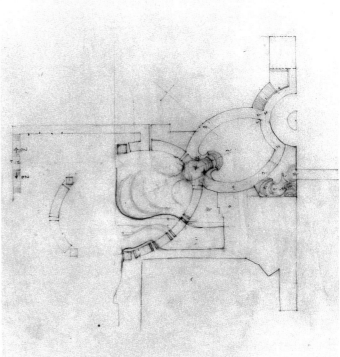

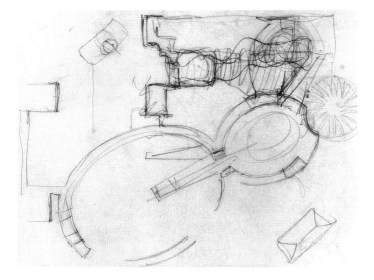

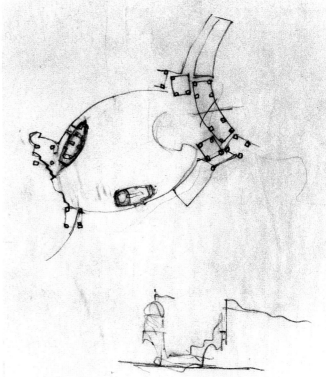

11. *Site plan*
    Pencil on yellow trace, 12" × 12"
    Drawing by Steven Harby

12. *Two elevations of fountain wall*
    Pencil on yellow trace, 12" × 26"
    Drawing on left by Charles W. Moore

13. *Elevation, entrance*
    Ink and watercolor on paper

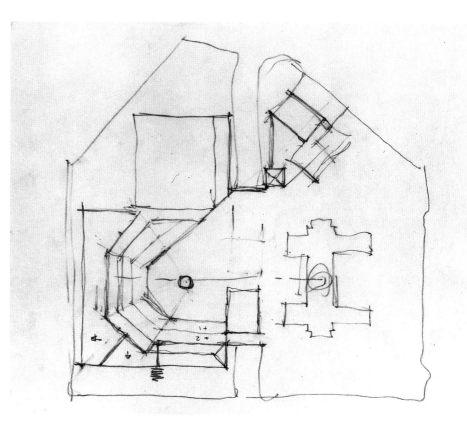

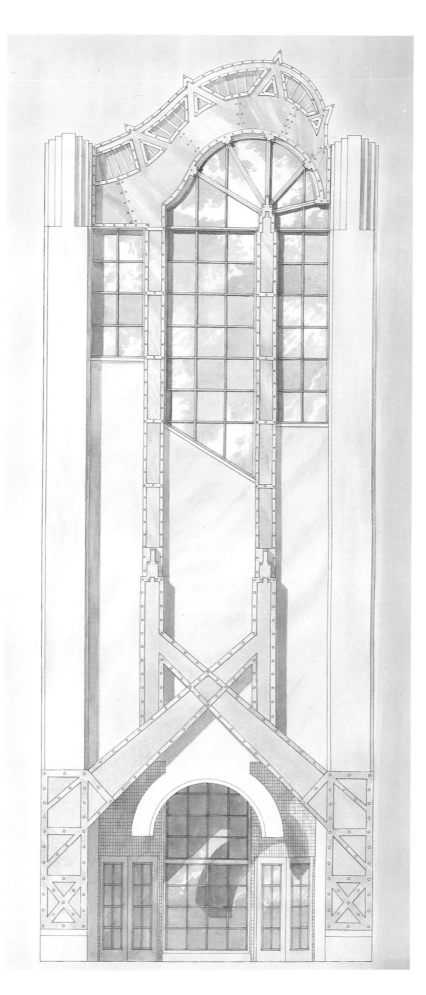

14. *Plan of police station*
   Pencil on paper, 11" × 18"
   Drawing by Charles W. Moore

15. *Competition model*
   Charles W. Moore with
   Urban Innovations Group
   (Courtesy City of Beverly Hills)

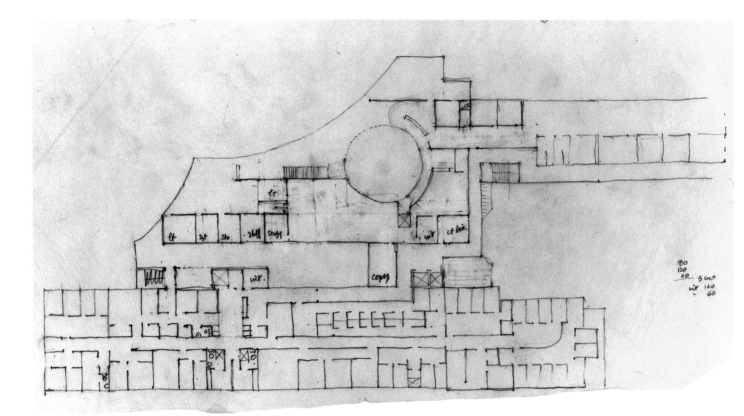

16. *Plan of library*
   Pencil on paper, 20" × 24"
   Drawing by Charles W. Moore

17. *Site plan*
   Ink and watercolor on paper, 30" × 35"

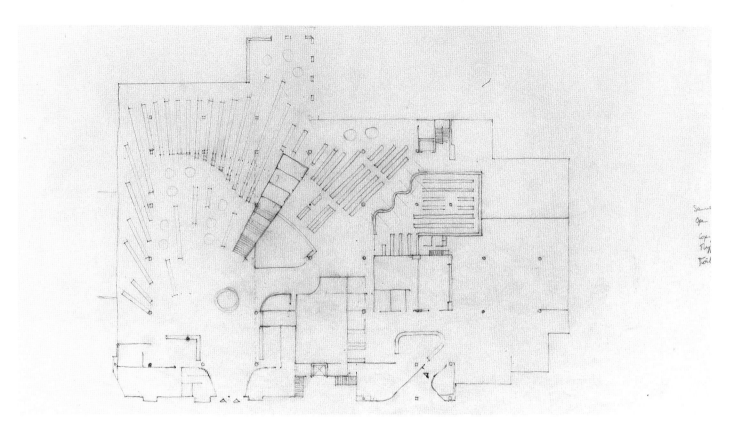

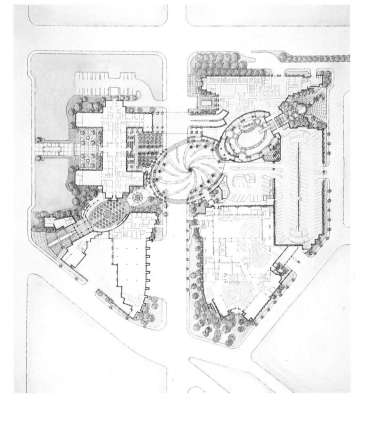

18–20. Details of competition drawing
Ink and watercolor on paper, full size
4' × 4'
Drawing by William Hersey
(Courtesy City of Beverly Hills)

56. Hood Museum, Dartmouth College
1981–1985
Hanover, New Hampshire
Art museum
Centerbrook with J. P. C. Floyd and Glenn Arbonies

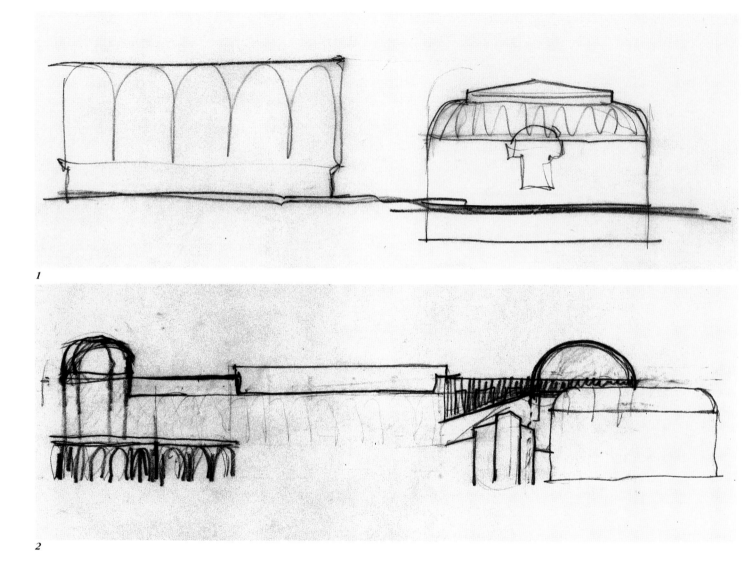

1

2

1. *Elevation of Hopkins Center with Hood*
   Museum to the west
   Pencil on yellow trace, 14" × 29"
   Drawing by Charles W. Moore

2. *Elevation of Hopkins Center with domes*
   Pencil on yellow trace, 14" × 22"
   Drawing by Charles W. Moore

3. *Elevation of Hopkins Center with domes*
   Red and black pencil on yellow trace,
   14" × 22"
   Drawing by Charles W. Moore

4. *Bird's-eye view of Hopkins Center and Hood*
   Museum; elevation of Hopkins Center, Hood
   Museum, and Hanover Inn
   Pencil on yellow trace, 14" × 35"
   Drawing by Charles W. Moore

5. *Sketch of plan, elevation, bird's-eye views,*
   and sections, September 9, 1981
   14" × 24"
   Drawing by Charles W. Moore

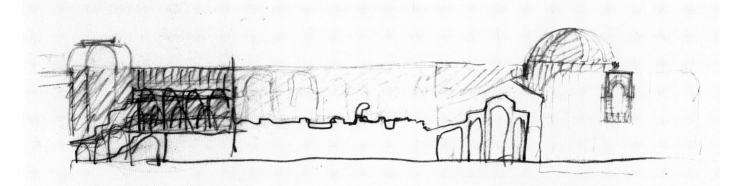

3

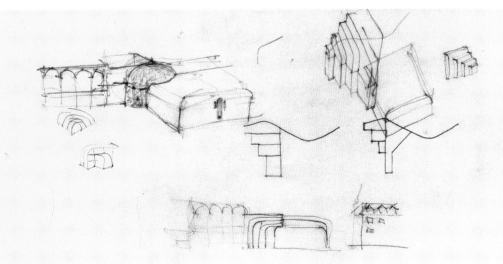

4

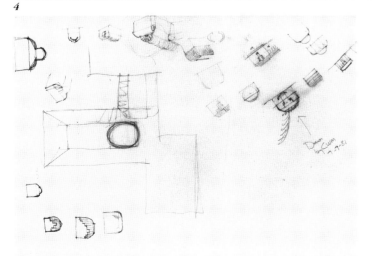

5

6–9. Model pieces
(Photographs by Amanda Merullo)

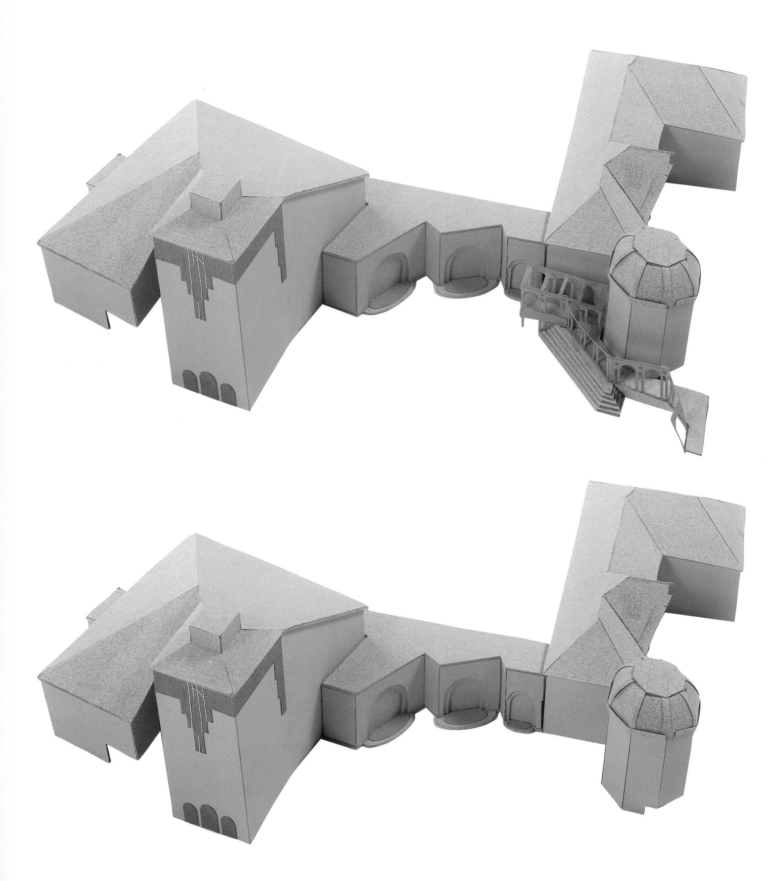

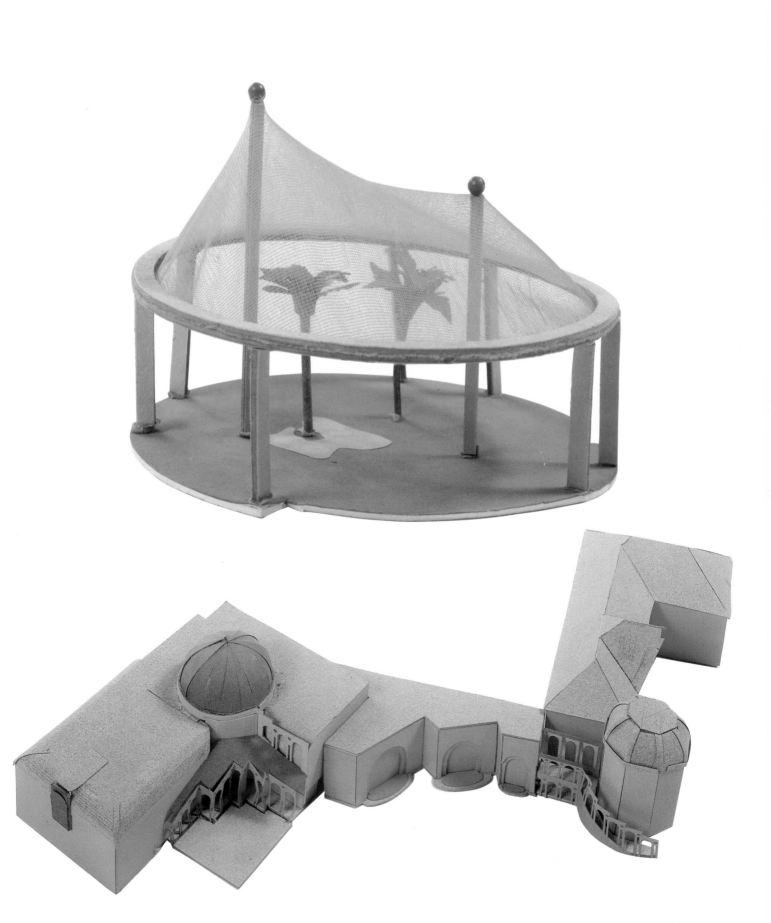

10. *Elevation of Wilson Hall with new screen wall and octagon*
    Colored pencil on yellow trace, 18″ × 18″
    Drawing by Charles W. Moore

11. *Plan, showing Hood Museum south of Wilson and east of Hopkins Center*
    Magic marker on yellow trace, 18″ × 22″
    Drawing by Charles W. Moore

12. *Elevation, plan and bird's-eye views of entrance tower to Hood Museum; word games exploring possible new names for Moore, Grover, Harper partnership*
    Blue pen on yellow sheet, 13″ × 8.5″
    Drawing by Charles W. Moore

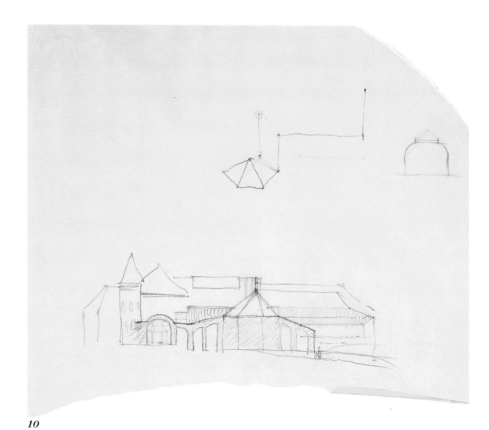

10

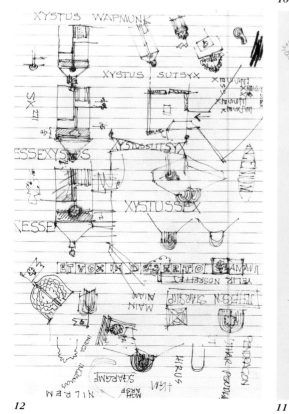

12

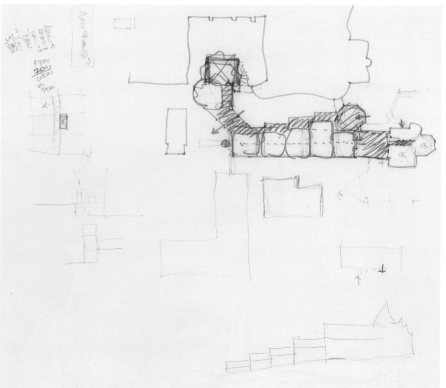

11

13. *Elevation, west, and sections*
   Ink on vellum, 19" x 33.5"

14. *Elevation, south*
   Ink on vellum, 19" x 33.5"

15. *Elevation, north*
   Ink on vellum, 8" x 19"

16. *Plan, entrance level*
   Ink on vellum, 24" × 18"

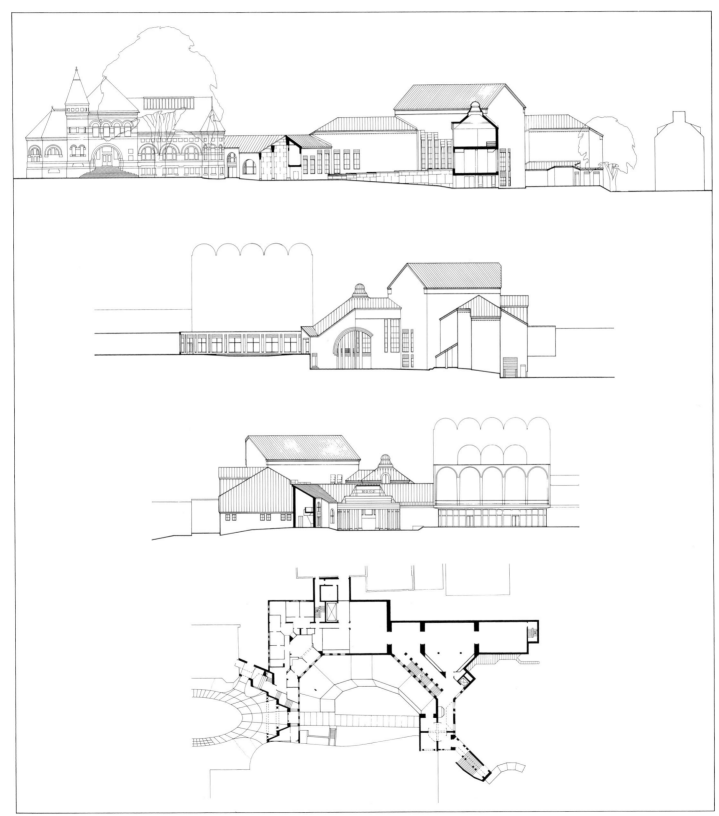

13–16

17. Model from southwest
(Photograph by Amanda Merullo)

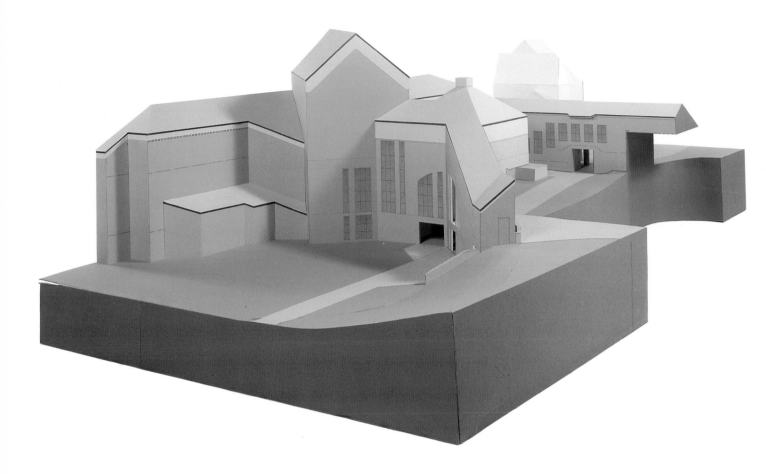

18. Model from northwest
  (Photograph by Amanda Merullo)

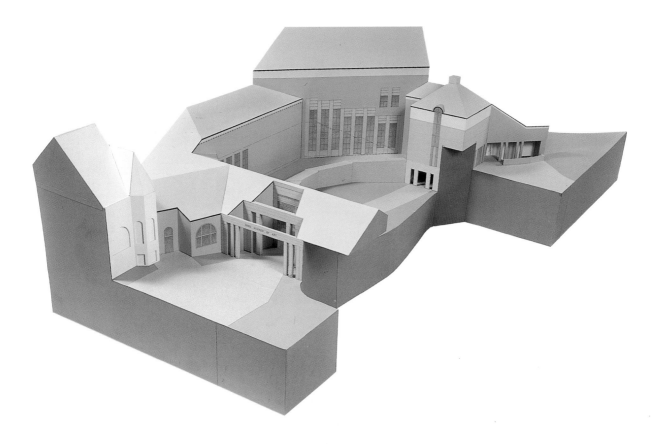

19. Exterior from southeast

20. Exterior from north

21. Exterior, museum court from north

22. Exterior from southwest

23. *Entrance*
   (Photograph © Steve Rosenthal)

24. *Detail of stairwell*
   (Photograph © Steve Rosenthal)

25. *Gallery*
   (Photograph © Steve Rosenthal)

23

24

25

57. Hermann Park 1982–
Houston, Texas
Public park
Charles W. Moore
with Urban Innovations Group
and Arthur Andersson

1. Elevation
Ink and watercolor on paper, 30" × 22.5"

HERMAN PARK CENTRAL FOVNTAIN   ·   CHARLES W. MOORE ARCHITECT

58. San Juan Capistrano Library
1982 *Project*
San Juan Capistrano, California
Moore, Ruble, Yudell

1. *Perspective of interior*
   Ink and watercolor on paper

2. *Competition model, roof removed*
   48" x 48" x 18"
   (Photograph by Amanda Merullo)

3. *Competition model*
   48" x 48" x 18"
   (Photograph by Amanda Merullo)

1

2

3

59. Alumni Center, University of California
1983–1985
Irvine, California
Charles W. Moore
with Urban Innovations Group

1

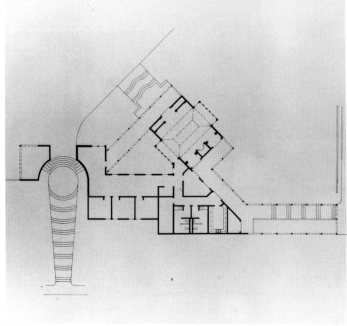

2

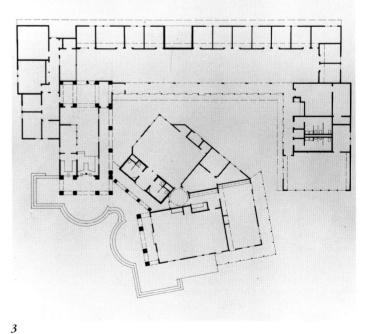

3

1. Exterior of extension building   4. Exterior of center

2. Plan of Alumni Center   5. Exterior of extension building

3. Plan of extension building

4

5

Fantasy Drawings

Fantasy Drawings

1. Fantasy with floating and tethered barge, 1985
Ink and watercolor on paper, 24" × 18"
Drawing by Charles W. Moore
(Collection of Mrs. Saul Weingarten)

2. *Architectural history of Texas (cover for*
   Center magazine), 1985
   Pencil, ink, and watercolor wash on paper,
   12.25" × 9"
   Drawing by Charles W. Moore

3. *Fantasy with towers, 1984*
   Ink and watercolor on paper
   Drawing by Charles W. Moore
   (Collection of Mrs. Saul Weingarten)

4. *The Spaniards Introduce Palm Trees*
   to Catalina Island, 1985
   Ink and watercolor on paper
   Drawing by Charles W. Moore

5. *Seaside*
   Hand-colored lithograph, 7" × 5"
   Drawing by Charles W. Moore

6. *Love to Mimi and Saul, Christmas 1981*
   Ink and watercolor on paper
   Drawing by Charles W. Moore
   (Collection of Mrs. Saul Weingarten)

4

5

6

7. *Barge on Bayou Lafourche*
   Hand-colored lithograph, 8.75" x 11.75"
   Drawing by Charles W. Moore

8. *Barge on the Carmel River, 1983*
   Hand-colored lithograph, 8.75" × 11.75"
   Drawing by Charles W. Moore

7

8

9. Eight decorated Christmas cookies, assorted
  sizes, 1983
  (Collection of Mrs. Saul Weingarten)

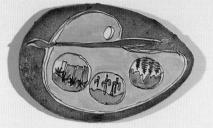

10. *Seven decorated Christmas cookies,*
    assorted sizes, 1983
    (Collection of Mrs. Saul Weingarten)

Bibliography and Chronology

Bibliography

1952

Moore, Charles W. "New Hope for Local Art." *The Forum*, April 23, 1952, 1–2.

1956

"Young Architect Sees Way to End Chaos, Emphasize Adobes." *Monterey Peninsula Herald*, September 7, 1956, 7.

1957

Moore, Charles W. *Water and Architecture*. Ph.D. Thesis. Princeton University, 1957.

"Visionary Plan for Monterey's Historic Sites." *Monterey Peninsula Herald*, January 4, 1957, 1.

1958

"Flexible Plan Provides for Present Needs, Future Expansion." *Book of Homes*, 14, 1958, 29.

Moore, Charles. "Environment and Industry, More Questions Than Answers: A Report on the Princeton Conference." *Architectural Record*, 124, July 1958, 159–162.

————. "Gospel According to Wright." *Architectural Record*, 124, February 1958, 58, 62.

————. "The Shapes of Our Time." Review of George Nelson, *Problems of Design*. In *Architectural Record*, 124, June 1958, 60, 64, 374.

1959

"Letter to Charles Moore re Monterey." *AIA Bulletin* (So. Cal.), 1959, 11.

Moore, Charles W. "The Architecture of Water." *Canadian Architect*, November 1959, 40–43.

————. "The Restoration of Old Monterey." *American Institute of Architects Journal*, 31, March 1959, 21–25.

————. Review of Alfred Proctor James and Charles Morse Stoltz, *Drums in the Forest: Decision at the Forks and Defense in the Wilderness*. In *Architectural Record*, 125, July 1959, 60, 63.

————. Review of David H. Pinkney, *Napoleon III and the Rebuilding of Paris*. In *Architectural Record*, 125, February 1959, 64, 374.

"New-Old Newport." *Architectural Record*, 125, February 1959, 189–192.

1960

Moore, Charles W. "Hadrian's Villa." *Perspecta*, 6, 1960, 16–27.

1961

"Hubbard Residence." *Sunset*, October 1961, 73.

"Merchant Built House in California." *AIA Sunset Western Home Awards*, 1961–1962.

Moore, Charles W. "Sagamore." *Journal of Architectural Education*, Summer 1961, 3–7.

"Technology with Circumspection." *Architectural Record*, August 1961, 9.

1962

"Casa per ospiti a Sobre Vista, Calif." *Casabella*, 269, November 1962, 39.

"Citation, Residential Design." *Progressive Architecture*, 43, January 1962, 146–149.

"Énfamiliehus for Mr. Moore." *Arkitektur*, 5 October 1962, 260–262.

Lyndon, Donlyn; Moore, Charles W.; Quinn, Patrick J.; and van der Ryn, Sim. "Toward Making Places." *Landscape*, 12, 1, Autumn 1962, 31–41. Reprinted as "Hacia La Creacion de Lugares," *Punto*, August–September 1964.

Moore, Charles W. Review of Konrad Wachsman, *The Turning Point of Building*. In *Landscape*, 12, 1, Autumn 1962, 44–45.

"Personalities." *Progressive Architecture*, 43, July 1962, 74.

"Powerful Design Sets Tract Pace." *Architectural Record*, 131, mid-May 1962, 66–69.

1963

"Architektur: USA, Zum Werk von Charles W. Moore." *Bauwelt*, June 1963, 653–659.

"Berkeley Firm Wins Design Award." *Oakland Tribune*, November 10, 1963, IL.

"A Bold New Shape Built with Familiar Materials." *House and Home*, 24, July 1963, 84–85.

"Citation, Residential Design." *Progressive Architecture*, 44, January 1963, 96–97.

"A Daylight Tower in the Redwoods." *AIA Sunset Western Home Awards*, 1963, 19.

"Designing Award Goes to a Cabin." *San Jose Mercury-News*, December 1, 1963, 14–15.

Escherick, Joseph; Hassid, Sami; and Moore, Charles W. "Graduate Programs. 1: The University of California." *American Institute of Architects Journal*, 40, September 1963, 95–98.

"Hard World Development." *Architectural Record*, 132, December 1963, 9.

"The Lair of the Lone Male." *San Francisco Examiner Pictorial Living*, November 3, 1963, 13–15.

Lyndon, Donlyn. "Filologia della architettura Americana." *Casabella*, 281, November 1963, 31.

Moore, Charles W. Review of Vincent Scully, *The Earth, The Temple and the Gods*, New Haven, 1962. In *Landscape*, 12, 1, Autumn 1963, 35–36.

"Private Residence." *Selected Houses—Progressive Architecture*, May 1963, 163–167.

"Private Residences." *Sunset*, November 1963, 103–104.

"Redwood Walls in a Redwood Canyon." *Progressive Architecture*, 44, June 1963, 126–131.

"Residence, Orinda, California." *Progressive Architecture*, 44, May 1963, 139, 171–175.

"San Francisco Bay Region AIA Awards." *Arts and Architecture*, May 1963, 29.

"A Simple Wood House." *AIA Sunset Western Home Awards*, 1963, 15.

"USA, Charles Moore, California." *Architectural Design*, September 1963, 403.

1964

"Berkeley Firm Wins Design Award." *Oakland Tribune*, January 26, 1964, 3C.

"Berkeley Students Plan City Study." *Santa Barbara News-Press*, September 3, 1964, A-10.

"Citation, Residential Design." *Progressive Architecture*, 45, January 1964, 114–117.

" 'Disaster Center' Designs at U.K. Guide for Future?" *Louisville Courier-Journal*, November 22, 1964, 2.

Gebhard, David. "The Bay Area Tradition in Architecture." *Art in America*, 52, June 1964, 60–63.

"Hacia la Creacion de Lugares." *Punto* (Venezuela), 19, August/September 1964, 20–23.

"Human Needs in Housing." *Savings and Loan News*, May 1964, 40–46.

"Model 'Toys' Are Really Tools." *Oakland Tribune*, March 29, 1964, 2C.

Moore, Charles W. Review of Esther McCoy, *Modern California Houses: Case Study Houses*. In *Progressive Architecture*, June 1964, 238, 244, 245.

"Nel Canyon di Palo Colorado." *Abitare*, November 1964, 38–39.

"A New Way to Create a Wide-Open House." *House Beautiful*, July 1964, 82–87.

"A Special Place." *Progressive Architecture*, 45, May 1964, 154–159.

"Vacation Houses." *Sunset*, May 1964, 106–109, 112–113.

"Visual Boundaries Extended." *Progressive Architecture*, 45, August 1964, 124–127.

1965

"AIA Honor Awards: Awards of Merit." *Architectural Record*, 138, July 1965, 74–75.

Architectural League of New York. *40 under 40*, exhibition catalog, 1965.

"The Architectural League's Sixty-Third Gold Medal Exhibition." *Interiors*, 125, December 1965, 102–105.

"Award of Merit." *House and Home*, June 1965, 86.

"Berkeley Résumé." *Architectural Forum*, 122, May 1965, 9.

Boyd, R. *The Puzzle of Architecture*, London, 1965, 154–155.

"Casa nel Canyon di Paolo Colorado." *Vitrum*, March–April 1965, 65–66.

"Citation, Residential Design." *Progressive Architecture*, 46, January 1965, 162–163.

"Coast Architect to Head School at Yale." *New York Times*, May 14, 1965, 39.

Delong, James. "The Sand Castle." *House Beautiful*, February 1965, 126–129.

"Designed to Serve the Land It Uses." *Architectural Record*, 138, November 1965, 152–155.

"Easy Extra Home." *Life*, 58, 18, May 7, 1965, 124–130.

Gebhard, David. "Charles Moore: Architecture and the New Vernacular." *Artforum*, 3, May 1965, 52–53.

"Holiday Homes." *Ameryka* (America Illustrated for USSR by USIA), 111, 1965, 39–41. [In Russian. Repeated for *Poland*, 85, 1965, 41–43 (in Polish).]

Lyndon, Donlyn. "Sea Ranch: The Process of Design." *World Architecture*, 2 1965, 30–39.

McCoy, Esther. "Avant-Garde Architecture." *Arts in Society*, III, 2, 1965, 164–168.

Misawa, Hiroshi; Ehira, Kanji; and Sugawara, Michio. "Charles W. Moore and his Partners." *Japan Architect*, 112, September 1965, 75–86.

Moore, Charles W. "Action House." *Architectural Forum*, 122, April 1965, 52–57.

———. "Architecture—Art and Science." *American Institute of Architects Journal*, 43, June 1965, 77–82.

Moore, Charles W. "In San Francisco, a Renewal Effort Based on Civic Pride Falls Short of Expectation." *Architectural Forum*, 123, July 1965, 58–63.

———. "The San Francisco Skyline: Hard to Spoil, but They're Working on It." *Architectural Forum*, 123, November 1965, 40–47.

———. "You Have to Pay for the Public Life." *Perspecta*, 9–10, 1965, 57–87.

"Moore Takes Yale Post." *Progressive Architecture*, 46, June 1965, 49.

"Noble Concept at Sea Ranch." *San Francisco Chronicle*, February 12, 1965.

"Portfolio of Recent Work." *Perspecta*, 9–10, 1965, 98–106.

"The Sea Ranch." *San Francisco Examiner, California Living*, August 1, 1965, 12–14, 16–19.

"Ten Buildings That Point to the Future." *Fortune*, December 1965, 179.

Whitaker, R. "Toward an Educated Architect." *American Institute of Architects Journal*, October 1965, 10.

1966

"13 Award Winning Apartments and Townhouses." *House and Home*, 29, August 1966, 64–81.

"40 under 40, Young Designs in Living." *New York Times Magazine*, April 24, 1966, 96–97, 99.

"Architectural Americana." *California Architecture*, October 1966, 20.

"Award of Merit." *House and Home*, August 1966, 68–69.

"Away from It All-Together." *Venture*, June/July 1966, 130–133.

"Building Types Study 364, The Changing Role of the Office Building." *Architectural Review*, 140, November 1966, 159–182.

"California: Second Homes Spare the Land." *Look*, June 28, 1966, 84–85.

"Citation, Recreation." *Progressive Architecture*, 47, January 1966, 150–153.

"A Condominium Castle for Week-End Living." *Fortune*, 73, May 1966, 135–137.

"Easy Living in a Rugged Country." *San Francisco Examiner*, May 22, 1966, 25.

"Ecological Architecture: Planning the Organic Environment." *Progressive Architecture*, 47, May 1966, 120–137.

"Eminent Domains." *California, The Sunday Oakland Tribune Home Magazine*, February 20, 1966, 12–13, 15.

"Environment: The California Concern." *Interiors*, 126, August 1966, 127–132.

The Faculty Club, University of California, Santa Barbara, and a Selection of Other Recent Buildings by Charles W. Moore and William Turnbull, Jr. (MLTW): An Exhibition at the Art Gallery, UCSB, November 16 through December 11, 1966, exhibtion catalog, Santa Barbara, 1966.

"Home Away from Home." *Newsweek*, January 3, 1966, 50.

"In Solitary Splendor." *Los Angeles Times Home Magazine*, June 19, 1966, 18–21.

"Introverted League Exhibit." *Progressive Architecture*, 48, June 1966, 52.

Jacobus, John. "New Forms in Architecture: The Skeleton Becomes a Frank Part of the Exterior Volume...." *Artforum*, 4, 9, May 1966, 35–39.

Lyndon, Donlyn. "Concrete Cascade in Portland." *Architectural Forum*, 125, July-August 1966, 74–79.

McCoy, E. Review of *Perspecta 9/10*, 1965. In *Arts & Architecture*, April 1966, 37–38.

"MLTW." Architectural League of New York, exhibition catalog, 1966.

Moholy-Nagy, S. "Architects without Architecture." Review of *Perspecta 9/10*, 1965. In *Progressive Architecture*, April 1966, 234, 236, 240, 246, 254, 258.

Moore, Charles W. "Creating of Place." *Image*, 4, 1966, 20–25.

————, and Canty, Donald. "The Establishment Invites You to Join in Hushed and Sumptuous Appreciation of the Several Arts LINCOLN CENTER Most Evenings Arrival Optional but Difficult." *Architectural Forum*, 125, September 1966, 71–79.

————. "New Shapes for Houses; Romantic Towers Soaring Skyward Offer One Answer to Difficult Sites," *House and Garden*, 129, January 1966, 92–99.

"New Faculty Club Drawings Shown." *Santa Barbara News-Press*, November 20, 1966.

"Redwood in the News." *Redwood News*, 2, June 1966, 15.

"The Sea Ranch." *San Francisco Magazine*, January 1966, 30–32.

"Sea Ranch Blends with Coastal Scenery." *Oakland Tribune*, August 14, 1966, 1C, 3C.

"Seeing Is Creating—Morley Baer's Art." *American Institute of Architects Journal*, 46, April 1966, 63.

"Shelter on a Scalloped Shore: Sea Ranch, California." *Sports Illustrated*, March 28, 1966, 24, 46–52.

"Superblock Points Way to New Building Type." *Architectural Record*, 140, November 1966, 180–182.

"Urban Design: Portland Parks Are Planned for People." *Architecture of the West*, November 1966, 36–37.

"Vinland Ranch." *Architectural Review*, 139, February 1966, 92.

"West Coast Casual." *New York Times Magazine*, June 26, 1966, 46–47.

1967

"5xSOM-oder die AIA-Ehrenpreise," *Bauwelt*, 27, July 1967, 666.

"The 1967 Honor Awards." *American Institute of Architects Journal*, 47, June 1967, 44–64.

"AIA Honors Six Western Projects." *Architecture West*, June 1967.

"AIA Honors 20 Buildings in National Awards Program." *Architectural Record*, 141, June 1967, 50–55.

"Architect Is Named for Project." *New Haven Journal Courier*, February 1, 1967.

"Award Winning Architect Loves His Work." *New Haven Journal Courier*, February 2, 1967.

"Award-Winning Homes." *California Architecture*, November 1967, A2–A3.

Baer, M. "Photographing Sea Ranch: An Adventure." *Innovations in Wood*, 3, 1, May 1967, 8–9.

"Bathhouse Graphics: Make It Happy Kid." *Progressive Architecture*, 48, March 1967, 156–161.

"A Box House Unboxed." *House and Garden*, 131, March 1967, 156–159.

Brown, D.S. " 'Team 10, Perspecta 10,' and the Present State of Architectural Theory." Review of *The Team 10 Primer* and *Perspecta 9/10*, 1965. In *AIP Journal*, January 1967, 46–47.

"The Designers." *Progressive Architecture*, 48, May 1967, 150–160.

"Expansive Living in One Room," *House and Garden*, 131, June 1967, 90–91.

"Experiments in Environment." *Progressive Architecture*, July 1967, 130–137.

"Un fortino a piedi nudi." *L'Architettura*, 12, January 1967, 600–601.

"Iconography and the Process of Architecture: The Jury's Conclusions." *Progressive Architecture*, 48, January 1967, 167–168.

"Implications of Giants." *Progressive Architecture*, 48, May 1967, 157–160.

"The Jewish Community Council Housing for the Elderly, New Haven." *Architectural Record*, 142, September 1967, 41.

"Karas House, Monterey, California." *Architectural Record*, 141, mid-May 1967, 112–114.

"The Lure of Living in Clustered Houses." *House and Garden*, 131, May 1967, 126–131.

Lyndon, Donlyn. "The Environment and the Market." *World Architecture*, 4, 1967, 35–36.

MLTW, exhibition catalog, University of Oregon, 1967.

Moore, Charles W. "Plug It in Rameses and See If It Lights Up, Because We Aren't Going to Keep It Unless It Works." *Perspecta*, 11, 1967, 32–43.

Moore, Charles W., and Lyndon, Donlyn. "Le Rôle de l'architecte: la création d'un lieu." *L'Architecture d'Aujourd'hui*, 60, January 1967, 72.

"Moore Designs Tower for Elderly." *Progressive Architecture*, 48, September 1967, 64.

"Moore Named Architect for Development Project." *Yale Daily News*, February 2, 1967, 1.

"A Neighborhood of Homes." *New Haven Journal-Courier*, February 7, 1967.

"Out of the Atelier and into Reality." *Progressive Architecture*, 48, September 1967, 166–169.

"Physical Sciences College, University of California, Santa Cruz." *Perspecta*, 11, 1967, 166–169.

Plumb, Barbara. "More Than Modern/Hip Baroque." *New York Times Magazine*, February 26, 1967, 79–81.

"Revolution in Architectural Education." *Progressive Architecture*, 48, March 1967, 136–147.

"Sea Ranch." *Palo Alto Times Peninsula Living*, November 18–19, 1967, 8–10, 30–31.

"Sea Ranch, Condominium I." *Deutsche Bauzeitung*, September 1967, 716–722.

"Sea Ranch, côte du pacifique États Unis." *L'Architecture d'Aujourd'hui*, 38, April 1967, 22–55.

"The Sea Ranch . . . Success Breeds Expansion." *Architecture/West*, February 1967, 9.

Smith, C. Ray. "The Permissiveness of Supermannerism." *Progressive Architecture*, 48, October 1967, 169–173.

Starlux Casts Light on a Rustic Retreat." *Creative Ideas in Glass*, 8, Spring 1967, 2–3.

"Super Graphics." *Progressive Architecture*, 48, November 1967, 133–136.

"Swim and Tennis Club." *Zodiac*, 17, 1967, 136–137.

"Ten Buildings That Point the Future." *Fortune*, December 6, 1967, 179.

"A Vacation House Where Space Is the Fun Element." *Los Angeles Times Home Magazine*, November 12, 1967, 32–35.

"Western Home Awards, Award of Merit: The Floor Rises in Four Levels." *Sunset*, October 1967, 80.

"Western Home Awards, Special Award: It's a 'Tent' Hung on Poles." *Sunset*, October 1967, 81.

1968

"6 Häuser in den U.S.A." *Deutsche Bauzeitung*, January 1968, 16–17.

"Architects at Play." *San Jose Mercury-News Magazine*, June 23, 1968, 22.

"Box Dorms for the University of Connecticut." *Progressive Architecture*, 49, June 1968, 133.

"Breaking the Rules . . . and Breaking Through." *Sunset*, April 1968, 88–95.

"Church St. So." *Connecticut Architect*, May-June 1968, 22.

"Dalla California—una finestra sull'oceano: Il 'Sea Ranch'." *Abitare*, September 1968, 20–31.

"En Californie un village neuf construit comme un paysage." *Elle*, April 1968, 110–115.

"Ferienclub am Meer, 'Sea Ranch'." *Schöner Wohnen*, November 1968, 104–109.

"Foyers bien dessinés." *Elle*, November 1968, 83, 175.

Gebhard, David, and Breton, H. von. *Architecture in California, 1868–1968*, exhibition catalog, University of California, Santa Barbara, 1968.

"In His Own House; A Noted Architect Plays Games." *House and Garden*, 133, January 1968, 110–115.

"It's Supergraphics." *Life*, May 3, 1968, 79–82.

"Die Kunst and das Heim (3). Architekt: Charles Moore, New Haven. Eigenes Haus in New Haven." *Deutsche Bauzeitung*, July 1968, 536–538.

Moore, Charles W. *The Ark Report*, January 1968.

————. "The Cannery: How It Looks to a Critic." *Architectural Forum*, 128, June 1968, 76–79.

————. "The Project at New Zion." *EYE*, 2, 1968, 18–21.

Plumb, Barbara. "Fiery Center." *New York Times Magazine*, March 17, 1968, 104.

"Portland Plaza: It's Like WOW." *Progressive Architecture*, 49, May 1968, 163–165.

"Revolution in Interior Design: The Bold New Poly-Expanded Mega-Decoration." *Progressive Architecture*, October 1968, 148–208.

"Sea Ranch California, USA." *Wood*, July 1968, 24–26.

"Seven Western Projects Honored in AIA National Awards Program." *Architecture/West*. June 1968, 22.

"Supergraphics." *Geijutsu Seikatsu*, 11, November 1968.

"Le Temps du grand soleil." *Elle*, July 1968, 88–89.

"UC Santa Cruz's Sixth College." *San Francisco Chronicle*, March 15, 1968, 6.

"Uninhibited Holiday Houses." *Interiors*, June 1968, 86.

"The Western House." *American Institute of Architects Journal*, 49, June 1968, 111–119.

"Yale Goes to Kentucky." *Interiors*, December 1968, 136–147.

1969

"Architecture without Fingerprints." *House Beautiful*, September 1969, 96.

"Arts and Architecture School Bandaged and Splinted Begins Another Year." *Yale Alumni Magazine*, October 1969, 18–19.

"Bilnachweis." *Deutsche Bauzeitung*, December 1969, 882–883.

"Citation, Rent-Supplemented Housing in Eastern Kentucky Keeps Costs Low, But Looks Like Conventional Construction." *Progressive Architecture*, 50, January 1969, 114–115.

"Club dell'Università di California, Santa Barbara, USA." *L'Architettura*, August 1969, 256–257.

"Coloniale + purismo + pop." *L'Architettura*, 15, August 1969, 256–257.

Drawings of Architectural Interiors, edited by J. Pile, New York, 1969, 108–111.

"Gallery House." *New York Times Magazine*, September 21, 1969, 82–83.

Gebhard, David. "Pop Scene for Profs." *Architectural Forum*, 130, March 1969, 78–85.

"House of Our Time, Latticed with Light." *House and Garden*, 136, October 1969, 118–123.

"McElrath House, Santa Cruz, Calif." *Architectural Record*, 145, May 1969, 46–47.

Moore, Charles W. "Dream House in the Country." *New York Times Real Estate Section*, November 23, 1969, 1, 10.

————. "Greatest Advance in 200 Years: The Nail." *House and Garden*, 136, October 1969, 30, 32, 38.

————. "Toward a New Spirit of '76." *Avant Garde*, July 1969.

"New Haven Haven." *Playboy*, October 1969, 126.

"New Pow with Paint." *American Home*, April 1969, 56–57.

Plumb, B. *Young Designs in Living*, New York, 1969.

Scully, Vincent. *American Architecture and Urbanism*, New York, 1969.

Stern, Robert A. M. *New Directions in American Architecture*, New York, 1969.

"Student Architects Show How." *House and Garden Guide for Young Living*, Spring-Summer 1969, 48–51.

Thompson, Elizabeth K. "College Buildings and Planning." *Architectural Record*, 145, May 1969, 145–154.

"Town Houses, Four Major Currents: The Geometrical Abstract Movement." *Realities*, October 1969, 42–43.

"USA. Faculty Club. Santa Barbara Calif. Moore/Turnbull. Bravo Mister Moore . . . ." *L'Architecture d'Aujourd'hui*, 145, September 1969, xx.

"Western Home Awards Jury." *Sunset*, October 1969, 86–87.

"Winning Western Homes." *Progressive Architecture*, October 1969, 67.

"Yale Changes." *Connecticut Architect*, 6, November/December 1969, 27.

"Yale School of Arts and Architecture Reorganized." *Architectural Record*, 10, October 1969, 36.

1970

"70 Talets Sommar-Noje For Alla." *VI*, September 1970, 16–21.

Aloi, R. *Nuove Ville*, Milan, 1970.

"Award of Merit." *House and Home*, July 1970, 70.

"Charles Moore." *Korea Architect*, November 1970, 44–61.

"Citation, MLTW/Moore, Turnbull, Project: The University of California at Santa Cruz, College 6, Santa Cruz, California." *Progressive Architecture*, 51, January 1970, 82–83.

"Il Colore è Un Segnale." *Domus*, November 1970, 21–25.

Connecticut Architect, May–June 1970, 22.

"Connecticut Honor Award Winners." *Connecticut Architect*, November 1970, 7–9.

"Cost-Cutting Supergraphics." *American Home*, October 1970, 62–63.

"A Custom House That Budget Built." *American Home*, July 1970, 52–53.

"Extensions of a Design Device." *Progressive Architecture*, 51, April 1970, 88–93.

"Filmmilieu: Klubhaus der Architektur—Facultät der University of California, Santa Barbara." *Baumeister*, 67, October 1970, 1151–1153.

"First Design Award, MLTW/Moore, Lyndon, Turnbull, Project: Pembroke College Dormitories, Brown University, Providence, Rhode Island." *Progressive Architecture*, 51 January 1970, 130–135.

"Four Centuries of American Style: Communal Living, Cloistered and Convivial, Spans Two Centuries." *American Home*, February 1970, 42–43.

Gebhard, David. "West Coast Report: L.A.—The Stuccoed Box." *Art In America*, 58, May–June 1970, 130–133.

Gilliatt, M. *Kitchens and Dining Rooms*, New York, 1970.

"Heirs to the Coming Age." *Japan Architect*, July 1970, 50–51.

"How Architect and Owner Create the Personal House." *House and Garden*, 137, January 1970, 64–75.

"Laurence Halprin Makes the City Scene." *Design and Environment*, Fall 1970, 56–58.

"Lots of Character in New Project." *The Hartford Courant Real Estate and Home*, September 27, 1970, 1–2.

"Middletown." *House and Home*, March 1970, 79.

MLTW/Moore, Lyndon, Turnbull and Whitaker: The Sea Ranch, California. 1966–. Edited and photographed by Yukio Futagawa. Text by William Turnbull, Jr. Tokyo, 1970 (Global Architecture Series, 3).

"Mathematics at Yale." *Architectural Forum*, 133, July/August 1970, 62–67.

"Mathematics at Yale: Readers Respond." *Architectural Forum*, 133, October 1970, 64–66.

"Naff House, Pajero Dunes, Calif." *Architectural Record*, 147, mid-May 1970, 30–31.

"Pleasantness Made to Order." *Fortune*, February 1970, 137–143.

Plumb, Barbara. "Playing the Angles." *New York Times Magazine*, February 15, 1970, 94–95.

"Rep Theatre Painted." *Yale Daily News*, October 8, 1970.

Schulze, Franz. "Chaos as Architecture." *Art in America*, 58, July 1970, 88–96.

"Show Worlds for Osaka." U.S. Pavilion Exhibition, Osaka World's Fair, 1970.

"Star-Struck Environments." *New York Times Magazine, Part 2, The Home*, September 27, 1970, 56–57.

"Supergraphics Are Good for You." *Ameryka*, 168, October 1970, 28–29. [USIA for USSR. Also published in *Ameryka*, 141, October 1970, 28–29 (USIA for Poland).]

"A View of Contemporary World Architecture." *Japan Architect*, 45, July 1970, special issue.

"Yale A and A: Restructured and Still Going Strong." *Architectural Record*, March 1970, 37.

"Your Point of View." *Progressive Architecture*, May 1970, 6.

1971

"Adventures for the Eye in a Young Family's Hilltop House." *House and Garden*, September 1971.

"Charles W. Moore." *Kenchiku Bunka*, 26, April 1971, 86–106.

"Factory/House Charles W. Moore Centerbrook." *A + U*, January 1971, 89.

"Grandeur and Intimacy." *On the Sound*, March 1971, 98–100.

"Honor Award: Name for It Is Barnhouse." *Sunset*, October 1971, 88.

"Houses in U.S.A." *Global Interiors*, 1, 1971, 128–135.

Jencks, Charles. *Architecture 2000: Predictions and Methods*, New York, 1971.,

Moore, Charles W. "Eleven Agonies and One Euphoria." *Michigan Society of Architects Monthly Bulletin*, February 1971, 2–3. [Also published in *Environmental Design/West*, May-June 1972, 14–15.]

———. and Allen, Gerald. "Church Street South Housing In New Haven." *Architect's Yearbook*, 13, 1971, 208–215.

"More Competitions." *Architectural Forum*, March 1971, 22.

"Some Homes Are 'Shrines'." *The Nashville Tennessean*, June 27, 1971, 3.

"Two New Haven Area Architects Win New England Region Awards." *New Haven Register*, January 24, 1971, 1–2.

Wauthier, Bernard, "Faculty Club, Université de California, Santa Barbara," *L'Architecture d'Aujourd'hui*, 157, August–September 1971, 60–61.

———. "Klotz House, Westerly, Rhode Island." *L'Architecture d'Aujourd'hui*, 157, August–September 1971, 62–63.

———. "Koizim House, Westport, Connecticut." *L'Architecture d'Aujourd'hui*, 157, August–September 1971, 64–65.

1972

"1972 Design Awards for Non-Profit Sponsored Low and Moderate Income Housing." *AIA Journal*, November 1972, 38–42.

Chermayeff, I. *Observations in American Architecture*, New York, 1972.

Crandall, Chuck. *They Chose to Be Different: Unusual California Homes*, San Francisco, 1972, 55–58, 107–110, 115–118.

"Housing: Low-Moderate Baroque." *Progressive Architecture*, 53, May 1972, 74–83.

Jencks, Charles, and Silver, N. *Adhocism: The Case for Improvisation*, New York, 1972, 166.

"Living with Light." *House and Garden Building Guide*, Fall/Winter 1972, 150–155.

"Metaphors of Habitation." Exhibition catalog, School of Architecture, University of Maryland, March-April 1972.

Moore, Charles W. "How Much Is a Monument Worth?" *Society of Architectural Historians Journal.*, 31, October 1972, 225.

"Private Residence." *Architectural Record*, 151, mid-May 1972, 60–63.

"The Seat in the Window." *Sunset*, February 1972, 75–77.

Sharp, D. *A Visual History of Twentieth-Century Architecture*, New York, 1972, 278–279, 294.

Skurka, N., and Gili, O. *Underground Interiors, Decorating for Alternative Life Styles*, London, 1972, 86–89.

"Yale Repertory Theater." *Connecticut*, February 1972, cover.

1973

Allen, Gerald. "Mapping Out Realms for the Body and Mind and Memory." *Architectural Record*, 154, September 1973, 133–135.

"An Apartment Complex That Rejuvenates." *House Beautiful* (special issue, *Decorating for Brides*), Spring/Summer 1973, 74–77.

"Beach House, Santa Cruz County." *American Institute of Architects Journal*, 59, May 1973, 46–47.

"Binker Barn." *Architectural Record*, 153, mid-May 1973, 74–75.

"Church Street South Housing." *Architecture and Urbanism*, June 1973, 47–50.

"Church Street South, New Haven." *Baumeister*, 70, January 1973, 33–35.

"Church Street South Housing Square, New Haven." *Architecture and Urbanism*, August 1973, 110.

Cook John, and Klotz, Heinrich. *Conversations with Architects*, New York, 1973.

Gebhard, David; Montgomery, R.; Woodbridge, J.; and Woodbridge, S. *A Guide to Architecture in San Francisco and Northern California*, Santa Barbara, 1973.

"A House on Monterey Bay, California." *L'Architecture d'Aujourd'hui,*, 45, May-June 1973, XVII.

Jencks, Charles. *Modern Movements in Architecture*, Garden City, 1973, 222–225.

Moore, Charles W. "In Similar States of Undress." *Architectural Forum*, 138, May 1973, 53-54.

————. "Schindler: Vulnerable and Powerful." *Progressive Architecture*, 54, January 1973, 132, 136.

"Out of the Blue." *Progressive Architecture*, 54, May 1973, 106–107.

"Portland Center, Lovejoy Plaza." *Architecture and Urbanism*, August 1973, 23–25.

"Vacation House of the Month." *American Home*, June 1973, 30–32.

1974

Allen, Gerald. "Found: The World as a Candy Box." *Architectural Record*, 156, December 1974, 126–131.

"Another America, Kresge College, University of California, Santa Cruz." *Architectural Review* 156, July 1974, 28–31.

"Architect and Owner Develop Solar Energy Systems for New Home." *Architectural Record*, 155, February 1974, 36.

"Barn House." *Architecture and Urbanism*, October 1974, 48–57.

"Berichte-USA East." *Architektur Aktuell*, 1974, 16–18.

"Centerbrook House." *Toshi Jutaku*, January 1974, 84–86.

"Einrichtungshaus in San Francisco." *Baumeister*, 71, August 1974, 895–897, 909.

Ellis, W. "Forum: Stocktaking." *Oppositions* 4, 1974, 165–167.

Fitzgibbons, Ruth Miller. "On-Campus Living: A Test of Multiple Choice." *Interiors*, 134, November 1974, 86–89.

"A Funky Village with Elegant Piazzas." *Interiors*, 134, October 1974, 122R-127R.

Goldberger, Paul. "Should Anyone Care about the 'New York Five'? . . . or about their Critics, the 'Five on Five'?" *Architectural Record*, 155, February 1974, 113–116.

Houses in USA, edited by Yukio Futagawa, Tokyo, 1974 (Global Interior Series, 6).

Moore, Charles W. "After a New Architecture: The Best Shape for a Chimera." *Oppositions*, 3, 1974, 1–16.

————; Allen, Gerald; and Lyndon, Donlyn. *The Place of Houses*, New York, 1974. An excerpt was also published in *Lotus* 8, September 1974, 8–37.

————. "Sea Ranch: A Second Look." *Architectural Record*, 156, November 1974, 129–132.

Schmertz, M. "Vincent Scully versus Charles Moore." Review of Charles W. Moore, Gerald Allen, and Donlyn Lyndon, *The Place of Houses*, 1974, and Vincent Scully, *The Shingle Style Today or the Historian's Revenge*, 1974. In *Architectural Record*, 156, December 1974, 45.

Scully, Vincent. *The Shingle Style Today or the Historian's Revenge*, New York, 1974.

"Sculpted for Space." *House Beautiful Building Manual*, Spring/Summer 1974, 126–131.

"Solar Thermos House." *Architectural Forum*, 140 January–February, 1974, 16–17.

"Sunpower." *Architecture Plus*, September/October 1974, 90.

Villecco, Marguerite. "Sun Power." *Architecture Plus*, 2, September–October 1974, 85–89.

"Whitman Village, Kresge College." *Toshi Jutaku*, September 1974, 93.

Woodbridge, Sally. "How to Make a Place." *Progressive Architecture*, 55, May 1974, 76–83, 118.

The Yale Mathematics Building Competition: Architecture for a Time of Questioning, edited by Charles W. Moore and Nicholas Pyle, New Haven, 1974.

1975

Allen, Gerald. "Discrimination in Housing Design." *Architectural Record*, 157, March 1975, 141–156.

"Un attualità dell'architettura U.S.A." *Controspazio*, 7, September 1975, 2–75.

"The Bay Window Idea Gets a Pushing Around." *Sunset*, February 1975, 70–72.

"Charles W. Moore, Project, Condominium Hotel/Project, Goodman House/Housing, Middletown/Lovejoy Plaza." In "Special Feature. White and Gray: Eleven Modern American Architects," edited by Peter D. Eisenman and Robert A. M. Stern, *Architecture and Urbanism*, April 1975, 91, 115–124.

"Concept: Building in Tune to the Environment." *Möbel Interior Design*, 21, December 1975, 30–33.

Davis, Jack. "The Dazzling Piazza That Might Have Been," *New Orleans States-Item*, January 29, 1975.

"A Flight of Fancy." *House Beautiful Home Remodeling*, Fall/Winter 1975, 181–183.

Goldberger, Paul. "Collage of a House." *New York Times Magazine*, November 9, 1975, 74–76.

"Kresge College, Santa Cruz, USA." *Baumeister*, 72, September 1975, 797–800.

Lyndon, Donlyn, "5 Ways to People Places." *Architectural Record*, 158, September 1975, 89–94.

MLTW: Houses by MLTW: Moore, Lyndon, Turnbull & Whitaker, Vol. One, 1959–1975, text by Donlyn Lyndon, edited and photographed by Yukiuo Futagawa, Tokyo, 1975.

MacMasters, Dan. "The Dream Expressed." *Los Angeles Times Home Magazine*, April 20, 1975, 12–15.

Moore Charles W. "How to Get More House for Your Money." *House and Garden*, 147, January 1975, 60.

————. Review of James F. O'Gorman, *Selected Drawings: H. H. Richardson and his Office*, Boston, 1975. In *Society of Architectural Historians Journal*, 34, December 1975, 323–324.

————. Review of Vincent Scully, *The Shingle Style Today, or the Historian's Revenge*, 1974, In *Progressive Architecture*, 56, April 1975, 112, 114.

————. "Southernness." *Perspecta*, 15, 1975, 9–17.

————. "Where Are We Now, Vincent Scully?" *Progressive Architecture*, 56, April 1975, 78–83.

"New Perspectives Open a Thirties Bungalow." *Interiors*, 134, July 1975, 78r–81r.

Newhouse, Nancy. "Little Egypt." *New York Magazine*, 8, May 26, 1975, 64–65.

"One Point of View." *Progressive Architecture*, 56, April 1975, 92–93.

"Prologue." In "Special Feature. White and Gray: Eleven Modern Architects," edited by Peter D. Eisenman and Robert A. M. Stern. *Architecture and Urbanism*, April 1975, 2–4.

Ryder, Sharon Lee. "One Point of View; Interior Architecture: Charles Moore House." *Progressive Architecture*, 56, April 1975, 92–93.

"School, Kresge College." *Architecture and Urbanism*, May 1975, 44–56.

Smith, C. Ray. "The House That's Inside Out." *Interiors*, 134, January 1975, 104R–107R, 137R, 139R.

Solomon, D. "Five and Dime Architects." *Design Quarterly*, 97, 1975, 18–19, 24.

Stern, Robert A. M. "Towards an Architecture of Symbolic Assemblage." *Progressive Architecture*, 56, April 1975, 72–77.

Sturgis, R. Review of Charles W. Moore, Gerald Allen, and Donlyn Lyndon, *The Place of Houses*, 1974. In *Landscape Architecture*, July 1975, 330–331.

"Sunworks." *Popular Science*, May 1975, 77–140.

1976

Agrest, Diana. "5. Portrait d'un artiste. Form Diggers (1)." Fifth of five essays in "Dossier: Charles W. Moore. Moore is More. Cinq portraits pour Chuck." *L'Architecture d'Aujourd'hui*, 184, March–April 1976, 54–57.

"Charles Moore." *Dortmunder Architekturausstellung 1976, Katalog* (May 1976), *Dortmunder Architeckturhefte no. 3*, Dortmund, 1976.

"Citation, August Perez & Associates." *Progressive Architecture*, January 1976, 82–83.

"Connecticut Solar Heated Armory Underway." *New England Construction*, November 15, 1976, 18–19.

"Country Federal Savings Bank, Green Farms, Connecticut, by Moore Grover Harper." *Architectural Record*, 159, January 1976, 94–95.

Creese, Walter L. Review of Charles Moore, Gerald Allen, and Donlyn Johnson, *The Place of Houses*, New York, 1974. In *Society of Architectural Historians Journal*, 35, March 1976, 64–65.

"A Decade of Dramatic Building with Redwood at Sea Ranch." *Redwood News*, Winter/Spring 1976, 3–4.

Gangneux, Marie-Christine. "3. Portrait d'un professeur: Fun and Frolics," Third of five essays in "Dossier: Charles W. Moore. Moore is More. Cinq portraits pour Chuck." *L'Architecture d'Aujourd'hui*, 184, March–April 1976, 24–25.

Gebhard, David, and King, Susan. *A View of California Architecture: 1960–1976*, San Francisco, 1976.

Ismet, S. "Réflexions sur l'œuvre et la pensée de Charles Moore." *L'Architecture d'Aujourd'hui*, 188, December 1976, vii–viii.

Israël, Franklin. "4. Portrait d'un acteur. Accommodating Ragtime." Fourth of five essays in "Dossier: Charles W. Moore. Moore is More. Cinq portraits pour Chuck." *L'Architecture d'Aujourd'hui*, 184, March–April 1976, 27–29.

Jordy, William H. "Making the Ordinary Extraordinary." *Progressive Architecture*, 57, February 1976, 47–53.

"Kresge College, University of California, Santa Cruz."
L'Architecture d'Aujourd'hui, 184, March 1976, 58–61.

Lewin, Susan Grant. "Gently It Sits There—but Step Inside and Shazam!" *House Beautiful*, 118, May 1976, 118–121.

Machado, Rodolfo. "Toward a Theory of Remodelling; Old Buildings as Palimpsest." *Progressive Architecture*, 57, November 1976, 46–49.

Moore, Charles W. "Après 'Roq' et 'Rob'." *L'Architecture d'Aujourd'hui*, 184, March–April 1976, 2–4.

———. "1. Autoportrait. Moore vs. Moore. " First of five essays in "Dossier: Charles W. Moore. Moore is More. Cinq portraits pour Chuck." *L'Architecture d'Aujourd'hui*, 184, March–April 1976, 2–4.

———. "Bad, Bad Bodie: Mines, Saloons, and Nightly Shoot-Outs Are of the Past; but What Remains Today Is Well Worth Visiting." *Americana*, 4, July 1976, 2–5.

———. "Conclusion." *Oppositions*, 6, 1976, 20–21.

———. "Foreword." *The Form of Housing*, edited by Sam Davis, New York, 1976, v–vi.

———. "I Think That All of Us . . ." *Lotus*, 13, December 1976, 36–37.

———, and Allen, Gerald. *Dimensions: Space, Shape, and Scale in Architecture*, New York, 1976. [Published in French as *L'architecture sensible: espace, echelle et forme*, translated by Ph. Deshayes and D. Duke, Paris, 1981.]

Morton, David, and Stephens, Suzanne. "Introduction; the House as a Relevant Object." *Progressive Architecture*, 57, August 1976, 37–39.

Quinn, Michael C., and Tucker, Paul H. "Drawings for Modern Public Architecture in New Haven." Yale University Art Gallery, 1976.

"Real Dream Houses." *Newsweek*, October 4, 1976, 66–69.

"Record Interiors of 1976." *Architectural Record*, January 1976, 94–95.

"Round-Up, More Moore. *L'Architecture d'Aujourd'hui*, March/April 76, *Architectural Design*, 46, July 1976, 438.

Stern, Robert A. M. "Gray Architecture: Quelques variations post-moderniste autour de l'orthodoxie," *L'Architecure d'Aujourd'hui*, 186, August–September 1976, 83.

Wauthier, Bernard, "2. Portrait d'un professional: Peppermint Twist." Second of five essays in "Dossier: Charles W. Moore. Moore is More. Cinq Portraits pour Chuck." *L'Architectrure d'Aujourd'hui*, 184, March–April 1976, 13–14.

1977

Andrews, Wayne. *Architecture in America*, New York, 1977.

"Armory for the Armed Forces Reserve." *Journal of Architectural Education*, February 1977, 51.

Bloomer, Kent C., and Moore, Charles W. *Body, Memory and Architecture*, New Haven, 1977.

Broadbent, Geoffrey. "A Plain Man's Guide to the Theory of Signs in Architecture." *Architectural Design*, 47, 7/8, 1977, 474–482.

"Charles Moore." *Architectural Design*, 47, 6, 1977, 405–406, 435.

"Citation, Moore Grover Harper/Lorenz Williams, Lively Likens & Partners." *Progressive Architecture*, January 1977, 84–85.

"Community Design: by the People." *Progressive Architecture*, 3, December 1977, 150–164.

"Educators Round Table." *Journal of Architectural Education*, February 1977, 2–5.

Filler, Martin. "They Knew What They Wanted, but Got More Than That, Too," *Progressive Architecture*, 58, September 1977, 80–83.

Goldberger, Paul. "More Than Meets the Eye." *New York Times Magazine*, January 16, 1977, 46–47.

———. "Post-Modernism: An Introduction." In "AD Profiles 4: Post Modernism." *Architectural Design*, 47, 4, 1977, 256–260.

Hoekema, James. "Drawing toward Architectural Drawings." *Artforum*, 16, December 1977, 44–47.

Jencks, Charles. *The Language of Post-Modern Architecture*, New York, 1977.

Moore, Charles W. "Alcoves." *Global Architecture, Houses*, 2, 1977, 4–7.

———. "A Great Architect Looks At California Architecture," *Mademoiselle*, 83, April 1977, 100–102.

———. "Charles Moore on Post-Modernism." In "AD Profiles 4: Post Modernism." *Architectural Design*, 47, 4, 1977, 255.

———, and Oliver, Richard B. "Magic, Nostalgia and a Hint of Greatness in the Workaday World of the Building Types Study." *Architectural Record*, 161, April 1977, 118–137.

Oliver, Richard B. "In 1923 Le Corsbusier..." In "AD Profiles 6: America Now, Drawing Toward a More Modern Architecture," edited by Robert A. M. Stern. *Architectural Design*, 47, 1977, 444–446.

"Norwich Armory Maintenance Shop." *Design Quarterly*, 103, 1977, 28.

Plumb, Barbara. *Houses Architects Live In*, New York, 1977.

Princeton's Beaux Arts and Its New Academicism: From Labatut to the Program of Geddes, exhibition catalog, Institute for Architecture and Urban Studies, New York, 1977.

Schuler, Stanley. *How to Design and Build a Fireplace*, New York, 1977.

Skuda, Fleming. "American Impulses 1965–1975." *Arkitekten*, 79, February 22, 1977, 61–67.

Smith, C. Ray. *Supermannerism, New Attitudes in Post-Modern Architecture*, New York, 1977.

Schmertz, Mildred F. "Two Houses by Charles Moore." *Architectural Record*, 161, June 1977, 109–116.

Stern, Robert A. M. "Something Borrowed, Something New." *Horizon*, 20, December 1977, 50–57.

Tanizaki, Jun'ichiro. *In Praise of Shadows*, Connecticut, 1977. Foreword by Charles Moore.

"Under Victorian Wraps a Riot of Color." *House Beautiful Home Remodeling*, Summer 1977, 136–139.

"Whitman Village, Huntington, N.Y." *Baumeister*, 74, January 1977. 40–41.

1978

"Active/Passive Systems and Eclectic Touches Combine with Ease in Connecticut Armory." *Architectural Record*, 164, mid-August, 1978, 88–89.

"Airslie House, Cold Spring Harbor Laboratory, New York, 1974." *Global Architecture, Houses*, 5, December 1978, 142–147.

Allen, Gerald. "Benign Perversity." *Extra Issue: The Work of Charles W. Moore, Architecture and Urbanism*, May 1978, 41–46.

Allende, Gabriel. "Del encanto de los geodos y huevos de pascua rusos a la correcta *sorpresa* en la arquitectura; Charles W. Moore." *Arquitectura*, 215, November–December 1978, 66–68, 81.

"Art: Architectural Drawings." *Architectural Digest*, 35, March 1978, 78–83.

"Barn Renovation." *Architectural Record*, 163, mid-May 1978, 56–57.

Bletter, Rosemarie Haag. "Rite of Passage and Place." *Extra Issue: The Work of Charles W. Moore, Architecture and Urbanism*, May 1978, 60–67.

Burns, Leland S. "Distance in Space and Time in a House Design—On Burns House." *Extra Issue: The Work of Charles W. Moore, Architecture and Urbanism*, May 1978, 53–59.

"By Design a Zoned House Saves Energy." *House and Garden Building Guide*, Winter 1978, 70–73.

Campbell, Craig S. *Water in Landscape Architecture*, New York, 1978.

"Charles Moore and Associates, Burns House." In "AD Profile 10: Post-Modern History." *Architectural Design*, 48, 1, 1978, 34–37.

"Charles Moore Has Been Named Head of the UCLA Architecture/Urban Design Program..." *Architectural Design*, 48, 8/9, 1978, 505.

"Convention '78 a Lively Discussion about Design." *AIA Journal*, July 1978, 22–90.

Cornell University. *Architecture and Media*, Riverdesign, video-tape.

Davis, Douglas. "Designs for Living." *Newsweek*, November 6, 1978, 82–91.

"D-zign Debated." *Progressive Architecture*, 59, June 1978, 23.

"Engineer, Architect Design Together." *House and Garden Building Guide*, Summer 1978, 76–78.

Filler, Martin. "Extra Sensory Perceptions." *Progressive Architecture*, 59, April 1978, 82–85.

———, "The Magic Fountain." *Progressive Architecture*, 59, November 1978, 81–87.

———. "Rooms for Improvement." *Progressive Architecture*, 59, December 1978, 76–77.

———. "Traveler from an Antique Land." *Extra Issue: The Work of Charles W. Moore, Architecture and Urbanism*, May 1978, 68–75.

Filson, Ronald. "The Magic Fountain of the Piazza d'Italia." *Arquitectura*, 215, November–December 1978, 59–65, 82.

Gebhard, David. "Charles Moore and the West Coast." *Extra Issue: The Work of Charles W. Moore, Architecture and Urbanism*, May 1978, 47–52.

Gropp, Louis. *Solar Houses*, New York, 1978.

Hines, Thomas. Review of *Bay Area Houses*. In *Progressive Architecture*, May 1978, 119–122.

Hoyt, Charles King. *Buildings for Commerce and Industry*, New York, 1978.

"In Tune with Nature." *House and Garden*, July 1978, 96–99.

Ishii, Kazuhiro. "Deliberate Regression from Modern Architecture: Eleven Points." *Extra Issue: The Work of Charles W. Moore, Architecture and Urbanism*, May 1978, 25–35.

Jencks, Charles. "AD Profile 10: Post Modern History." *Architectural Design*, 48, 1, 1978, 11–26, 48–56.

Klotz, Heinrich. "The Principles and the Context of Architecture: Two Projects by James Stirling and Charles Moore." *Lotus*, 18, March 1978, 42–51.

Lyndon, Donlyn. "Immanence: The Indwelling Spirit." *Extra Issue: The Work of Charles W. Moore, Architecture and Urbanism*, May 1978, 36–40.

"Maison Isham, Sagaponack, N.Y." *L'Architecture d'Aujourd'hui*, 200, December 1978, 73–75.

McGrath, Norman and Molly. *Children's Spaces*, New York, 1978.

Moore, Charles W. "As a Disneyland, We Already Had the Future: It Was the 50's." *American Institute of Architects Journal*, 67, mid-May 1978, 161.

———. "Faculty Club Universität von Californien Santa Barbara Calif." *Bauen und Wohnen*, 32, July–August 1978, 313–315.

———. "Impressions of Japanese Architecture." *Japan Architect*, 53, February 1978, 5–6.

———. "Introduction," In Alma and Deirdre McArdle, *Carpenter Gothic: Nineteenth Century Ornamented Houses of New England*, New York, 1978.

Moore, Charles W. "Introduction and Personal Statement." *Extra Issue: The Work of Charles W. Moore, Architecture and Urbanism*, May 1978, 5–25.

———. "A Post-Modernist Speaks, Or How to Feel Just Plain Good about Architecture." *North Carolina Architect*, 25, 6, November–December 1978, 20–21.

———. "Shinkenchiku Residential Design Competition, Judge: Charles W. Moore. Advice from the Judge." *Japan Architect*, 53, January 1978, 6–7.

"New Haven Senior Housing." *Progressive Architecture*, 59, April 1978, 54.

"Pembroke, Church Street South, Kresge." *Baumeister*, July 1978, 582.

Peters, Paulhans. "Aspekte einer neuen Freiheit in der Architektur." *Baumeister*, December 1978, 1041–1114.

"Setti e balconi a mare, anti-uragano." *L'Architettura*, 23, January 1978, 526–527.

"Shinefield House, San Francisco, California, USA, 1968–1978." *Global Architecture, Houses*, 5, December 1978, 148–155.

"Solar Armory Shows How to Cut Energy Use 30%." *Professional Builder*, July 1978, 131.

Solar Architecture, Process Architecture #6, Tokyo, 1978.

"Tech House." *Spinoff* (NASA Annual Report), 1978, 46–47.

Trends in Contemporary Architecture, exhibition catalog, New Gallery of Contemporary Art, Cleveland, 1978.

"Uninhibited Holiday Houses." *Architecture and Urbanism*, May 1978, 85–88.

1979

Abercrombie, Stanley. "Rooms for the Federal Design Assembly, Washington, D.C." *Interiors*, 138, January 1979, 90–95.

American Academy and Institute of Arts and Letters, *Exhibition of Work by Newly Elected Members and Recipients of Honors and Awards*, exhibition catalog, New York, 1979.

"Architects Who Excel in Using Sunshine Wisely." *Building: A House and Garden Guide*, Spring, 1979, 84–85 +.

"Bad Men and Architecture." *Co-Evolution Quarterly*, Spring 1979, 137.

"Barn in Maryland, Converted into a Second Home." *Global Architecture, Houses*, 6, 1979, 132–141.

"Baths Go High Style." *House and Garden Kitchen and Bath Guide*, 1979, 138–139.

"Bewegliche Wandeverandern Licht und Raum." *Architektur und Wohnen*, March 1979, 8–15.

"Beyond Modernism, Book of Lists." *Progressive Architecture*, 60, December 1979, 56.

Bletter, Rosemarie Haag. Review of *Five Architects*, New York, 1975, and "Five on Five," *Architectural Forum*, 157, May 1973. In *Society of Architectural Historians Journal*, 38, May 1979, 205–207.

Blyth, Jeffrey. "Guinea Pig Residents: Test Occupation of a Prototype Experimental Low Energy House at the Langley Research Center." *Building Design*, 448, June 8, 1979, 26.

Buildings for Best Products, exhibition catalog, foreword by Philip Johnson, Museum of Modern Art, New York, ca. 1979.

Cameron, George. "Charles Moore at Plymouth." *Royal Institute of British Architects Journal*, 4, April 1979, 181.

"Carpenter Gothic: 19th Century Ornamented Houses of New England." *Royal Institute of British Architects Journal*, 1, January 1979, 11.

"Changing Spaces with Moving Walls." *House and Garden*, February 1979, 114–119.

Clark, Roger; Pause, Michael, et al. "Special Issue. Analysis of Precedent: An Investigation of Elements, Relationships, and Ordering Ideas in the Work of Eight Architects (Aalto, Kahn, Moore, Stirling, Mitchell Giurgola, Le Corbusier, Palladio, and Venturi & Rauch)." *North Carolina State University. The Student Publication of the School of Design*, 28, 1979, 1-228.

"Connecticut Architects Recieve Honor Awards. *Architectural Record*, March 1979, 44.

Davis, Douglas. "Architecture in the 1970's." *Dialogue*, December 1979, 47–57.

"Designing on TV: Charles Moore and Chad Floyd Prove It Can Be Done." *Architectural Record*, 166, December 1979, 101.

Douglas, Lake. "Piazza d'Italia." *Architectural Review*, 165, May 1979, 255–256.

Drexler, Arthur. *Transformations in Modern Architecture*, New York, 1979, 147, 155, 163.

"Erbe Verpflichtet zum Restaurieren." *Architektur & Wohnen*, January 1979, 8–11.

Filler, Martin, and Torre, Susanna. "Moore Ruble Yudell." *Design Quarterly*, 109, 1979, 24–31.

"Four Ways of Furnishing a Bathroom." *Casa Vogue*, June 1979, 135.

Goldberger, Paul. "Humanizing the House." *House and Garden*, February 1979, 108–150.

———. "New Orleans' New Plaza Is a Wild and Mad Vision." *New York Times*, February 9, 1979, 138.

"Grand Illusion." *Diversion*, May 1979, 229–232.

Gregory, Daniel; Pastier, John; Lym, Glen Robert. "UC Santa Cruz: Site and Planning, Architecture and Kresge College." *American Institute of Architects Journal*, 68, August 1979, 35–55, 70.

"Guide to Architect-Designed Houses, West." *Town and Country*, October 1979.

Hughes, Robert. "Mr. Architetto ad una svolte." *Casa Vogue*, June 1979, 168–176.

———. "Doing Their Own Thing (Post-Modernism in Architecture)." *Time*, 113, January 8, 1979, 52–58.

Irace, Fulvio. "Lasciatemi giocare in pace, l'architettura è una cosa seria." *Modo*, 3, 23, October 1979, 39–43.

"Isham Residence, Sagaponack, New York." *Architectural Record*, 165, mid-May 1979, 84–85.

Ishii, Kazuhiro. "Moore at Work, Less in the Drafting Room; Practical Education the Charles Moore Way." *Japan Architect*, 54, February 1979, 7.

Jencks, Charles. Reviews of Charles Moore, Gerald Allen, *Dimensions, Space, Shape, and Scale in Architecture*, and Kent C. Bloomer and Charles Moore, *Body, Memory, and Architecture*. In *Journal of the Society of Architectural Historians*, 38, March 1979, 50–52.

"Kaleidoscope." *AIA Journal*, mid-May 1979, 153.

Kallmeyer, Lothar. "Funktionalismus und Widerspruch." *Kunst und Kirche*, March 1979, 113–122.

LeCuyer, Annette. "Fountains of Pleasure: Charles Moore's Monument to New Orleans." *Building Design*, 464, September 21, 1979, 22–24.

———. "Scourge of the International Style: Charles Moore at the Architectural Association." *Building Design*, 431, February 2, 1979, 2.

McGuire, Penny. "Moore Goes Further." *Building Design*, 454, July 13, 1979, 22–23.

"A Mix That Suits Past and Present." *New York Times Magazine*, March 25, 1979, 66–80.

Moore, Charles W. "Charles Moore Says." *Japan Architect*, 54, February 1979, 64–66.

"Parole et Fatras." *L'Architecture d'Aujourd'hui*, September 1979, 66–70.

"Prime Time Programming to Spark Public Interest in Roanoke's Renewal Plan." *WDBJ-7-TV Produces*, April 1979.

"The Quiet Americans: Venturi and Moore in London." *International Architect*, 1, 5, 1979, 2.

"A Rebirth in Roanoke." *Commonwealth* (Va.), March 1979, 25–28.

"Rooms for the Federal Design Assembly." *Progressive Architecture*, 60, January 1979, 90–95.

Ross, M.F. "Local Color." *Residential Interiors*, 4 November 1979, 78–85.

Rubino, Luciano. "Il superamento del moderno." *Ville e Giardini*, 136, July–August 1979, 30–32.

"Shaping Space with Moving Walls." *Washington Star Home Life*, August 5, 1979, 8–11.

Taylor, Lisa, ed. *Urban Open Spaces*, exhibition catalog, Cooper-Hewitt Museum, New York, 1979.

"Three under One Roof." *House and Garden Building Guide*, Winter 1979, 74–75.

"Town Houses in the USA." *Toshi Jutaku*, April 1979, 52–55.

Turnbull, Jeff. "Morality and the Architecture of Charles Moore." *Transition*, 1, July 1979, 14–21.

"Vacationing Now Retiring Later." *House Beautiful Building Manual*, Spring/Summer 1979, 154–155.

Views. *Progressive Architecture*, February 1979, 8.

Views. *Progressive Architecture*, March 1979, 14.

Watson, Donald. "Insolutions." *Progressive Architecture*, November 1979, 102–107.

1980

Abercrombie, Stanley. "Ornament." *AIA Journal*, December 1980, 26–30.

Allen, Gerald. *Charles Moore*, New York, 1980.

———, and Pallasmaa, Juhani. *Creation and Recreation: America Draws*, exhibition catalog, Helsinki, 1980.

Archer, B. J., ed. *Houses for Sale*, exhibition catalog, Leo Castelli Gallery, New York, 1980.

Beebe, Tina. "Coloring Space." *Special Issue: Charles Moore and Company. Global Architecture, Houses*, 7, 1980, 158–165.

"Best." *Architecture Intérieure Crée*, 176, March–April 1980, 77–79.

Blyth, Jeffrey. "Supermarkets—Showrooms Designed for Best Products by Various Architects." *Building Design*, 483, February 15, 1980, 27–29.

Boissiere, Olivier. "Trois maisons à Bel Air." *Architecture Intérieure Crée*, 178, July–August 1980, 78–91.

"Buildings for BEST Products." *Progressive Architecture*, 61, February 1980, 24, 29.

"Buildings for Best Products." *Skyline*, February 1980, 4–5.

"Bunker Hill Architects Announced." *Progressive Architecture*, September 1980, 42.

Burr, F. Andrus. "Learning under Moore." *Special Issue: Charles Moore and Company. Global Architecture, Houses*, 7, 1980, 173–179.

Canty, Philip. "Six Ways to Decorate a Shed." *American Institute of Architects Journal*, 69, February 1980, 50–53.

"Casa in Vendita." *Domus*, 611, November 1980, 30–31.

"Centre de maintenance pour l'armée, Norwich, Connecticut." *L'Architecture d'Aujourd'hui*, 209, June 1980, 90–91.

"Centre mondial d'information." *Macadam*, no. 13–14, February/ March 1980, 12–13.

Cohen, Stuart. "Late Entries." *Progressive Architecture*, June 1980, 94–99.

Coote, James. "Eight for the Eighties." *Texas Architect*, July/ August 1980, 67–76.

Cortes, Juan Antonio, and Muñoz, Maria Teresa. "The Mirage of an Architectural Problem: The Buildings for Best Products Exhibition at MOMA." *Arquitectura*, 222, January–February 1980, 58–62, 72.

Diamonstein, Barbaralee. *American Architecture Now*, New York, 1980.

Dreyfuss, John. "Architecture: Charles Moore." *Architectural Digest*, 37, March 1980, 140–147.

Filler, Martin. "Charles Moore: House Vernacular." *Art in America*, 68, October 1980, 105–112.

Filson, Ronald. "Charles Moore & Company: Evolution." *Special Issue: Charles Moore and Company. Global Architecture Houses*, 7, 1980, 128–131.

Floyd, J. P. Chadwick. "Making a Splash in Paris." In "AD Profiles 30: Les Halles," *Architectural Design*, 50, 9/10, 1980, 37–39.

Freedman, Alex. "Architects Pick Outstanding Works." *New York Times*, December 7, 1980, sec. 23, 12.

Gandee, Charles K. "An Addition to a California Farmhouse by Charles Moore." *Architectural Record*, 167, January 1980, 125–132.

Goldberger, Paul. "Architect Plays with Symbols of the Home." *New York Times*, November 27, 1980, C1, C6.

———. "Exhibiting Dream Houses That Can Really Be Built." *New York Times Magazine*, 130, October 12, 1980, 129–130.

"Die grossen Architekten (3) Charles W. Moore." *Häuser* 3, 1980, 95–103.

Hathorn, George T. "Random Thoughts on the Architecture of Applied Image." *Special Issue: Charles Moore and Company. Global Architecture Houses*, 7, 1980, 228–233.

"Hexastyle Texas Style, Charles Moore." *Architecture and Urbanism*, November 1980, 89, 104–105.

Hoffer, Peter, "The New Commercialism." *Architectural Review*, 167, March 1980, 135–137.

Hubbard, William. *Complicity and Conviction: Steps toward an Architecture of Convention*, Cambridge, Mass. 1980.

Huxtable, Ada Louise. "Focus on the Museum Tower." *New York Times*, August 24, 1980, Sec. 2, 27–28.

"Isham Residence." *Toshi Jutaku*, February 1980, 34–38.

Jencks, Charles. "Introduction." In "AD Profile 28: Post-Modern Classicism," *Architectural Design*, 50, 5/6, 1980, 4–17.

———. *Post-Modern Classicism: The New Synthesis*, London, 1980.

———. "Toward Radical Eclecticism." In *The Presence of the Past, First International Exhibition of Architecture, la Biennale*, Milan, 1980, 30–37.

Joedicke, Jurgen. *Architektur in Umbruch*, Germany, 1980.

"Kings Road Elderly Housing, West Hollywood, California." *Progressive Architecture*, 61, January 1980, 29.

Lampugnani, Vittorio Magnago. *Architektur und Städtebau des 20. Jahrhunderts*, West Germany, 1980.

Low-Rise Housing in America—the Urban Scene, Process Architecture #14, Tokyo, 1980.

Moore, Charles W. "Eight Houses in Search of Their Owners." *House and Garden*, 152, December 1980, 104–106.

———. "Human Energy." *Architecture for People*, edited by B. Mikellides, London, 1980, 115–121.

———. " 'The Past' Lies in Everyone's Memory . . . ." In *The Presence of the Past, First International Exhibition of Architecture, la Biennale*, Milan, 1980, 240–245.

———. "A Personal View of Architecture." *Arquitectura*, 225, July–August 1980, 54–63.

———. "Piazza d'Italia." In "AD Profile 28: Post-Modern Classicism." *Architectural Design*, 50, 5/6, 1980, 20–25.

———. "Rodes House." In "AD Profile 28: Post-Modern Classicism," *Architectural Design*, 50, 5/6, 1980, 26–29.

"Moore Grover Harper." *L'Architecture d'Aujourd'hui*, September 1980, 78.

"Moore's Principles." *Skyline*, March 1980, 12.

"Museum of Modern Art Exhibits SITE's Inventive Building for Best—and Invites Six Architects to Design New Ones," *Architectural Record*, 167, February 1980, 39.

"Palladio Lives On." *Life*, December 1980, 112–113.

Peters, Richard C. "Lighting for Moore." *Special Issue: Charles Moore and Company. Global Architecture, Houses*, 7, 1980, 143–148.

"Pioneer Courthouse Square: Another Major Portland Competition," *Architectural Record*, 168, August 1980, 37.

"Playful Facades." *Newsweek*, January 28, 1980, 75–76.

Pommer, Richard. "Some Architectural Ideologies after the Fall." *Art Journal*, 40, Fall/Winter 1980, 353–361.

"Portland Square Competition Winner Announced." *Progressive Architecture*, September 1980, 42.

Portoghesi, Paolo. *Post-Modern Architecture*, New York, 1983.

"Report from the Venice Biennale." *Progressive Architecture*, September 1980, 39.

Ross, Michael Franklin. "Classical Allusions." *Residential Interiors*, 5, September–October 1980, 108–113.

Sands, Olivia. "Free Thinking Art and Functional Design on Show." *Building Design*, 521, November 14, 1980, 30–31.

Scully, Vincent. "How Things Got to Be the Way They Are Now." In *The Presence of the Past, First International Exhibition of Architecture, la Biennale*, Milan, 1980, 15–20.

"Selling Houses as Art." *Newsweek*, 96, October 27, 1980, 14.

"Shelton House Bel Air, California/1979." *Architecture and Urbanism*, July 1980, 34–38.

Simon, Mark. "The Halcyon Days of Now or the Desparate Hours." *Special Issue: Charles Moore and Company. Global Architecture, Houses*, 7, 1980, 76–77.

Skorneck, A. Jeffrey. "Bunker Hill Development Competition: The Jury's Still Out." *LA Architect*, 6, April 1980, 2–3.

Slesin, Suzanne. "The Postmodern Interior: A Collage of Times Gone By." *New York Times*, September 18, 1980, C1, C6.

Special Issue: Charles Moore and Company. Global Architecture Houses, 7, 1980.

Stern, Robert A. M. "The Doubles Of Post-Modern." *Harvard Architectural Reivew*, 1, Spring 1980, 75–87.

"The 'Strada Novissima'." *The Presence of the Past, First International Exhibition of Architecture, la Biennale*, Milan, 1980, 38.

Sudjic, Deyan. "Latest Best." *Architectural Review*, 167, April 1980, 221–225.

"Tegeler Hafen Competition: Residential and Recreation Facilities in Berlin. Charles Moore Wins First European Commission." *Architectural Design, New Supplement*, November 1980, 1–3.

Urban Encounters: Art, Architecture, Audience, exhibition catalog, Philadelphia, Institute of Contemporary Art, University of Pennsylvania, March–August 1980.

"Urban Innovations Group; Charles Moore, Ron Filson, UIG; House in Ventura County [sic]/1978," *Architecture and Urbanism*, July 1980, 27–33.

"The Utopian and the Pragmatic." *Art News*, 79, November 1980, 14–15.

Viladas, Pilar. "Nothing but the Best." *Interiors*, 139, March 1980, 18, 26.

"A Villa for Karl." *Japan Architect*, 55, February 1980, 46–47.

Whitaker, Richard R., Jr. "Connections," *Special Issue: Charles Moore and Company. Global Architecture Houses*, 7, 1980, 7–11.

"Winners in the Shinkenchiku Residential Design Competition 1979: Honorable Mention." *Japan Architect*, 55, February 1980, 46–47.

"Wohnen und Freizeit am Tegeler Hafen." *Bauwelt*, 42, November 1980, 1894–1897.

Yudell, Buzz. "Moore in Progress." *Special Issue: Charles Moore and Company. Global Architecture Houses*, 7 1980, 112–119.

1981

"AIA Honor Awards." *Progressive Architecture*, May 1981, 32.

"Abbiamo in contrata Charles Moore." *Casa Vogue*, April 1981, 178–179.

Allen, G., and Oliver, R. *Architectural Drawing: The Art and the Process*, London, New York, 1981.

"Award Winning Architecture." *Connecticut Architect*, January 1981, 118.

"Awards for Extended Use: 6. Jones Laboratory, Cold Spring Harbor, New York." *Architectural Record*, 169, May 1981, 49.

Boddy, Trevor. "Charles Moore: Recent Projects." *Architectural Review*, 170, August 1981, 94–101.

Beebe, Tina. "An Expert's Guide to Color." *House and Garden*, September 1981, 146–150.

Bognar, Botond. *Cultural Patterns and the Role of History in Recent Pluralistic Architectural Intentions*, M.A. Thesis, University of California, Los Angeles, 1981.

Boissière, Olivier. "C. W. Moore—The Gift of Ubiquity." *Architectes (Révue de l'Ordre des Architectes)*, 23, March 1981, 18–23.

Broadbent, Geoffrey. "The Pests Strike Back!" *Royal Institute of British Architects Journal*, November 1981, unpaginated (4 pages).

Busch, Akiko. "The Decorated Surface." *Metropolis*, December 1981, 14–17.

"Charles Moore: el máximo de vida posible." *Summa*, 61, April 1981, 55–59.

"The Classical Transformed." *Progressive Architecture*, October 1981, 105–107.

Collaboration. Artists and Architects. The Centennial Project of the Architectural League, edited by Barbaralee Diamonstein, New York, 1981.

"Color in Texas Architecture." *Texas Architect*, May/June 1981, 60–65.

Davis, Douglas. "Back to the Classics." *Newsweek*, 98, September 1981, 76–78.

Doll, Larry. "Inclusivism." *Texas Architect*, November/December 1981, 40–45.

Dubow, Neville. "Houses for Sale. Architecture as Art." *Architecture SA (South Africa)*, 15, October 1981, 52–55.

Eriksson, Eva. "Internationell tävling i Berlin." *Arkitektur (Stockholm)*, 81, January–February 1981, 30–31.

"Everything in Its Place." *House and Garden*, January 1981, 118.

Filler, Martin. "Transition Transformed: Amazing Spaces." *House and Garden*, 153, April 1981, 170–175.

Five Years of Record Houses, special issue of *Architectural Record*, New York, 1981.

Foster, Hal. "Pastiche/Prototype/Purity: 'Houses for Sale'." *Artforum*, 19, March 1981, 77–79.

"Gleaming Laboratory Cubes in a Rustic 19th Century Shell." *American Institute of Architects Journal*, 70, mid-May 1981, 252–253.

Goldstein, Barbara. "Graves Wins Library Competition." *Progressive Architecture*, 62, March 1981, 25–26.

"Guest Speaker: Charles Moore on Color in Architecture." *House Beautiful*, 122, May 1981, 28–29.

Huxtable, Ada Louise. "The Troubled State of Modern Architecture." *Architectural Design*, 51, 1/2, 1981, 9–17.

"Interview One: Charles Moore." *Transition*, 2, 2, June 1981, 4–6.

Johnson, Eugene J. "United States of America." In *International Handbook of Contemporary Developments in Architecture*, edited by Warren Sanderson, Westport, Connecticut, 1981, 501–524.

"Kingsmill, 1974; Owen Brown Village, 1974." In 'AD Profile 37: The Anglo-American Suburb," edited by Robert A. M. Stern and John Montague Massengale, *Architectural Design*, 51, 10/11, 1981, 90–91.

Kulterman, Udo. "Space, Time and the New Architecture—about the 1980 Architecture Biennale in Venice." *Architecture and Urbanism*, February 1981, 14–38.

Maerker, C. "Wohnhäuser wie Skulpturen—wer will sie?" *Art: das Kunstmagazin*, 2, February 1981, 86–91.

"A Meeting of Artistic Minds." *New York Times Magazine*, 130, March 1981, 70–74.

Miller, Nory. "Sweet and Sour: House, Southern California," *Progressive Architecture*, 62, September 1981, 182–183.

"Mixed Marriages of Art." *Newsweek*, 97, March 1981, 71.

"Moore Confidence." *Architect's Journal*, 174, July 1981, 90.

Moore, Charles W. "Moore is More." *Royal Institute of British Architects Journal*, November 1981, unpaginated (4 pages).

———. "On Getting Things Built." In 'AD Profile 38: Current Projects," *Architectural Design*, 51, 12, 1981, 114.

———. "Ort, Erinnerung und Architektur." *Deutsches Architektenblatt*, 13, December 1981, 1715–1724.

"Moore, Ruble, Yudell, Rodes House, Los Angeles, California." *Architectural Record*, 169, mid-May 1981, 126–128.

Myers, Barton. "A Grand Avenue: Design Process." *Architecture and Urbanism*, August 1981, 24–58.

Oliver, Richard (ed.). *The Making of an Architect*, New York, 1981.

Pommer, Richard, and Hubert, Christine. *Idea as Model*, New York, 1981.

"Post Modernism: Piazza D'Italia." *Huset Sum Billede*, September–October 1981, 58–59.

"Reconnaissance, Houses for Sale." *Architectural Review*, 169, 1981, 5–8.

"Red Cedar Shingle and Handsplit Shake Bureau Awards." *Architectural Record*, 169, November 1981, 45–48.

Reed, Rochelle. "California by Design." *California Magazine*, October 1981, 82–83.

"Restoration of Things Past." *Newsweek*, March 23, 1981, 84–87.

Review of Tom Wolfe, *From Bauhaus to Our House*. In *Progressive Architecture*, December 1981, 108.

Russell, John. "Jackie Ferrara and Charles Moore." *New York Times*, February 27, 1981.

Sadfie, Moshe. "Private Jokes in Public Places." *Atlantic*, 248, December 1981, 62–69.

"San Juan Capistrano Public Library Design Competition." *Architectural Record*, 169, March 1981, 46–49.

Scully, Vincent. "The Shingle Style Revival." *House Beautiful*, August 1981, 76–79. Reprinted in *House Beautiful's Building Manual*, Winter 1982, 53.

Skude, F. "Om symbolisme og ornamentik i post modernismen." *Louisiana Revy (Denmark)*, 22, 1, October 1981, 61–64.

Speaking a New Classicism: American Architecture Now, with essays by Helen Searing and Henry Hope Reed, exhibition catalog, Smith College Museum of Art, Northampton, Massachusetts, 1981.

Special Issue: American Architecture after Modernism, Architecture and Urbanism, supplement, March 1981.

Spring, Martin. "Literally Superficial: Robert Venturi and Charles Moore Made a Winning Combination for This Year's RIBA Annual Discourse Fixture." *Building*, 241, 7199 (29), July 1981, 25.

"Tegel Harbor Design Competition." *Global Architecture, Document*, 4, 1981, 88–89.

Three Centuries of Notable American Architects, New York, 1981.

"The Town Square." *Texas Architect*, May/June 1981, 56–59.

Viladas, Pilar. "A Smart Investment." *Interiors*, 141, October 1981, 98–99.

Wagner, Walter F., Jr. "Moore Ruble Yudell." *Architectural Record*, 169, May 15, 1981, 126.

Walden, Russell. "Charles Moore, Educator and Architect." *New Zealand Architect*, 2, 1981, 4–7.

Walker, Lester. *American Shelter*, Woodstock, New York, 1981. Preface by Charles Moore.

Werner, Frank. *Neues Wohnon in Alten Hausern*, Germany, 1981.

"White River Park is a 250-acre recreational park for Indianapolis." *Architectural Record*, 169, December 1981, 40.

1982

Barnett, Jonathan. *An Introduction to Urban Design*, New York, 1982.

"Bauen für den Einpragsamen Ort." *Architektur und Wöhnen*, March 1982, 52–57.

"Beverly Hills: The Jury Speaks." *LA Architect*, 8, November 1982, 4–5.

Boudon, Philippe. "L'architecture n'est pas la géométrie: à propos d'un livre d'architecture de Ch. Moore et Gerald Allen." *L'Architecture d'Aujourd'hui*, 220, April 1982, XII-XIII.

Brolin, Brent, and Richards, Jean. *Sourcebook of Architectural Ornament*, New York, 1982.

"Casa-Teatro per Spiriti Puri." *Casa Vogue*, July/August 1982, 74–79.

"Charles Moore on Color in Architecture." *House Beautiful's Building Manual*, Winter 1982, 52.

Climate, Nature and House, Process Architecture #29, Tokyo, 1982.

Dardi, Costantino. "Verde pensiero in un'ombra verde." *Domus*, 628, May 1982, 2–29.

Dreyfuss, John. "How Capistrano's Library Stacks Up." *Los Angeles Times*, April 23, 1982, 1, 10–11.

Duffy, Glen. "A Good Man Is Hard to Find." *New Jersey Monthly*, 6, June 1982, 46.

Filler, Martin. "History Reinvented: Adam and His Heirs." *Art in America*, 70, 6, Summer 1982, 86–97.

"A Flowering of Museums." *United*, September 1982, 64.

Furer, René. "Robert Venturi, Charles Moore—Auf der Such nach einer amerikanischen Architektur." *Werk, Bauen und Wohnen*, 69, 37, May 1982, 24–27.

Gandee, Charles K. "Preserving the Quietude." *Architectural Record*, 170, April 1982, 95–103.

Goldstein, Barbara. "Moore Awarded Beverly Hills Civic Center." *Progressive Architecture*, 63, December 1982, 21–22.

Harvard University Graduate School of Design. *Charles Moore: Exhibition Checklist*, Cambridge, Mass., 1982.

Heyne, Pamela. *Today's Architectural Mirror*, New York, 1982.

"IBA '84: Exhibition/Collection." *Progressive Architecture*, January 1982, 197–204.

Ichinowatari, Katsuhiko. *Special Issue: Climate, Nature and House: Climate and the American House, Process: Architecture*, 29, May 1982.

"In Competition: Beverly Hills, California, Civic Center." *Skyline*, November 1982.

"In Good Form, Housebuilder and the New Place of Houses." *Chicago*, 31, August 1982. 124–127.

"In Progress." *Progressive Architecture*, March 1982, 32.

"Infill and Outreach at Dartmouth." *Architectural Record*, 170, July 1982, 55.

"Isham House, Eastern Long Island, New York." *Process: Architecture*, 29, 1982, 46–49.

Jencks, Charles. *Architecture Today*, New York, ca. 1982.

———. "Free Style Classicism, The Wider Tradition." In "AD Profile 39: Free Style Classicism," edited by Charles Jencks, *Architectural Design*, 52, 1/2, 1982, 5–21.

Jensen, Robert, and Conway, Patricia. *Ornamentalism*, New York, 1982.

Joly, Pierre. "Les livres d'architecture: La ville comme société et signification (suite)." *L'Oeil*, 322, May 1982, 82–85.

Kaufman, Jacob. *"Post-Modern Architecture": An Ideology*. Ph.D. Thesis, University of California, Los Angeles, 1982.

Kay, Jane Holtz. "Museums: An Architect's Canvas." *Christian Science Monitor*, August 20, 1982.

Kirsch, Jonathan. "Hot Profs." *California Magazine*, 7, September 1982, 82–86.

Knox, Marion. "8 Einsichten an 16 Beispielen." *Bauwelt*, 89, 1/2, January 8, 1982, 22–55.

———. "Brief aus New York." *Bauwelt*, 89, 1/2, January 8, 1982, 16–21.

Kuspit, Donald. "New American Art Museums." *Artforum*, 21, December 1982, 78–79.

May, S. W. "On the Importance of Charles Moore." *The Architect* (Perth), 22, 1, 1982, 29–30.

Moore, Charles W. "Building Club Sandwiches." *Design Quarterly*, 118–119, Summer 1982, 42–51.

———. "Schinkel's Free Style Pavilion and the Berlin Tegeler Hafen Scheme." In "AD Profile 39: Free Style Classicism," edited by Charles Jencks, *Architectural Design*, 52, 1/2, 1982, 22–23.

"Moore, Grover, Harper, Sammis Hall, 1978–1981, and Rudolph House, 1978–1981." In "AD Profile 39: Free Style Classicism," Charles Jencks, ed., *Architectural Design*, 52, 1/2, 1982, 80–83.

"The Moore House." *National Parks and Conservation*, 56, January–February 1982, 39.

New American Museums, exhibition catalog, Whitney Museum, New York, 1982.

"Pencil Points." *Progressive Architecture*, March 1982, 23.

Peters, Paulhans, and Henn, Ursula. *Einfamilienhauser*, Germany, 1982.

Ruthenfranz, E. "Das Berlin von Morgen." *Art: das Kunstmagazin*, 7, July 1982, 34–45.

———. "Die Wilden vom Bau." *Art: das Kunstmagazin*, 3 March 1982, 48–55.

"Sammis Hall Guest House, Banbury Conference Center, Long Island." *Baumeister*, 79, April 1982, 367–369.

Searing, Helen. "New American Art Museums." *Skyline*, June 1982, 16–21.

"Seven Buildings: A Sampling of Recent Fort Worth Architecture." *Texas Architecture*, September/October 1982, 40.

Shapiro, Brenda. "In Good Form, Housebuilders and the New Place of Houses." *Chicago*, 31, August 1982, 124.

Special Issue: The Presence of the Past, Archetype, 3, Spring 1982.

"Stage Set—High Art." In "AD Profiles 40: Los Angeles—Part 2," edited by Derek Walker, *Architectural Design*, 52, 3/4, 1982, 108–111.

"Strada Novissima." *Architectural Record*, 170, July 1982, 55.

Strodthoff, W. "Some Pros and Cons of Beautiful Appearances." *Daidalos*, 6, December 15, 1982, 103–109.

1983

Allies, Bob. "Architectural Import: Report of an Exhibition at the ICA in Their Series of Exhibitions 'Art and Architecture'." *Architect's Journal*, 177, 4, January 26, 1983, 30–33.

"American Architecture Exhibit at Various Locations." *Los Angeles Times*, December 8, 1983, VI, 1.

"Baby Boom Architects/Connecticut." *Metropolitan Home*, July 1983, 62–63.

"Backstreet Restaurant, New Haven, Conn.; Sammis Hall, Cold Spring Harbor Laboratory, Long Island, New York." *American Institute of Architects Journal*, 72, April 1983, 56–57.

"Baroque Beverly Hills." *Domus*, 644, November 1983, 31.

"Battery Park's grand design; architects Charles Moore, Gruzen & Partners, Bond Ryder James, Conklin & Rossant, Ulrich Franzen & Associates, Davis Brody & Associates, Rothzeid Kaiserman Thompson & Bee, and others." *Progressive Architecture*, 64, 12, December 1983, 25.

"Beverly Hills Adds to Civic Core: New Construction Will Reflect City Hall's Style." *Los Angeles Times*, July 17, 1983.

"Beverly Hills Civic Center: Charles Moore in Zusammenarbeit mit Albert C. Martin." *Bauen und Wohnen*, 38, October 1983, 62.

"Beverly Hills Civic Center Design Competition." *Architectural Record*, 171, January 1983, 72–74.

"Cabin, Temple, Trailer." *Artweek*, 14, December 17, 1983, 12.

Campbell, Robert, et al. "Special issue. The sixth annual review of new American architecture." *American Institute of Architects Journal*, 72, 5, May 1983, 149–359.

"Charles Moore: Licht House." *Arts and Architecture*, January–February 1983, 30–31.

"A Church Is not a Home." *Newsweek*, 101, March 28, 1983, 76–78.

"Corner Cupboard." *Architectural Record*, 171, August 1983, 135.

"Dolls' Houses: Charles Moore." *Architectural Design*, 53, 3/4, 1983, 56.

Douglas, William Lake. "WonderWall, '84 World Exposition; New Orleans, Louisiana." *Landscape Architecture*, July/August 1983, 70–71.

Filler, Martin. "Is Consensus Next to Godliness?" *House and Garden*, August 1983, 155.

Fox, Stephen. "New Texas Country Clubs." *Cite*, Fall 1983, 6–7.

Giovannini, Joseph. "Beverly Hills Panel Chooses Design for a Civic Center to Fit City's Image." *New York Times*, January 18, 1983.

———. "Personable Interiors: There Are Rooms That Are Remarkable for Reasons That Are Not Architectural." *New York Times*, September 1983, 6, S40.

Hansen, Jorgen Peder. "The Work of Charles Moore." *Arkitekten* (Copenhagen), 85, 14, August 9, 1983, 273–284.

Home Sweet Home American Domestic Vernacular Architecture, edited by Charles W. Moore, Kathryn Smith, Peter Becker, New York, 1983.

"'Home Sweet Home', Craft and Folk Art Museum." *Los Angeles Times*, November 14, 1983, VI, 1.

Ianco-Starrels, Josine. "Charles Moore." *Los Angeles Times*, October 30, 1983, C, 92.

Ingwerson, Marshall. "Architect Charles Moore: Searching for a Fresh Sense of Place." *Christian Science Monitor*, February 3, 1983, B1-B3, B9.

Jencks, Charles. "Architecture: Charles Jencks/Buzz Yudell." *Architectural Digest*, 40, November 1983, 106–113.

Jodido, P. "Tout oser." *Connaissance des Arts*, 379, September 1983, 80–81.

Kingsley, Karen. "A New Twist in Design." *Louisiana Life*, 2, January/February 1983, 117+.

Lewin, Susan Grant. "Palladio in America." *House Beautiful*, 125, January 1983, 62–65.

Littlejohn, David. "A Fair to Remember." *TWA Ambassador*, October 1983, 47–58.

Maxwell, Robert. "The Ten New Buildings Exhibition at the ICA—Aiming to Amend Popular Preconceptions about Modern Architecture." *Building Design*, 626, January 28, 1983, 15–17.

Moore, Charles W. "Inclusive and Exclusive." *Immagini del poste-moderno: il dibattito sulla società post-industriale e l'architettura*, edited by C. Aldegheri and M. Sabini, Venice, 1983.

———. "John Soane." *House and Garden*, 155, March 1983, 38–40.

———. "Tegel Harbour, Berlin." *Architectural Design*, 53, 1/2, 1983, 42–43.

"Moore Ruble Yudell, Rodes House." *GA Document*, October 1983, 112–117.

"New Ornamentalism is American Architecture." *Christian Science Monitor*, March 4, 1983, 15.

Pastier, John. "The People's Architect." *PSA Magazine*, May 1983, 86.

"People and Projects." *Skyline*, January 1983, 26.

"Personable Interiors." *New York Times Magazine*, 133, September 25, 1983, S40–S42.

Russell, Frank, et al. "AD Profile: 45. Architecture in progress. The Internationale Bauausstellung Berlin." *Architectural Design*, 53, 1/2, 1983, 1–127 (after p. 8).

Searing, Helen. *New American Art Museums*, Berkeley, 1983.

"Special Issue. Houses." *GA Houses*, 13, March 1983, 16–173.

"Special Issue. International Architecture: The Generation of 1925." *Hinterland*, 6, no. 27, September 1983, 1–68.

"St. Matthew's Church, Pacific Palisades, California. 1983." *GA Document*, 8, October 1983, 112–117.

Whitcomb, Claire. "Saluting America's Town Spirit: In Thibodaux, Louisiana, an Architectural Competition Turns into a Catalyzing Event." *House Beautiful*, 125, March 1983, 39.

1984

"AIA Honor Awards/St. Matthew's Church." *Architecture California*, May/June 1984.

"AIA Honor Awards: No Duds, No Surprises." *Progressive Architecture*, 65, 5, May 1984, 22–23.

Abrams, Janet. "On the Banks of the Mississippi: The World of Rivers Is the Theme for the 1984 Louisiana World Exposition—a Report on the Architecture." *Building Design*, 693, 8 June 1984, 32–33.

Betsky, A. "Designs for Living (illustrated houses by Charles Moore, Frank Gehry, Steven Hall, Robert Stern, Charles Gwathmey, Stanley Tigerman and Batey and Mack)." *Horizon*, 27, 9, 1984, 49–55.

"The Blendo Manifesto: California Designers Are Rethinking Everything. The New Rule Is No Rules." *California Magazine*, 9, March 1984, 78.

Bletter, Rosemarie Haag. "Dekonstrucktionen." *Werk Bauen Wohnen*, 71/38[39], July/August 1984, 22–23.

Bognar, Botond. "The Church and Its Spirit of Place, Note on the Latest Work of Moore Ruble Yudell Partnership (St. Matthew's Parish Church)." *A + U—Architecture and Urbanism*, 160, 1984, 104–108.

Boles, Darlice Donkervoet. "Mixed Metaphors: The New Orleans Fair." *Progressive Architecture*, 65, 5, May 1984, 19–20.

"Books Exploring Architecture from 12th Century to Present." *Los Angeles Times*, February 5, 1984, Book Review, 3.

Burns, Jim. "Sea Ranch: Resisting Suburbia: After 20 Years a Framed Development in Turmoil." *Architecture*, 73, December 1984, 56–63.

"The City Observed: Los Angeles." *Newsweek*, 104, December 10, 1984, 90, Review.

"The City Observed: Los Angeles: A Guide to Its Architecture and Landscapes." *Los Angeles*, 29, August 1984, 56. Review.

" 'City Observed: LA,' by Moore, Becker and Campbell." *Los Angeles Times*, July 1, 1984, Book Review, 2.

"Country Club, Sweetwater; Interiors by Morris and Aubry; Near Houston, Texas." *Interior Design*, August 1984, 170–177.

"Country House, Massachusetts." *Builder*, October 1984, 137.

Crosbie, Michael J. "Television as a Tool of Urban Design: The Renewal of Downtown Roanoke, Virginia." *Architecture (AIA)*, 73, November 1984, 54–61.

"Culture Swapping: The New International Style." *Vogue*, 174, April 1984, 336.

Curtis, W. "Principle versus Pastiche: Perspectives on Some Recent Classicism." *Architectural Review*, 176, August 1984, 16–17.

Davis, Douglas. "Return to Religious Symbolism." *Dialogue*, February 1984, 7–15.

"Designs for living." *Horizon*, 27, November 1984, 49.

"For Fitness, Food and Informality de Luxe." *Interior Design*, August 1984, 170–177.

Gandee, C. K. "Design by Congregation." *Architectural Record*, 172, 2, 1984, 94–101.

Giovannini, J. "Charles Moore Comes to Austin." *Ultra*, November 1984, 112–115.

———. Review of David Littlejohn, *Architect: The Life and Work of Charles W. Moore*, in *New York Times Book Review*, October 28, 1984, 27.

Gleye, Paul, review of David Littlejohn, *Architect: The Life and Work of Charles W. Moore*. In *Los Angeles Times*, July 1, 1984, Books, 2.

Glusberg, Jorge. "AD Profile: 56. Cairo International Exhibition." *Architectural Design*, 54, 11/12, 1984, 5–88.

Goldberger, Paul. "Reality Squeezes Out Fantasy in Louisiana Fair's Architecture." *New York Times*, May 13, 1984, 1, 24.

Gordon, Alastair. "L.I.'s Architectural Winners." *New York Times*, December 9, 1984, XXI, 39.

Guenther, Robert. "No Light in the Piazza: An Architectural Joke." *Wall Street Journal*, February 24, 1984.

Hansen, Jorgen Peder. "1984 Louisiana World Exposition." *Arkitekten* (Copenhagen), 86, 13, 24 July 1984, 274–275.

Hart, C. "Spray-on America." *Industrial Design Magazine*, 31, July/August 1984, 20–29.

Hines, Thomas S. "He's Serious about Whimsy on the Job." *The Philadelphia Inquirer*, July 8, 1984, 1-H, 12-H.

———. "Charles Moore and William Turnbull (architectural collaboration for house design in Colorado Rockies)." *Architectural Digest*, 41, July 1984, 118–125, 150.

"Housing, Leisure and Cultural Buildings: Tegeler Hafen." *Architectural Review*, 176, September 1984, 64–65.

Isozaki, Shinji. "Plan for a House of God (St. Matthew's Parish Church by Moore Ruble Yudell architects and planners)." *A + U, Architecture and Urbanism*, 160, January 1984, 99–103.

Ivy, R. A. "In New Orleans, Warehouses and Forms From an Ideal World." *Architecture*, 73, July 1984, 10–12.

Jencks, Charles. "The Building as Scenario: Elemental House, Los Angeles, California." *Architectural Record*, 172, 9 (8), August 1984, 118–125.

———. "Hunt the Symbol." *Domus*, 655, November 1984, 44–47.

Kingsley, Karen. "Designing a Wall of Wonder." *Louisiana Life*, 4, May/June 1984, 106–111.

Klotz, Heinrich. *Moderne und Postmoderne Architektur der Gegenwart 1960–1980*, Weisbaden, 1984.

Knight, Carleton. "Built on Religious, Regional Traditions." *Architecture—The AIA Journal*, 73, 5, May 1984, 178–185.

Kohn, M. "Mannerism and Contemporary Art: The Style and Its Critics." *Arts Magazine*, 58, March 1984, 72–77.

Lemoine, B. Review of David Littlejohn, *Architect: The Life and Work of Charles W. Moore*. In *L'Architecture d'Aujourd'hui*, 235, October 1984, R65.

Littlejohn, David. *Architect: The Life and Work of Charles W. Moore*, New York, 1984.

———. "The Wild, Wondrous Imagination of Charles W. Moore." *Smithsonian*, 15, June 1984, 54–61.

Moore, Charles W. *The City Observed, Los Angeles: A Guide to Its Architecture and Landscapes*, New York, 1984.

———. "Food for Thought." *New York Times Book Review*, 89, October 14, 1984, 47.

———. "For All the Talk about the So-called International Style …," *Vogue*, April 1984, 338.

———. "Working Together to Make Something." *Architectural Record*, 172, 2, February 1984, 102–103.

———, et al. "Building Type Study: 597. Religious Buildings. Design by Congregation: St. Matthew's Parish Church, Pacific Palisades; and, Working Together to Make Something; Architects Moore Ruble Yudell." *Architectural Record*, 172, 2, February 1984, 94–103.

Nairn, J. "Conference Dissects Works of Five Very Different Architects." *Architecture*, 73, October 1984, 18.

"Never Say Too Small to Remodel." *Sunset*, March 1984, 99.

Papademetriou, Peter C. "A Seaside Hideaway," *Ultra*, November 1984, 106–111.

"The Parish of St. Matthew's Episcopal Church in Pacific Palisades, California." *Sun/Coast Architect/Builder*, August 1984, 16–18.

"Practice of Setting Up Designs Review Boards to Okay Projects." *Christian Science Monitor*, April 23, 1984, 4.

Radovic, Ranko. "Text Architects." *Architektura Urbanizam*, 24, (supplement), 1984, 2–68.

Regina, Kate, review of David Littlejohn, *Architect: The Life and Work of Charles W. Moore*. In *San Francisco Chronicle*, September 3, 1984, 37.

Revision der Moderne Postmoderne Architektur 1960–1980, Herausgegeben von Heinrich Klotz, Munich, 1984.

"Revitalized Riverfront Is Legacy of New Orleans Fair." *Architectural Record*, 172, 3, March 1984, 61.

"St. Matthew's Episcopal Church: Tradition and Typology Come Together." *LA Architect*, May 1984, 1.

"St. Matthew's Parish Church, Pacific Palisades, California, USA, 1983, Moore, Ruble, Yudell, Architects and Planners." *A + U— Architecture and Urbanism*, 160, 1984, 95–98.

Smith, H. L. "New Life for Old Memories." *Architectural Record*, 172, 1, January 1984, 132–137.

"Special Issue. Houses." *GA Houses*, 16, July 1984, 7–175.

"Temple, Cabin, Trailer (installation)." *Progressive Architecture*, 65, February 1984, 26.

"Williams College Museum of Art." *American School and University*, November 1984, 110.

"The Wonderwall, New Orleans, Louisiana." *Architectural Design*, 54, 3/4, 1984, 60.

"World's Fair Charettes: A Look at Concepts for 1992." *Inland Architect*, 28, 2, March/April 1984, 42–46.

1985

"Architectural Design of the New Hood Museum at Dartmouth." *Christian Science Monitor*, October 16, 1985, A&L, 23.

"Art Museum Opening at Dartmouth." *New York Times*, September 26, 1985, C17.

Bonetti, David. "Moore, Stirling and Sir John Soane." *Art New England*, October 1985, 3–4.

"Campus Americana." *Newsweek*, April 1985, 22–27.

"Centerbrook Architects and Planners." *Architecture in Greece*, 19, 1985, 105–106.

The Critical Edge: Controversy in Recent American Architecture, edited by Todd A. Marder, Cambridge, Mass., 1985.

Crosbie, Michael J. "Television as a Tool of Urban Design." *Architectural Quarterly*, introductory issue, 1985, 54–61.

"Dartmouth Celebrates Its New Museum." *Architectural Record*, 173, November 1985, 71.

"Dartmouth's New Museum." *Wall Street Journal*, November 1, 1985, 28.

"Frankfurt: Culture and Urban Politics." *Techniques and Architecture*, no. 359, April/May 1985, 84–111.

Gill, Brendan. "Architecture: Moore, Ruble, Yudell." *Architectural Design*, 42, 8, August 1985, 58–65, 148.

Goldberger, Paul. "Museums Designed for Tight Quarters." *New York Times*, October 20, 1985, II, 28.

———. "Museums Set the Tone in Architecture." *New York Times*, September 8, 1985, II, 43, 45.

———. "There's Fun in the Fair's Architecture, but Not Quite Enough." *New York Times*, May 13, 1985, I, 24.

Hines, Thomas S. "Windows into Their Work: Architects as Writers." *New York Times Books Review*, September 8, 1985, 1, 32, 34.

"A House for All Seasons." *Diversion*, March 1985, 275–278.

Hubbard, William. Review of David Littlejohn, *Architect: The Life and Work of Charles W. Moore*. In *Architectural Record*, 173, January 1985, 73.

"Mixed Use Complexes." *Center: A Journal for Architecture in America*, 1985, 72–78.

Moore, Charles W. "Planning the Hood Museum of Art."

Dedication, Hood Museum of Art, Dartmouth College, September 26–28, 1985, 11–13.

———. "Planning the Hood Museum of Art." In *Treasures of the Hood Museum of Art, Dartmouth College*, New York and Hanover, 1985, 22–27.

———. Review of Ada Louise Huxtable, *The Tall Building Artistically Reconsidered: The Search for a Skyscraper Style*. In *New York Times Book Review*, June 23, 1985, 22.

Morgenthaler, Anne. "Rejuvenation Plans Unveiled for SM Pier." *Outlook Mail*, May 16, 1985, 1.

"On New Winds of Art." *Yankee*, December 1985, 40–41.

"A Post-Modern Palladian." *House Beautiful Building Manual*, Fall/Winter 1984–1985, 58–59.

"When New Is Old," *Newsday Magazine*, September 15, 1985, 47.

"Whites and Grays." *Toshi Jutaku*, November 1985, 52–59.

Wilson, R. G. Review of David Littlejohn, *Architect: The Life and Work of Charles W. Moore*. In *Architecture—The AIA Journal*, 74, 3, 1985, 163.

Chronology

1925
Born in Benton Harbor, Michigan

1946–1947
Jones Cottage, Torch Lake, Michigan

1947
Received Bachelor of Architecture degree, University of Michigan, Ann Arbor

1949
Jones House   *Project*, Eugene, Oregon

1947–1949
Worked in offices of Mario Corbett, Joseph Allen Stein, and Clark and Beuttler, San Francisco, California

1949–1950
Awarded George Booth Traveling Fellowship in Europe and in the Near East

1950–1952
Assistant Professor of Architecture, University of Utah, Salt Lake City

1952–1954
Lieutenant, U.S. Army Corps of Engineers in the United States, Japan, and Korea

1953
Weingarten House, Pebble Beach, California

1954
Khan House   *Project*, Carmel Highlands, California
Arnold House   *Project*, Carmel, California
Farr Professional Building   *Project*, Seaside, California
Yun Chon Chapel   *Project*,
Chung Wha Girls' Middle and High School   *Destroyed*, Seoul, Korea

1954–1955
Moore House, Pebble Beach, California

1956
Received Master of Fine Arts degree, Princeton University
Seaside Professional Building I, Seaside, California
Stores and offices   *Project*, Seaside, California
Twohig House, Monterey, California
Weingarten House addition and alteration, Pebble Beach, California
Cultural Center   *Project*, Chichén Itzá, Mexico

1957
Ph.D Project, Princeton University
Awarded Doctor of Philosophy degree, Princeton University
Jewish Community Center   *Project*, Seaside, California
Hubbard House I, Monterey, California

1958
Awarded Council of the Humanities Post-doctoral Fellowship, Princeton University
Matterson House, Monterey, California (with William Turnbull and Donlyn Lyndon)
Martin Studio, San Francisco, California
Inn at Cannery Row   *Project*, Monterey, California
(Wallace Holm, Architect with Charles W. Moore)

1958–1959
Assistant Professor, Princeton University

1959–1960
Hubbard House II, Corral de Tierra, California, with Richard C. Peters

1959–1962
Associate Professor, University of California, Berkeley
Worked independently and in offices of Clark and Beuttler, San Francisco, California

1960
Retail Mail Products Drive-in   *Project*, Pacific Grove, California

1960–1961
Citizens Federal Savings and Loan Building, San Francisco, California
(Charles W. Moore with Alan Morgan for Clark Beuttler Architects)

1961
Porte Cochere for Dr. and Mrs. Seymour Pastron, Los Angeles, California
Jenkins House   *Project*, St. Helena, California
Jobson House, Paolo Colorado Canyon, California (with Peter Hopkinson

1961–1962
Bonham House, Boulder Creek, California (with Warren Fuller)

1962
Moore House, Orinda, California
West Plaza Condominium   *Project*, Coronado, California (with Donlyn Lyndon and William Turnbull)
Cortese House   *Project*, Orinda, California (with Donlyn Lyndon)

1962–1965
Chairman, Department of Architecture, University of California, Berkeley
Worked with Moore, Lyndon, Turnbull, Whitaker in Berkeley, California

1963
Fremont Professional Center, Seaside, California (with Moore, Lyndon, Turnbull, Whitaker)
Jewell House, Orinda, California (with Moore, Lyndon, Turnbull, Whitaker)
Monte Vista Apartments, Monterey, California (with Moore, Lyndon, Turnbull, Whitaker)

Turner-Hall House *Project*, Pebble Beach, California (with Moore, Lyndon, Turnbull, Whitaker)

Jenkins House, St. Helena, California (with Moore, Lyndon, Turnbull, Whitaker)

Otus House I, II, and III, Berkeley, California (Moore, Lyndon, Turnbull, Whitaker/Charles Moore with Warren Fuller)

1963–1965
Sea Ranch Condominium, Sea Ranch, California (with Moore, Lyndon, Turnbull, Whitaker)

Moore House, Sea Ranch, California (with Moore, Lyndon, Turnbull, Whitaker

1964
Cudaback House Remodeling *Project*, Oakland, California (with Moore, Lyndon, Turnbull, Whitaker)

Slater House, Stinson Beach, California (with Moore, Lyndon, Turnbull, Whitaker)

Talbert House, Oakland, California (with Moore, Lyndon, Turnbull, Whitaker)

Seaside Professional Building II, Seaside, California (with Moore, Turnbull, Whitaker)

1964–1974
Kresge College, University of California at Santa Cruz (with Moore, Lyndon, Turnbull, Whitaker/Moore-Turnbull and Marvin Buchanan, Robert Calderwood, Robert Simpson, and Richard C. Peters)

1965
Alcoa Prefabricated Housing *Project* (with Moore, Lyndon, Turnbull, Whitaker/Moore-Turnbull)

Carmel Knolls Housing *Project*, Carmel, California (with Moore, Lyndon, Turnbull, Whitaker/Moore-Turnbull)

Johnson House, Sea Ranch, California (with Moore, Lyndon, Turnbull, Whitaker/Moore-Turnbull)

1965–1966
Karas House, Monterey, California (with Moore, Lyndon, Turnbull, Whitaker/Moore-Turnbull)

Lawrence House, Sea Ranch, California (with Moore, Lyndon, Turnbull, Whitaker/Moore-Turnbull)

Lovejoy Fountain, Portland, Oregon (with Moore, Lyndon, Turnbull, Whitaker/Moore-Turnbull as consultants to Lawrence Halprin and Associates)

1965–1969
Chairman, Department of Architecture, Yale University Worked with Moore, Lyndon, Turnbull, Whitaker/Moore-Turnbull, New Haven, Connecticut, and San Francisco, California

1966
Sea Ranch Athletic Club I, Sea Ranch, California (with Moore, Lyndon, Turnbull, Whitaker/Moore-Turnbull; pool and tennis courts by Lawrence Halprin and Associates; graphics by Barbara Stauffacher)

Thomasian House, Orinda, California (with Moore, Lyndon, Turnbull, Whitaker/Moore-Turnbull)

Sea Ranch Corporation Yard, Sea Ranch, California (with Moore, Lyndon, Turnbull, Whitaker/Moore-Turnbull),

Harrison House *Project*, Santa Barbara, California (with Moore, Lyndon, Turnbull, Whitaker/Moore-Turnbull)

Moore House *Renovation*, New Haven, Connecticut

Savin Rock Urban Renewal Project No. 2 *Project*, New Haven, Connecticut (with Moore, Lyndon, Turnbull, Whitaker)

Bransten House Remodeling *Project*, San Francisco, California (with Moore, Lyndon, Turnbull, Whitaker/Moore-Turnbull)

Halprin House, Sea Ranch, California (with Moore, Lyndon, Turnbull, Whitaker/Moore-Turnbull)

Knutsen House, Sonoma, California (with Moore, Lyndon, Turnbull, Whitaker/Moore-Turnbull)

Saltzman House, Carmel, California (with Moore, Lyndon, Turnbull, Whitaker/Moore-Turnbull)

Sea Ranch, Condominum, Hillside Unit *Project*, Sea Ranch, California (with Moore, Lyndon, Turnbull, Whitaker/Moore-Turnbull)

Akron Cascade Urban Renewal *Project*, Akron, Ohio (with Moore, Lyndon, Whitaker/Moore-Turnbull with Lawrence Halprin and Associates)

1966-1967
Boas House, Stinson Beach, California (with Moore, Lyndon, Turnbull, Whitaker/Moore-Turnbull)

Budge House, Healdsburg, California (with Moore, Lyndon, Turnbull, Whitaker/Moore-Turnbull)

1966-1968
Faculty Club, University of California, Santa Barbara, California (with Moore, Lyndon, Turnbull, Whitaker/Moore-Turnbull and Donlyn Lyndon, Marvin Buchanan, and Bruce Beebe)

1966-1969
Church Street South, New Haven, Connecticut (with Moore, Lyndon, Turnbull, Whitaker/Moore-Turnbull with Marvin Buchanan and Donald Whitaker)

1967
Bankes House *Project*, Brewster, New York (with Moore, Lyndon, Turnbull, Whitaker/Moore-Turnbull)

Seaside Housing for the Elderly, Seaside, California (with Moore, Lyndon, Turnbull, Whitaker/Moore-Turnbull and Sabastian Bordonaro Associates)

Pirofski House *Project*, Palo Alto, California (with Moore, Lyndon, Turnbull, Whitaker/Moore-Turnbull)

1976–1969
Sea Ranch Barn Houses, Sea Ranch, California (with Moore, Lyndon, Turnbull, Whitaker/Moore-Turnbull)

1967–1970
Tower One, Jewish Community Council Housing, New Haven, Connecticut (with Moore, Lyndon, Turnbull, Whitaker/Moore-Turnbull, Marvin Buchanan, Edward Johnson, and Mary Ann Rumney)

Klotz House, Westerly, Rhode Island, (with Moore, Lyndon, Turnbull, Whitaker/Moore-Turnbull and William Grover and Marvin Buchanan)

1968

Tric-Pac Housing   *Project*, Vernon, Connecticut (with Moore, Lyndon, Turnbull, Whitaker/Moore-Turnbull)

Navy Lodge Officers Housing   *Project*, New London, Connecticut and Newport, Rhode Island (with Moore, Lyndon, Turnbull, Whitaker/Moore-Turnbull and Larry Linder)

New Haven College Student Housing   *Project*, New Haven, Connecticut (with Moore, Lyndon, Turnbull, Whitaker/Moore-Turnbull)

University of Connecticut Staff Housing   *Project*, Storrs, Connecticut (with Moore, Lyndon, Turnbull, Whitaker/Moore-Turnbull)

Wooster Street Housing and Shops   *Project*, New Haven, Connecticut (with Moore, Lyndon, Turnbull, Whitaker/Moore-Turnbull)

Sea Ranch Spec House   *Project*, Sea Ranch, California (with Moore, Lyndon, Turnbull, Whitaker/Moore-Turnbull)

1968–1969

Pearson House Addition, Branford, Connecticut (with Moore, Lyndon, Turnbull, Whitaker/Moore-Turnbull and Steven Izenour)

Tempchin House, Bethesda, Maryland (with Moore, Lyndon, Turnbull, Whitaker/Moore-Turnbull and Rik Ekstrom)

Weyerhauser Demonstration House, Kansas City, Missouri (with Moore, Lyndon, Turnbull, Whitaker/Moore-Turnbull)

1968–1970

Robert T. Wolfe Housing for the Elderly, New Haven, Connecticut (with Moore, Lyndon, Turnbull, Whitaker/Moore-Turnbull and Robert Harper and Marvin Buchanan)

1968–1971

Psychoanalytic Associates Building, Los Angeles, California (with Moore, Lyndon, Turnbull, Whitaker/Moore-Turnbull and Arthur Ballman and Richard Chylinski)

1968–1976

Shinefield House, San Francisco, California (with Dmitri Vedensky)

1968–1976

Shinefield House, Sea Ranch, California (with Dmitri Vedensky)

1969

American Shakespeare Theater   *Project*, Stratford, Connecticut (with Moore, Lyndon, Turnbull, Whitaker/Moore-Turnbull)

Cornuelle House   *Project*, New Hampshire (with Moore, Lyndon, Turnbull, Whitaker/Moore-Turnbull)

Eastern Kentucky Housing Development Corporation   *Project*, Whitesburg, Kentucky (with Moore, Lyndon, Turnbull, Whitaker/Moore-Turnbull and Ron Filson and Thomas Rapp)

Essex Point Housing   *Project*, Deep River, Connecticut (with Moore, Lyndon, Turnbull, Whitaker/Moore-Turnbull)

Schub House   *Project*, Sag Harbor, New York, (with Moore, Lyndon, Turnbull, Whitaker/Moore-Turnbull)

Goodman House   *Project*, Montauk, New York (with Moore, Lyndon, Turnbull, Whitaker/Moore-Turnbull)

1969–1970

Dean, School of Architecture and Planning, Yale University

Stern House, Woodbridge, Connecticut (with Charles W. Moore Associates)

1969–1971

Koizim House, Westport, Connecticut (with Moore, Lyndon, Turnbull, Whitaker/Moore-Turnbull and Arthur Ballman)

Orono Housing, Orono, Maine (with Charles W. Moore, Associates and Marvin Buchanan and Robert Harper)

Saz House, Woods Hole, Massachusetts (with Charles W. Moore Associates)

Sea Ranch Athletic Club II, Sea Ranch, California (with Moore, Lyndon, Turnbull, Whitaker/Turnbull Associates and Donlyn Lyndon; graphics by Martha and Jerry Wagner)

1969–1972

Gagarin House, Peru, Vermont (with Moore, Lyndon, Turnbull, Whitaker/Moore-Turnbull and Arthur Ballman)

1969–1975

Murray House   *Renovation*, Cambridge, Massachusetts (with Charles W. Moore Associates)

1970

Essex Point, Scheme II   *Project*, Deep River, Connecticut (with Charles W. Moore Associates and Larry Linder and Marvin Buchanan)

Main Street Partnership, stores and offices (partially built in 1971), Essex, Connecticut (with Charles W. Moore Associates)

Middletown Inn and Renewal   *Project*, Middletown, Connecticut (with Charles W. Moore Associates and Robert Renfro)

Middletown Low-income Housing for the Elderly, Middletown, Connecticut (with Charles W. Moore Associates)

Moore House   *Project*, Essex, Connecticut (with Charles W. Moore Associates and Marvin Buchanan)

Southern Illinois University   *Project*, Carbondale, Illinois (with Charles W. Moore Associates)

Station Plaza   *Project*, Huntington, New York (with Charles W. Moore Associates and Gilbert Hoffman)

Worcester Polytecnic Institute   *Project*, Worcester, Massachusetts (with Charles W. Moore Associates and Donald Whitaker)

1970–1971

Maplewood Terrace Low-income Housing, Middletown, Connecticut (with Charles W. Moore and Frank Gravino)

Rudolph House I, Captiva Island, Florida (with Charles W. Moore Associates and James V. Righter)

1970–1975

Professor, School of Architecture, Yale University

Moore House   *Renovation*, Essex, Connecticut (with Charles W. Moore Associates)

1971

Clarke House, Old Lyme, Connecticut (with Charles W. Moore Associates and William Grover)

Heritage Harbor   *Project*, Annapolis, Maryland (with Charles W. Moore Associates)

Klotz Development *Project*, Westhampton Beach, New York (with Charles W. Moore Associates)
Orlando Housing *Project*, Orlando Florida (with Charles W. Moore Associates)
RAVAL Planning Study, Huntington, New York (with Charles W. Moore Associates)

1971–1972
McCall's House, Ocala, Florida (with Charles W. Moore Associates)
Taylor Town Houses, Norwalk, Connecticut (with Charles W. Moore Associates and William Grover, Robert Harper, and Mary Ann Rumney)

1971–1973
Magra's Drive-in, New London, Connecticut (with Charles W. Moore Associates)

1971–1975
Whitman Village, Huntington, New York (with Charles W. Moore Associates and Robert Harper)

1972
Antioch College, South Hall *Project*, Yellow Springs, Ohio (with Charles W. Moore Associates)
Chester Diversified Products *Project*, Chester, Connecticut (with Charles W. Moore Associates)
Dauntless Yacht Club *Project*, Essex, Connecticut (with Charles W. Associates and Carl Wies)
E.M.I. Reception Center *Project*, St. Simons Island, Georgia (with Charles W. Moore Associates)
Essex Point, Scheme III *Project*, Deep River, Connecticut (with Charles W. Moore Associates and Carl Wies, Robert Harper, and Robert Yudell)
Hindman Pool *Project*, New Zion, Kentucky (with Charles W. Moore Associates and Thomas Dryer)
Malibu Apartments *Project*, Malibu, California (with Charles W. Moore Associates and Richard Chylinski)
Indian Springs Ranch *Project*, Salinas, California (with Charles W. Moore Associates and Thomas Dryer)
Xanadune *Project*, St. Simons Island, Georgia (with Charles W. Moore Associates and Richard Oliver, Mary Ann Rumney, and Robert Yudell)

1972–1973
Ambro House, Schemes I–II, East Hampton, New York (with Charles W. Moore Associates and Robert Harper)
Kansas City Graphics, Kansas City, Kansas (with Charles W. Moore Associates and Mary Ann Rumney and Thomas Dryer)

1972-1974
Burns House, Santa Monica, California (with Richard Chylinski; colors by Christine Beebe; lighting by Richard C. Peters)

1973
Anderson Housing Development *Project*, Springfield, Massachusetts (with Charles W. Moore Associates and Thomas Dryer)

Country Federal Savings Bank, Green Farms, Connecticut (with Charles W. Moore Associates and William Grover, Mary Ann Rumney, and Richard Oliver)

1973–1974
Levin House, Little Falls, New York (with Charles W. Moore Associates and Marvin Buchanan and Jefferson Riley)
Old Farm *Project*, Mt. Holly, New Jersey (with Charles W. Moore Associates and Richard Oliver and Wing Hung Wong)
Tuscan Doll House, (with Charles W. Moore Associates and Rober Harper)
Doll Castle, (with Robert Yudell and Christine Beebe)
Kingsmill On the James Housing *Project*, Williamsburg, Virginia (with Charles W. Moore Associates and Robert Harper, William Grover, and Glenn Arbonies)
Owen Brown Village *Project*, Columbia, Maryland (with MLTW/ Moore-Turnbull Associates and Charles W. Moore Associates and Richard Oliver)
Stonington Development *Project*, Stonington, Connecticut (with Charles W. Moore Associates)
Taft-Adams Renovation *Project*, New Haven, Connecticut (with Charles W. Moore Associates and Edward Johnson and J.P.C. Floyd)
Temple of Understanding *Project*, St. Mary's County, Maryland (with Charles W. Moore Associates)
Paumanack Manor Housing for the Elderly *Project*, Huntington, New York (with Charles W. Moore Associates)

1973–1976
House near New York (with Richard Oliver)

1974–1975
Madras Consulate-General's Residence *Renovation*, Madras, India (with Charles W. Moore Associates and Jefferson Riley)

1974–1976
Barber House, Guilford, Connecticut (with Charles W. Moore Associates and Richard Oliver; colors by Christine Beebe)

1974–1977
Jones Laboratory, Cold Spring Harbor, New York (with Moore, Grover, Harper)

1975
Professor, University of California at Los Angeles, and Visiting Professor, School of Architecture, Yale University
Cold Spring Harbor Laboratories, Waste Treatment Building, and Airslie House, Cold Spring Harbor, New York (with Moore, Grover, Harper)
Cranbury Road Housing *Project*, Hightstown, New Jersey (with Moore, Grover, Harper)
Heady House, addition for former Moore House *Project*, Orinda, California (with Urban Innovations Group and Ron Filson and John Ruble)
Kuhio Shores Mauka *Project*, Kauai, Hawaii (with MLTW/ Moore-Turnbull Associates and Urban Innovations Group)

1975–1976
Swan House, Southhold, New York (with Moore, Grover, Harper and Mark Simon)

1975–1977
Isham House, Sagaponak, New York (with Moore, Grover, Harper and Mark Simon)
Rubenstein House, Trappe, Maryland (with Moore, Grover, Harper and Mark Simon; landscape by Lester Collins)

1975–1978
Moore, Rogger, Hofflander Condominium, Los Angeles, California (with Richard Chylinski)
Norwich Armed Forces Reserve Center, Norwich, Connecticut (with Moore, Grover, Harper and Arthur D. Little)
Abel House, Los Angeles, California (with Urban Innovations Group and Ron Filson and Robert Yudell)

1976
Riverdesign *Project*, Dayton, Ohio (with Moore, Grover, Harper and Lorenz and Williams)

1977
Minnesota II State Capitol Competition *Project*, St. Paul, Minnesota (with William Turnbull, Ron Filson, Barton Phelps, and Nicholas Pyle)
Wilheim House *Project*, Los Angeles, California (with Urban Innovations Group and Elias Torres and John Ruble)
Meyer Duplexes *Project*, Redondo Beach, California (with Moore, Grover, Harper)
Kaprelian House, Reedy, California (with Ron Filson, Urban Innovations Group and Cheryl Kaprelian)
House in Ojai, Ojai, California (with John Ruble, Barton Phelps, and Urban Innovations Group)

1977–1978
Piazza d'Italia, New Orleans, Louisiana (with Charles W. Moore Associates, Urban Innovations Group and Ron Filson, August Perez, Malcolm Heard, and Allen Eskew; colors by Christine Beebe)

1977–1979
Licht House, Mill Valley, California (with Urban Innovations Group and Nicholas Pyle)
Larson House, Angwin, California (with Robert Yudell)

1977–1983
Williams College Museum of Art (additions to Lawrence Hall, 1977–1986), Williamstown, Massachusetts (with Moore, Grover, Harper/Centerbrook with Robert Harper and Richard King)

1978
R. P. I. Fountain *Project*, Troy, New York, (with Moore, Grover, Harper and William Grover and Jefferson Riley)
Kings Road Housing for the Elderly, Los Angeles, California (Ron Filson, Urban Innovations Group, and Bobrow Thomas)
Fourney House, Malibu, California (with Ron Filson and Urban Innovations Group)
Shelton House, Belair, California (with Ron Filson and Urban Innoviations Group)
Best Products Show For The Museum Of Modern Art (with Urban Innovations Group and Jim Winkler)
Rodes House, Los Angeles, California (with Robert Yudell)

Del Rey Oaks *Project*, Monterey, California (with John Ruble and Robert Yudell)
Central Business District Plan *Project*, Buena Park, California (with Moore, Ruble, Yudell and Doug Campbell and Regula Campbell)

1978–1979
Stanwood House, Bloomfield, Connecticut (with Moore, Grover, Harper and Mark Simon)

1978–1981
Sammis Hall, Cold Spring Harbor, New York (with Moore, Grover, Harper)

1979
Roanoke Design '79 *Project*, Roanoke, Virginia (with Moore, Grover, Harper and J.P.C. Floyd)
Bunker Hill *Project*, Los Angeles, California, (with Barton Myers, Urban Innovations Group, Cesar Pelli, Robert Kinnard, Hardy Holtzman Pfeiffer, Frank Gehry, Ricardo Legorreta, and Lawrence Halprin)
Restoration Plan, Seal Beach, California (with Moore, Ruble, Yudell, Tim Felchlin, and Regula Campbell)
Beverly House, Santa Monica, California (with Robert Yudell, Charles Jencks, and Peter Zingg)

1979–1980
Gunwyn Offices, Princeton, New Jersey (with Moore, Grover, Harper and Mark Simon)

1979–1981
Rudolph House II, Williamstown, Massachusetts (with Moore, Grover, Harper and Robert Harper)

1979–1983
St. Matthew's Episcopal Church Pacific Palisades, California (with John Ruble, Robert Yudell, Tim Felchlin, Shinji Isozaki)

1980
House in Aspen, Aspen, Colorado (with William Turnbull, Jim Winkler, Urban Innovations Group)
Hancock Bank Plaza, Gulfport, Mississippi (with Ron Filson, Urban Innovaitons Group, Allen Eskew, and Perez Associates)

1981
Sweetwater Houses, Sugarland, Texas (with William Turnbull, George Harris, and Urban Innovations Group)
Knapp Center *Project*, Los Angeles, California (with John Ruble, Robert Yudell, and Stephen Harby)
Huntington Museum *Project*, San Marino, California (with Jim Winkler and Brian Lyons)
Tegel Harbor Housing, Berlin, West Germany (with Moore, Ruble, Yudell, Thomas Nagel, Leon Glodt, and Regina Pizzinini)

1981–1982
Indiana Landing *Project*, Indianapolis, Indiana (with Stephen Harby, Jim Winkler, George Harris, and Urban Innovations Group)

Sweetwater Country Clubhouse, Sugarland, Texas (with William Turnbull, Stephen Harby, George Harris, Jim Winkler, Morris Aubry Associates, and Richard Fitzgerald Associates; lighting by Richard C. Peters)
Glorietta Bay Beautification, Coronado, California (with Moore, Ruble, Yudell)

1981–1984
Kwee House, Singapore, (with Moore, Ruble, Yudell; colors by Christine Beebe)

1981–1985
Hood Museum Of Art, Dartmouth College, Hanover, New Hampshire (with Centerbrook, J.P.C. Floyd, Glenn Arbonies)

1982
Eola Hotel, Natchez, Mississippi (with Ron Filson, Urban Innovations Group, Allen Eskew, and Perez Associates)
Watkins Glen   *Project*, Watkins Glen, New York (with J.P.C. Floyd, Mark Denton, and Moore, Grover, Harper)
San Juan Capistrano Public Library   *Project*, San Juan Capistrano, California (with John Ruble, Robert Yudell, and Peter Zingg)
Parador Hotel   *Project*, San Juan Capistrano, California (with John Ruble and Robert Yudell)

1982–1984
Wonderwall (World's Fair), New Orleans, Louisiana (with William Turnbull, August Perez Associates, Kent Bloomer, Leonard Salvato, Arthur Andersson, and Urban Innovations Group; lighting by Richard C. Peters; colors by Christine Beebe)
Centennial Pavilion (World's Fair), New Orleans, Louisiana (with William Turnbull, August Perez Associates, and Arthur Andersson)

1982–
Hermann Park, Houston, Texas (with Arthur Andersson, Bart Phelps, and Urban Innovations Group)
Beverly Hills Civic Center, Beverly Hills, California (with Urban Innovations Group in association with Albert C. Martin and Associates, Edgardo Contini, James Morton, Stephen Harby, Richard Best, Shinji Isozaki and Renzo Zechetto; lighting by Richard C. Peters)

1983
Battery Park City South Facade New York, New York (with George Harris, Rothzeid, Kaiserman, Thomson, and Bee)
Breacans   *Project*, Steamboat Springs, Colorado (with Robin Leavitt, Stephen Harby and Robert DeHaven)
Stamford Center For The Performing Arts, Stamford, Connecticut (with J.P.C. Floyd, James Coan, and Centerbrook)

1983–1985
University of California at Irvine Extension Center and Alumni House, Irvine, California (with Urban Innovations Group, Bill Hubbard, Michael Bernard, Bart Phelps, and Jerry Radin)

1984
Burke House, Greenwich, Connecticut (with Centerbrook and J.P.C. Floyd)

Cedar Rapids Museum of Art, Cedar Rapids, Iowa (with Centerbrook, Glenn Arbonies, and Richard King)
Embassy Hotel, Los Angeles, California (with Marty Borko, Urban Innovations Group, and Pam Woodbridge; colors by Christine Beebe)
Sweetwater Cottages   *Project*, Sugarland, Texas (with Shinji Isozaki)
Austin City Hall   *Project*, Austin, Texas (with Robert Yudell, Ming Kae Yang, Arthur Andersson, Stephen Harby, and Shefelman & Nix)
Languna Gloria Art Museum Block   *Project*, Austin, Texas (with Robert Yudell, Ming Kae Yang, Arthur Andersson, Stephen Harby, and Shefelman & Nix)
Victoria Beach Hotel   *Project*, Coronado, California (with Moore, Ruble, Yudell and Urban Innovations Group, Rex Lottery, and Brian Croeni)
Turtle Creek Condominiums, Dallas, Texas (with Arthur Andersson, Mell Lawrence, Paul Lamb, and John Echlin)
Piazza d'Italia Hotel   *Project*, New Orleans, Louisiana (with Arthur Andersson and August Perez Associates)
Atlantixenter   *Project*, Philadelphia, Pennsylvania (with Robert DeHaven, Arthur Andersson, and D. P. Kopple and Associates Architects)

1984–1986
Miglio House, Sea Ranch, California (with Urban Innovations Group, John Echlin, and Mike Burch)

1985
Inman House, Atlanta, Georgia (with Moore, Ruble, Yudell, and Peter Zingg)
Pynoos House, Beverly Hills, California (with Moore, Ruble, Yudell, Peter Zingg, and Stephen Harby)
Highlands Hotel   *Project*, Steamboat Springs, Colorado (with Robert DeHaven)
Houston Decorative Center, Houston, Texas (with Marty Borko and Urban Innovations Group)
Buffalo Bayou   *Project*, Houston, Texas (with Arthur Andersson and Charles Tapley Associates)
Furniture Designs for Festival of India, Cooper-Hewitt Museum, New York, New York (with Arthur Andersson and Paul Lamb)
Layered Tables For Stendig International (with Inner Images)
St. Louis Art Museum, West Wing, St. Louis, Missouri (with Moore, Ruble, Yudell, Mark Johnson, Dan Garness, and Thomas Nagel and Smith Entzeroth Architects)
All Saints Episcopal Church   *Project*, Pasadena, California (with Moore, Ruble, Yudell and Renzo Zechetto)
Bel-Air Presbyterian Church, Bel-Air, California (with Moore, Ruble, Yudell, Mark Johnson, and Renzo Zechetto)
University of Oregon Science Buildings, Eugene, Oregon (with Moore, Ruble, Yudell, James Morton, Neal Matsumo, and the Ratcliff Architects)
University of California at San Diego, Howard Hughes Medical Institute, San Diego, California (with Moore, Ruble, Yudell, Markku Kari, Stephen Harby, and the Ratcliff Architects)
Church of the Nativity, Rancho Santa Fe, California (with Moore, Ruble, Yudell, and Renzo Zechetto)
Plaza De Las Fuentas, Pasadena, California (with Moore, Ruble, Yudell, Dan Garness, and Miguel Escobar)
Oceanside Civic Center

Oceanside, California (with Urban Innovations Group, John Echlin, Robin Hayne, and Danielson Associates)
Phoenix House, Oak Mountain School, Escondido, California (with Arthur Andersson, Urban Innovations Group, and Robin Hayne)
Galveston Arch, Galveston, Texas (with Paul Lamb and Mell Lawrence)
Lafayette Town Center, Lafayette, California (with Arthur Andersson, Mell Lawrence, and Yutaka Masuda
Amusement Park, New Jersey (with Arthur Andersson, Charles Lamb, Centerbrook, J.P.C. Floyd, and James Childress)
1992 Chicago World's Fair *Project*, Chicago, Illinois (SOM, Stanley Tigerman, Thomas Beeby, Robert A.M. Stern, Jacquelin Robertson, with Renzo Zechetto)

1985–
O'Neil Ford Professor of Architecture at the University of Texas in Austin
Hoffman House, Dallas, Texas (with Arthur Andersson, Paul Lamb, and John Mullen)
San Antonio Art Institute, San Antonio, Texas (with Moore, Ruble, Yudell, Miguel Escobar, Steve Vitalich, Renzo Zechetto, Paul Nagashima, and George Nakatani)
Sanders House, Santa Monica, California (with Moore, Ruble, Yudell, Peter Zingg, and Steve Vitalich)

Credits

No architecture is made alone, and limited space has made it impossible to recount the many people who have contributed to the work at hand. I would like to make special note here of my partners and some others who have been involved in many projects.

The MLTW partnership was founded in Berkeley in 1962 with William Turnbull, Donlyn Lyndon, Richard Whitaker, and myself. It began to dissolve in 1964 when Lyndon and Whitaker moved away, but remained alive as MLTW Moore-Turnbull with offices in San Francisco and New Haven until 1970. The four of us have remained close to this day.

From 1970 until 1974 the office in Connecticut was called Charles W. Moore Associates, but in 1974, it was recast as Moore, Grover, Harper, with William Grover, Robert Harper, and myself. That office later came to include four more partners: Mark Simon, Glenn Arbonies, J.P. Chadwick Floyd, and Jefferson Riley, and is now called Centerbrook.

After 1974 I worked mostly in Los Angeles with the professional arm of the UCLA School of Architecture—the Urban Innovations Group, and after 1977 with Robert Yudell and John Ruble in Moore, Ruble, Yudell. In 1985 I moved to Austin, Texas where I have an office with Arthur Andersson, Mell Lawrence, Yutaka Masuda, and a very few others.

Some consultants too have been an important continuing part of this work. Patrick Morreau's structural engineering made possible the Sea Ranch Condominium in 1964. Richard C. Peters has been a valuable colleague and lighting consultant on most of the buildings since 1964. Tina Beebe designed the colors for the Burns House for her Yale University thesis in 1974 and has been responsible for almost all of our colors ever since.

Others who have been important include Marvin Buchanan and Edward B. Allen in Berkeley throughout the 1960s; Don Whitaker, Larry Linder, and Richard Oliver in the late 1960s; Ron Filson and Allen Eskew in the 1970s; more recently, Stephen Harby, George Harris, Shinji Isozaki, Renzo Zecchetto, and Richard Dodge; Among those who are indispensable are Kent Bloomer in Connecticut, Gerald Allen in New York, and Marilyn Zuber and Edgardo Contini in Los Angeles.

Charles W. Moore

New drawings prepared especially for this publication:

Moore House *Pebble Beach*
Oscar Cadena, Steve Dvorak, Robert Shemwell: pp. 98–99
Moore House *New Haven*
Robert Shemwell: p. 104
Moore House *Essex*
Robert Shemwell: p. 106
Moore, Rogger, Hofflander Condominium
Toby Greenbaum, Robert Shemwell: p. 108
Moore Cabin
Toby Greenbaum, Robert Shemwell: p. 112
Moore House *Austin*
Steve Dvorak, Robert Shemwell, Arthur Andersson: p. 113
Bonham House
Oscar Cadena, Robert Shemwell: p. 122
Jenkins House
Constantine Papavasiliou, Steve Dvorak, Robert Shemwell:
p. 125
Otus House
Ann Cuthbertson, Robert Shemwell: p. 126
Burns House
Greg Splinter, Steve Dvorak, Robert Shemwell: p. 142
Miglio House
Robert Shemwell: p. 156
Hoffman House
Toby Greenbaum, Robert Shemwell, Steve Dvorak: p. 157
Indiana Landing
Mell Lawrence, Steve Dvorak, Robert Shemwell,
Arthur Andersson: pp. 192–193
Wonderwall
Arthur Andersson, Robert Shemwell, Steve Dvorak:
pp. 194–195
Centennial Pavilion
Arthur Andersson: p. 200
1992 World's Fair
Renzo Zecchetto and Brian Tichenor: p. 203
St. Matthew's Church
Brian Tichenor, Sylvia Diely: pp. 230–237
Tegel Harbor Housing
Leon Glodt, Regina Pizzinini, Brian Tichenor, Raun Thorp,
George Nakatani: pp. 238–245
Beverly Hills Civic Center
Charles W. Moore, Renzo Zecchetto, Brian Tichenor:
pp. 246–255
Hermann Park
Arthur Andersson: p. 268